D0174445

"STRONG OF BODY,
BRAVE AND NOBLE"

"STRONG OF BODY, BRAVE AND NOBLE"

Chivalry and Society in Medieval France

Constance Brittain Bouchard

CORNELL UNIVERSITY PRESS

ITHACA AND LONDON

Copyright © 1998 by Cornell University

All rights reserved. Except for brief quotations in a review, this book, or parts thereof, must not be reproduced in any form without permission in writing from the publisher. For information, address Cornell University Press, Sage House, 512 East State Street, Ithaca, New York 14850.

First published 1998 by Cornell University Press

Printed in the United States of America

Library of Congress Cataloging-in-Publication Data

Bouchard, Constance Brittain.
"Strong of body, brave and noble" : chivalry and society in
medieval France / Constance Brittain Bouchard.
p.   cm.
Includes bibliographical references and index.
ISBN-13: 978-0-8014-8548-0 (pbk. : alk. paper)
1. France—Civilization—1000–1328.   2. Nobility—France—History.
3. Chivalry—France—History.   I. Title.
DC33.2.B59   1998
944'.02—dc21   97-38906

Cornell University Press strives to utilize environmentally responsible suppliers and materials to the fullest extent possible in the publishing of its books. Such materials include vegetable-based, low-VOC inks and acid-free papers that are also either recycled, totally chlorine-free, or partly composed of nonwood fibers. For further information, visit our website at www.cornellpress.cornell.edu.

Paperback printing   10   9   8   7   6   5   4   3

CONTENTS

ILLUSTRATIONS

PREFACE

"Strong of body, brave and noble," ran the description of an idealized lord in the twelfth-century epic "The Coronation of Louis."[1] Medieval aristocrats prided themselves on their prowess, their courage, and their noble birth. They wielded great power, and they were fascinated by what was required to acquire and keep that power. Repeatedly, especially in their fictional literature, almost all of which turned on exploits of the brave and wellborn, they tried to create an idealized image of nobility and knighthood—and yet kept discovering that every ideal was shot full of contradictions. In this book, I examine both the position of knights and nobles in the society of the High Middle Ages and the images of those positions created at that time.

The medieval aristocracy, especially that of France, has been the subject of a great deal of study during the last generation. Scholars have reexamined and redefined the roots of noble status, the relationship between nobles and knights, the part the aristocracy played in both rural and urban economies, the origins of chivalry, the meaning of "feudalism," the nobility's role in church reform, and the ties between kings and their great nobles. Regional and local studies have challenged older timetables and definitions. Yet while scholarly understanding of these topics has changed markedly, their presentation in general survey works has not. Most recent studies of chivalry and nobility are highly technical, very narrowly focused, and published in specialized journals, often in French and German. Such work is not always easily accessible to the English-speaking scholar. In addition, specialists in literature and specialists in history have sometimes been

---

[1] "The Coronation of Louis" 1, in *Guillaume d'Orange*, p. 63.

ignorant of each other's work. In this study of the nobility in high medieval France I hope to tie together many of these recent findings (including some of my own work) and to provide an introduction to medieval nobility and chivalry in a form accessible both to scholars and to students of medieval history and literature.

During the High Middle Ages, the eleventh through early thirteenth centuries, French aristocratic culture was especially influential, and not just in France. In England after the Norman Conquest of 1066, French culture permeated the highest social circles. The same was true, though to a lesser degree, in the Spanish peninsula as the *reconquista* against the Muslims gradually worked its way south; the first king of Portugal was descended from the dukes of Burgundy, and the twelfth-century kings of Spain were descended from the counts of Burgundy and Mâcon. Although German aristocrats had long-standing traditions of their own, they adopted many elements of French chivalry during this period.

This book's central focus is high medieval France, but in several instances I look back before the eleventh century or forward after the middle of the thirteenth century, and I sometimes compare developments in France with those in neighboring areas. The High Middle Ages was chosen both because it is the period with which I am most familiar and because this period has not received enough attention. Most other studies of chivalry still stress the late Middle Ages, but it is not safe to assume that one can read the twelfth century back from the fifteenth. The term "France" is used here roughly to describe that area of the Continent in which the population spoke French. Thus it corresponds neither to the modern-day French Republic, which includes some areas (such as Alsace) that were not French speaking in the Middle Ages, nor to the medieval Kingdom of the Franks, which did include French-speaking Flanders (now part of Belgium) but not some other areas (such as the Jura) where French *was* spoken. Southern France, or Occitania, separated linguistically but not politically from the French kingdom, is included, but only peripherally.

Throughout this book I work from a conviction that one cannot create tidy definitions and then attempt to apply them to the past. In the late twentieth century many social institutions, such as "the middle class," cannot be explained in twenty-five words or fewer, and yet everyone knows them when they see them. In just the same way, there were no consistent definitions in the High Middle Ages of such key institutions as nobility, chivalry, fief holding, or the church, even though contemporaries certainly recognized and discussed them. It is also important to keep in mind that what people "recognized when they saw it" changed over time, so that one set of definitions cannot be applied to the 250 years covered by this book, much less to the entire Middle Ages. The study of medieval nobility and chivalry has sometimes bogged down in rather sterile semantic discussions about, for example, whether "classic feudalism" reached an area "late," or whether a poem "reflects the ethos of courtly love"—questions that presume preexisting and essentially unchanging standards to which one can compare local political institutions or a particular poet's use of imagery. Rather than try to create or impose simple models of medieval institutions, I believe, one should try to understand the people of the past and what they thought they were doing in a vital and ever-shifting social context.

Because this book is meant to be an introduction, I have for the most part done no more than suggest the complex historiographical debates that swirl around many of the topics I am addressing. I have made no attempt to be exhaustive in citing the extensive scholarly literature. To keep down the bulk of footnotes, I have reserved full references for the bibliography, where I have also added a few annotations to signal some of the most significant studies. Similarly, I have where possible cited works—both primary and secondary—in easily accessible English translations.

This book begins with an attempt to define the nobility: who were they, how were they recognized, what functions did they fill, and how were they different from knights? In the second chapter, I put the nobles in their social context, including their relations with kings at one end of the social spectrum and with peasants at the other. Previous studies of nobility and chivalry have done little more than hint at the rural economy in which lords functioned; yet I think it is important to discuss at least briefly those from whom noble wealth derived. In this chapter I also deal with the thorny question of the nature of "feudalism." In Chapter 3 I address the structure of noble families more fully, including their marriages and the round of their lives. Chapter 4 is devoted to the literature that nobles read and responded to, especially works that involved chivalrous behavior and love. The book ends with a chapter on the interactions between the nobility and the church, a topic that has attracted intensive scholarly attention in recent years.

In graduate school I was greatly influenced by Sidney Painter's *French Chivalry*, first published in 1940, and the present book is to some degree a tribute to that work. A recent survey done by the Consortium for the Teaching of the Middle Ages indicates that it is still the most commonly assigned book on the topic of chivalry.[2] Nearly sixty years have passed since Painter's book first appeared, however, and during that time, scholars have drastically redefined both nobility and chivalry. Though Painter's book is no longer an adequate introduction to the topic, its wit and clarity have kept it continuously in print. If my own work is not always as lively, I hope that at least I have learned Painter's lesson to keep the telling of history as interesting as the subject matter.

The writing of this book was assisted by a 1993 National Endowment for the Humanities Summer Stipend, FT-38322. My husband, Bob, read the manuscript as he has read all my work, asking the insightful questions that helped me to determine what I really wanted to say. I wish especially to thank John G. Ackerman, director of Cornell University Press, for persuading me that this book needed to be written and that I was the person to write it.

CONSTANCE BRITTAIN BOUCHARD

Wooster, Ohio

[2] Elizabeth B. Keiser and Bonnie Wheeler, "Teaching Chivalry: From Footnote to Foreground," in Howell Chickering and Thomas H. Seiler, eds., *The Study of Chivalry*, p. 128.

Abbreviations

AHR	*American Historical Review*
MGH SS	*Monumenta Germaniae Historica, Scriptores*
PL	J.-P. Migne, ed., *Patrologiae cursus completus, Series Latina*
RHGF	*Recueil des historiens des Gaules et de la France*

"STRONG OF BODY,
BRAVE AND NOBLE"

CHAPTER ONE

Nobles and Knights

How to define the medieval nobility? This is an especially difficult task for modern scholars because the people of the High Middle Ages, the eleventh through thirteenth centuries, did not have a definition themselves. They did not talk about "the nobility" as a social unit, even though they might discuss "noble attributes" (*nobilitas*) at great length. *Nobilis*, the medieval Latin term usually translated as "nobleman," was not, strictly speaking, a noun but an adjective. By the time criteria for nobility were finally established in the late thirteenth century, it was on bases that would have made no sense to nobles of earlier generations. And yet medieval nobles always knew who they were.

For a long time scholars tried to create simple, straightforward definitions of the medieval nobility. Nobles, some said, were exactly the same as free men. Others, remarking the existence throughout medieval history of free peasants, said instead that the nobility was a closed social caste composed of those descended from the noble senatorial class of Rome or (alternatively) from the noble Germanic warlords who had settled in the Roman Empire. Some maintained that nobility was determined only by the father's noble blood; others that only the mother's blood counted. Still other historians, noting that the nobles of the High Middle Ages themselves often pointed to upwardly mobile men in their ancestry, decided that the nobility of the eleventh and subsequent centuries was an entirely new group, perhaps to be equated with knights or with feudal vassals.

All these tidy definitions have recently been discarded. Instead, scholars have come to agree that many different elements went into making a medieval man or woman someone both they and their contemporaries would recognize as noble. There were continuities, certainly, from the time of the Roman Empire; yet there was also an evolution in noble status.[1] All nobles of the High Middle Ages doubtless carried both the blood of upstarts and noble bloodlines that went back centuries, for in every generation the upwardly mobile sought to marry into noble ranks.

Part of the difficulty in defining the nobility derives from the lack of a single medieval word to designate members of the group. Theoretical discussions of social structures from the period (discussed more fully in Chapter 2) did not attempt to break society down into "nobles" and "non-nobles." Of course both modern scholars and people of the time would consider noble someone designated as *nobilis vir* or *nobilis femina* in contemporary charters, or by such related adjectives as *praeclarus, venerabilis,* or *illuster,* but these terms were not applied universally. Indeed, the term *nobilis* itself was fairly unusual until the eleventh century, when it began to replace the previously more common term *illuster.*[2] Someone designated as a count or duke in the documents—that is, someone who held an important office— or someone referred to as "lord," *domnus,* would generally not also be called "noble." The latter term may indeed have been reserved for those whose status was *not* immediately obvious from their titles.[3]

While it is certainly possible to discern the general attributes of members of the medieval nobility, it is therefore important to keep in mind that this nobility did not in the eleventh and twelfth centuries constitute a distinct or even clearly definable group. Calling someone "noble" meant only that he or she was distinguished and from a distinguished family, not that the person was a member of any "noble class." Nobles were members of an aristocracy—that is, the small seg-

---

[1] Theodore Evergates, *Feudal Society in the Bailliage of Troyes under the Counts of Champagne,* pp. 144–47. Martin Heinzelmann, "La noblesse du haut moyen âge." Gerd Tellenbach, "Zur Erforschung des hochmittelalterlichen Adels," pp. 320–24. Léopold Genicot, "La noblesse médiévale: Pans de lumière et zones obscures." T. N. Bisson, "Nobility and Family in Medieval France."

[2] Régine Le Jan-Hennebique, "*Domnus, illuster, nobilis,*" pp. 439–48. Stephen Weinberger, "The Ennoblement of the Aristocracy in Medieval Provence." Theodore Evergates, "Nobles and Knights in Twelfth-Century France," in Thomas N. Bisson, ed., *Cultures of Power,* pp. 11–17. Dominique Barthélemy, *La société dans le comté de Vendôme,* pp. 508–9.

[3] George Beech, "Prosopography," pp. 206–7.

ment of a society which stands above the rest—and yet aristocracy and nobility are not strictly synonymous. When knights first appeared in the late tenth and eleventh centuries, for example, they were not considered noble, and yet they were certainly aristocratic, in that they were different from the great mass of society. The term "aristocracy" now implies a social class; yet nothing like modern consciousness of social class existed before the fourteenth century.[4]

Even without any easily stated set of criteria, medieval men and women could recognize nobles operationally. There is broad scholarly consensus that from at least the ninth century onward, nobles were characterized by a combination of wealth, power, and noble birth.[5] In the eleventh century there was an enormous gap between the wealthy nobles and everybody else. Although by the thirteenth century some merchants in the rapidly growing towns had accumulated substantial fortunes, and some nobles had lost theirs, it was generally taken for granted that a nobleman would be rich. In the same way, nobles were assumed to have the power to command: they might hold an important office, such as that of duke or count, might control a castle or, at a minimum, have a group of followers, servants, and clients. But even more important than wealth and power was the possession of noble blood.[6]

Noble Blood

The chivalric romances that medieval French nobles enjoyed always stressed the importance of family. Noble birth, with its glorious attributes, always emerged in these stories no matter how much someone tried to hide it. Someone like the hero Perceval, a nobleman's son brought up like a peasant because his mother wanted to

[4] Joachim Bumke, *The Concept of Knighthood in the Middle Ages*, pp. 116–19. Johanna Maria van Winter, "The Knightly Aristocracy of the Middle Ages as a 'Social Class,' " in Timothy Reuter, ed. and trans., *The Medieval Nobility*, pp. 313–29.

[5] Jane Martindale, "The French Aristocracy in the Early Middle Ages." Régine Le Jan, *Famille et pouvoir dans le monde franc*, pp. 9–12. Wilhelm Störmer, *Früher Adel*, pp. 13–28. E. Warlop, *The Flemish Nobility before 1300*, 1:40, 101, 332. Stuart Airlie, "Bonds of Power and Bonds of Association in the Court Circle of Louis the Pious," pp. 191–204.

[6] Karl Ferdinand Werner, "Adel: Fränkisches Reich, Imperium, Frankreich," in *Vom Frankenreich zur Entfaltung Deutschlands und Frankreichs*, p. 12. Léopold Genicot, "Recent Research on the Medieval Nobility," in Reuter, *The Medieval Nobility*, pp. 23–24.

save him from the dangers of a warrior's life, nonetheless learned chivalric behavior and elaborate fighting skills virtually overnight once he was given a chance. Queen Guinevere was able to deduce that Galahad was Lancelot's son after only a brief conversation with him; she recognized that he must be "descended on both sides from kings and queens and from the noblest lineage known to man."[7]

In reality, of course, noble blood did not reveal itself quite so conveniently. And indeed there was always a tension between nobility of blood and nobility of spirit or soul, with the full awareness that the first did not necessarily imply the second. Bishop Adalbero of Laon wrote to the French king in the early eleventh century, "Noble birth is a source of high praise for kings and dukes, but enough has been said of beauty and strength: the strength of the soul is more important than that of the body." The same sentiment was echoed nearly two and half centuries later by a secular author in the vulgate *Lancelot* cycle, when the hero tells the Lady of the Lake, "I don't know on what grounds some are more noble than others, unless they gain nobility through prowess."[8] This *topos* was repeatedly invoked throughout the Middle Ages, but the nobles, like Adalbero's king and, for that matter, most churchmen, continued to treat noble birth as deserving of "high praise."

During the eleventh century, the first attempts were made to construct family histories, *genealogiae* as they were called, linking living nobles with their glorious dead ancestors, and this literary form became more common in the twelfth century.[9] It was especially important for noble families to find a biological connection with early kings, who represented noble blood most unequivocally. Bishop Adalbero stated flatly, "Noble lineages descend from the blood of

---

[7] Perceval's parentage allows him easily to overcome his boorish upbringing in both the twelfth-century French romance *Perceval* and the German *Parzival*, written at the beginning of the thirteenth century. Chrétien de Troyes, "The Story of the Grail (Perceval),"·in *Arthurian Romances*, pp. 399–402. Wolfram von Eschenbach, *Parzival*, pp. 95–98. *The Quest of the Holy Grail*, p. 47.

[8] Adalbero, "Carmen ad Rotbertum regum," lines 23–25, p. 2. *Lancelot* 1.15, p. 46.

[9] Georges Duby, "French Genealogical Literature: The Eleventh and Twelfth Centuries," in *The Chivalrous Society*, pp. 149–57. Fernand Vercauteren, "A Kindred in France in the Eleventh and Twelfth Centuries," in Reuter, *The Medieval Nobility*, pp. 87–103. Léopold Genicot, *Les généalogies*. Idem, "Princes territoriaux et sang carolingien: La *Genealogia Comitum Buloniensium*," in *Études sur les principautés lotharingiennes*, pp. 217–306.

kings."[10] Indeed, although Charlemagne's descendants had been multiplying for two hundred years, it was only in the eleventh century that people (other than the Carolingian kings themselves) consciously attempted to glorify themselves by means of their Carolingian blood (the Capetian kings of France had reigned too briefly in the early eleventh century to show up in anyone's glorious and distant ancestry).[11]

But noble birth was crucial long before the eleventh century, and a glorious noble ancestor was still noble even if he was not actually a king. In practice, most nobles *were* descended from kings by the twelfth century, because of a long-standing pattern of intermarriage among the upper aristocracy, including the kings. In spite of Adalbero's flattering remarks to his own king, it was not that nobility had to flow directly from kings but that a king was simply the most powerful and important noble. Although it is difficult to construct family trees from scanty evidence, modern scholars have been able to demonstrate convincingly that the nobles of the eleventh and twelfth centuries were descended from the nobles of the ninth and tenth centuries, who were in turn descended from even earlier nobles.[12] Long before noble families began commissioning *genealogiae*, then, descent from the gloriously born was a key element in noble status.

The nobility was not a closed caste, however, and an eleventh-century noble who was able to trace his ancestry, fairly plausibly, to a count of the ninth century would also have had plenty of non-noble ancestors. In France someone really needed only one demonstrably noble ancestor in order to claim noble birth, and nobility might come either through the mother's or the father's side. Perhaps ironically, at the same time as many nobles were claiming (or creating) biological links with earlier kings, others were pointing proudly to ancestors whose strength and virtue—though not their birth—had given them

[10] Adalbero, "Carmen," line 22, p. 2. See also Genicot, "La noblesse médiévale," p. 343.

[11] The definitive study of Charlemagne's descendants is that by Karl Ferdinand Werner, "Die Nachkommen Karls des Großen bis um das Jahr 1000," pp. 403–82. For the importance of Carolingian ancestors in the eleventh century, see also Heinz Thomas, "Zur Kritik an der Ehe Heinrichs III. mit Agnes von Poitou," pp. 224–35.

[12] Karl Ferdinand Werner, "Untersuchungen zur Frühzeit des französischen Fürstentums."

authority at a time when kings were weak. The twelfth-century legends of the origins of the county of Catalonia, founded three centuries earlier, tried to have it both ways, stressing *both* the legitimate appointment of the first count by the French king and Count Wifred the Hairy's independence, recognized when he conquered the Saracens with no help from the king.[13]

In fact new men were constantly joining the nobility, marrying women of longer-established families and thus giving their children ancestors both among ancient kings and among parvenus. By the late eleventh century, as discussed more fully in Chapter 3, lords of castles sometimes tried to strengthen their ties to their non-noble followers by marrying their daughters to them. These men would not become noble themselves merely by marrying a noble girl, but their children would indubitably have noble birth. Scholars who have pointed to the new men in the ancestry of high medieval nobles as evidence that there was a turnover in the aristocracy, and scholars who have used the long-established nobles in this ancestry to argue that the aristocracy was unchanging, have both missed the point. The group of men and women who constituted the high medieval nobility had many ties to the aristocracy of centuries earlier and yet constantly took on new members as well. As much as the nobles themselves liked to stress their noble birth, the same noble ancestors might be found in the family trees of men of a variety of status.[14] For all practical purposes, purity of blood, assuming there were at least some nobles in one's ancestry, was less important than wealth and power.

Wealth and Power

Early medieval nobles had been enormously wealthy and enormously powerful—and also very few. Monasteries in the seventh and eighth centuries might be established by a single individual who had

---

[13] Paul Freedman, "Cowardice, Heroism, and the Legendary Origins of Catalonia," pp. 14–19. More generally, see Éric Bournazel, "Mémoire et parenté," in Robert Delort and Dominique Iogna-Prat, eds., *La France de l'an mil*, pp. 114–24.

[14] Constance B. Bouchard, "The Origins of the French Nobility." Idem, "Consanguinity and Noble Marriages in the Tenth and Eleventh Centuries." The nobility continued to recruit new members in the late Middle Ages, even while trying to find ways to prove or demonstrate that only those with long pedigrees were real nobles. See Howard Kaminsky, "Estate, Nobility, and the Exhibition of Estate in the Later Middle Ages," pp. 695–98.

enough disposable wealth to endow a church at a single stroke with property scattered over many miles.[15] The nobles of the High Middle Ages, more numerous and not so wealthy (either in absolute terms or in comparison to the rest of the population), nevertheless stood out in their ability to buy luxury goods, build castles (always an expensive proposition), and make gifts of land to holy monks with whose prayers they wished to be associated. In one of the late twelfth-century *Lais* of Marie de France, an infant wrapped in expensive brocade from Constantinople, with a gold and ruby ring tied to her arm, could be recognized at once as being of "noble birth."[16]

The power that nobles exercised could be nothing more than the might of a strong sword arm, multiplied by those of many retainers, but it would be a mistake to see medieval nobles, brutish as many doubtless were, only as powerful louts. Nobles, like other members of medieval society, believed very strongly in the rule of law (even if they were not always entirely sure what that law was), and in the force of tradition. The offices held by the powerful were in most cases derived from public power, and the incumbents (at least theoretically) exercised these offices for the good of the downtrodden as well as for other nobles and themselves. Truly egregious abuse of such power could bring down a sanction worse than any available legal penalty: the scorn of one's fellow nobles.

Throughout the Middle Ages, many nobles were closely related to the kings, and even those who were not actually of royal blood could rise in power through association with the royal court (a strategy German scholars call *Königsnähe*). Kings had ruled France since even before it was France, since the latter days of the Roman Empire, through men called counts. The term *comes*, Latin for "count" (*comites* in the plural), is derived from the same root as "companion," and the first counts were indeed the king's trusted companions. Without these rich and powerful associates, it would have been impossible to rule over a world where the population was scattered and communication and transportation were at best difficult.[17] To the very few nobles who

---

[15] For example, see the testament of Abbo, who made the abbey of Novalesa the heir to his considerable fortune in 739, and that of Wideradus, who founded Flavigny in 717 by making extremely generous gifts. Patrick J. Geary, *Aristocracy in Provence*, pp. 38–79; *The Cartulary of Flavigny*, pp. 19–28, no. 1.

[16] Marie de France, *Lais* 3, p. 62.

[17] Karl Ferdinand Werner, "Missus—Marchio—Comes," pp. 191–239.

had the opportunity to be counts the office brought both responsibilities and great opportunities for personal advancement. An understanding of the powers granted to counts and how those powers changed can give some sense of the authority wielded by the most powerful members of the nobility.

The count was the lord of a county, an administrative unit whose name we still use more than a millennium after its original appearance. The count did not actually *own* the county any more than the head of the county commissioners in a modern American district owns his or her county, but the early medieval count was the chief administrative, judicial, financial, and military official in the area. He administered laws and rulings on behalf of the king, brought criminals to justice in his own court, collected the king's taxes, and raised the army when necessary.[18]

The county he ruled was the direct descendant of the *pagus*, the unit of provincial administration under the Roman Empire, and indeed many charters continued to call counties *pagi* into the tenth century. Since Rome had been an urban civilization, its administrative units were always centered on cities, at least small cities, after which the *pagi* (and hence the counties) were usually named. Thus the French county of Maine (after which the American state is named) is the region surrounding the city of Le Mans. There was always some slippage; that is, several *pagi* were often combined into a single county, and a count might simultaneously hold several counties. Overall, however, there were remarkable continuities between late Roman and medieval administration in France.[19]

In the late ninth or early tenth century, viscounts began to be common, men acting as the counts' representatives but sometimes functioning independently, serving almost the same functions as the counts but in smaller areas (usually one portion of a county).[20] At about the same time, the new title of duke (*dux* in Latin) also began to be used. A duke was essentially a very powerful count, usually one who held a number of counties, often with other counts under him. Dukes wielded a great deal of authority within duchies that had once been the principal subdivisions of Carolingian kingdoms *(regna)*; a

[18] Jean Dunbabin, *France in the Making*, pp. 44–58, 226–32.
[19] Patrick J. Geary, *Before France and Germany*, pp. 88–95, 158–62.
[20] Jean-Pierre Poly, *La Provence et la société féodale*, pp. 41–43.

duke might even be considered the equivalent of a king in his own territory. According to the chronicler Raoul Glaber, Duke Conan I of Brittany celebrated his consolidation of power over the duchy in the eleventh century by putting a diadem on his head, "in the manner of kings."[21] Indeed, in the early twelfth century the duke of Aquitaine, who controlled most of the counties in southwestern France, was more powerful than the French king himself. The dukes of Normandy were called *dux* and *comes* almost interchangeably in the eleventh and twelfth centuries, even after they had also become kings of England.[22]

Counts were originally appointed by the kings for shorter or longer periods, and kings could and did remove and replace counts at will until the ninth century. In the second half of the ninth century, however, counties gradually became hereditary offices, held no longer at the king's will but by the count's own hereditary right.[23] Even after counties became hereditary, the counts continued to exercise what might be considered public power for the next century or so (although it is important to realize that medieval people did not draw nearly as sharp a distinction between public and private power as does modern society). Although the Carolingian kings after the middle of the ninth century did not have the centralized authority of Charlemagne or even his son Louis the Pious, it was their counts, not other kings, who replaced them as major political figures. These counts may have acted in their own right rather than at a king's direction as royal power weakened, but like earlier kings, they directed the armies, protected monasteries, and administered justice.[24]

But then in many areas even comital power began to disintegrate. By the year 1000 in many cases counts had ceased to hold the public courts at which all free men of the region had assembled for five cen-

[21] Raoul Glaber, *Historia* 2.3.4, p. 59. See also Karl Ferdinand Werner, "La genèse des duchés en France et en Allemagne," in *Vom Frankenreich zur Entfaltung Deutschlands und Frankreichs*, pp. 278–310; idem, "Kingdom and Principality in Twelfth-Century France," in Reuter, *The Medieval Nobility*, pp. 243–90; and Benjamin Arnold, *Princes and Territories in Medieval Germany*, pp. 88–95.

[22] Karl Ferdinand Werner, "Quelques observations au sujet des débuts du 'duché' de Normandie," in *Droit privé et institutions régionales*, pp. 691–709.

[23] Janet L. Nelson, *Charles the Bald*, pp. 248–49.

[24] Tellenbach, "Zur Erforschung des hochmittelalterlichen Adels," p. 331. Jean-Pierre Poly and Eric Bournazel, *The Feudal Transformation*, pp. 18–25.

turies.[25] Increasingly, conflicts had to be resolved not by definitive ruling of the count's court but through negotiation that often merely reduced the level of disagreement.[26] Although in some areas the counts held onto their functions longer than in others, generally by the eleventh century justice was no longer in the hands of men appointed, ultimately, by the kings. Instead, just as tenth-century counts had gradually come to exercise in their own names functions their ancestors had exercised in the name of the king, so in the eleventh century many of the counts' former functions were taken over by a new group of men, the castellans (lords of castles).

Even after public authority was no longer seen as proceeding directly from the king, all contemporary sources agreed that a good noble was one who ruled well. Of course, such a consensus carried with it the implication that a great many nobles ruled badly. A twelfth-century biographer of Count Geoffrey V of Anjou described him as "a lover of law, a guardian of peace, a conqueror of his enemies, and helper of the oppressed," whose only real problem was not keeping a tight enough rein on the apparently quite serious abuses of his agents, who were here blamed for any shortcoming in comital rule.[27] In spite of all the difficulties that the great mass of of the population must have had with warlike nobles in their midst, these same nobles were their only source of justice and order.

Knighthood and Warfare

The operational definition of nobility I have given here, as characterized by wealth, power, and birth, leaves out what some might consider the chief attribute of a medieval noble: fighting on horseback with sword and armor. Indeed, this vision is no mere modern construct; twelfth- and thirteenth-century romances also put an enormous stress on such fighting. But it was *not* originally part of any

[25] Bisson, "Nobility and Family," pp. 600–601. This disintegration of comital power at the end of the tenth century was first noted by Georges Duby for the Mâconnais in *La société aux XIe et XIIe siècles dans la région mâconnaise*, pp. 137–41. It has since been confirmed in many other regions, though not all. Some counts, such as the count of Anjou, in fact increased their power in this period. See Bernard S. Bachrach, *Fulk Nerra*.

[26] Patrick J. Geary, *Living with the Dead in the Middle Ages*, pp. 125–60.

[27] Jim Bradbury, "Geoffrey V of Anjou, Count and Knight," in Christopher Harper-Bill and Ruth Harvey, eds., *The Ideals and Practice of Medieval Knighthood III*, p. 30.

"Strong of Body, Brave and Noble"

description of nobility, and nobles existed, wealthy, powerful, and proud of their ancestors, long before the romances. In the early Middle Ages, when most fighting was done on foot (as had also been the case in the Roman Empire), all free men were expected to participate in royal wars.[28] It was only in the High Middle Ages that warfare, or at least mounted warfare, became a specifically aristocratic pursuit, and even so, all armies were accompanied by crowds of men on foot, some of whom did fight as well as make camp, cook, and take care of the horses.

Scholars, extrapolating backward from the late Middle Ages, once assumed that knighthood (implying warfare on horseback) was identical with nobility in the High Middle Ages.[29] In fact, however, although the terms "knight" and "noble" could be used almost interchangeably by the fourteenth century, when the knights first appeared they were sharply differentiated from the noble lords they served.[30]

There is today a rough consensus on the role and position of knights; and here again, it is no static picture. Knights emerged as a new group around the year 1000.[31] The term *miles*, meaning knight (*milites* in the plural), is first found in the documents in the final decades of the tenth century. Centuries earlier, the word applied to the Roman foot soldier, but it had not been used for generations, and the scribes of the year 1000 meant something quite different when they used it. For them a *miles* was a fighting professional, not a noble himself but one who served the nobility. Most commonly knights fought on horseback, and indeed, the documents sometimes used the term *caballarius* (from a late Latin word for horse) as a synonym for

[28] Philippe Contamine, *War in the Middle Ages*, p. 17.

[29] This was the view of Marc Bloch, *Feudal Society*, pp. 293–355.

[30] Evergates, *Feudal Society*, pp. 113–27. Warlop, *The Flemish Nobility*, 1:11–17. Bumke, *The Concept of Knighthood*, pp. 22–45. Georges Duby, "La diffusion du titre chevaleresque sur le versant méditerranéen de la Chrétienté latine," in Philippe Contamine, ed., *La noblesse au moyen âge*, pp. 39–70. Jean Flori, "Chevalerie, noblesse et lutte de classes au moyen âge." Jean Scammell, "The Formation of the English Social Structure." Léopold Genicot, "La noblesse médiévale: Encore!" pp. 184–87.

[31] Even Karl Ferdinand Werner, who has attempted to establish unbroken continuity in noble lineages and noble rule from Carolingian times to the High Middle Ages, still considers the rise of the knights "revolutionary." "Important Noble Families in the Kingdom of Charlemagne," in Reuter, *The Medieval Nobility*, p. 180. One of the few scholars who still equates nobility and knighthood is Barthélemy, doing so because of their shared power over the rest of society, and even he notes that eleventh-century knights were of lower social status than the nobles; *La société dans le comté de Vendôme*, pp. 507–13.

A rather ferocious mustached knight stands on guard as one of the twelfth-century pillars of the church of Notre-Dame-en-Vaux at Châlons-sur-Marne. He carries a long, triangular shield emblazoned with the sign of the cross, perhaps indicating a Crusader. He wears mail gloves and boots as well as a long chain mail shirt.

"Strong of Body, Brave and Noble"

miles. The chronicler Richer, writing at the end of the tenth century, distinguished between *pedites,* foot soldiers, and *milites,* whom he also called *equites.*[32]

It should be stressed that the earliest "knights" formed no uniform class, for there was a great deal of social inequality among them. What identified them was their warrior function, even when that function was temporary. A man was a knight only as long as he wielded the arms his lord had issued to him, often briefly. Nor was eleventh-century knighthood synonymous with chivalry, which did not develop until the twelfth century, or, indeed, with any particular standard of behavior.[33] Robbers and mercenaries could be described as knights as easily as honorable and loyal soldiers. There was no equation between knights and vassals either. Nevertheless, knights, cavalry fighters of fairly undistinguished backgrounds, quickly became an important part of the medieval social landscape. From the first, the idea of service was integral to the concept of knighthood. Knights followed their lords to war, to regional councils, and on excursions to cities and monasteries.[34]

In many ways these knights of the eleventh century were closer to peasants than they were to their noble lords. Many seem to have been servile, legally unfree. In France the social status of knights and nobles drew closer together in the twelfth century until they eventually fused as a single group in the thirteenth century, but in some other areas, knights continued to be of low social or legal status. Until the late Middle Ages, in the German Empire, serf-knights, *ministeriales,* had to gain the permission of their lords to marry, as did any serf, even after they had become the de facto nobility of their regions.[35] A similar social gulf also persisted in some French-speaking areas that bordered the Empire.

[32] Richer, *Histoire de France* 4.23, 2:180.

[33] Jean Flori, *L'essor de la chevalerie,* p. 6. For English parallels, see Richard Barber, "When Is a Knight Not a Knight?" in Stephen Church and Ruth Harvey, eds., *Medieval Knighthood V,* pp. 1–17; David Crouch, *The Image of the Aristocracy in Britain,* pp. 120–68; and Matthew Strickland, *War and Chivalry,* pp. 19–28.

[34] Georges Duby, *La société mâconnaise,* pp. 191–201. Idem, "The Origins of Knighthood," in *The Chivalrous Society,* pp. 158–70. Lucien Musset, "L'aristocratie normande au XIe siècle," in Contamine, *La noblesse au moyen âge,* pp. 71–96. Tony Hunt, "The Emergence of the Knight in France and England." Jean Flori, *L'idéologie du glaive,* pp. 24–28.

[35] Flori, *L'idéologie du glaive,* pp. 55–57. John B. Freed, *Noble Bondsmen,* pp. 30–32. Benjamin Arnold, "Instruments of Power: The Profile and Profession of *Ministeriales*

Why should knights, men who fought for their lords on horseback rather than on foot, men armed by these lords with high-quality weapons, have first appeared when they did at the very end of the tenth century? Part of the answer is certainly the improvements in horse breeding and the development of metallurgical techniques that made possible fine swords, good armor, and large numbers of horseshoes. The spread of the stirrup, which was unknown in the ancient world but seems to have become relatively common in the West in the tenth century, made fighting on horseback a much more realistic possibility than it had been when the rider was always in danger of slipping off.[36]

The military equipment of the mounted warrior and the training and practice needed to master its use were so expensive and time-consuming that they were out of the question for ordinary people.[37] The foot soldier armed with an axe was no match for the armored warrior on horseback, and fighting became increasingly restricted to a group of professionals who put all their energies into it and either could afford to buy their equipment themselves (the nobles) or else, as was the case with the knights, had it provided to them by their lords. It should be stressed again that fighting with expensive knightly weapons did not automatically raise the social status of a lowborn knight, for the weapons only reflected the power and wealth of his lord.

We can see this increased professionalization of warfare in the poem Bishop Adalbero of Laon wrote for King Robert II in the 1020s, in which he divided society into three groups, the fighters, the workers, and those who pray.[38] Although, as I discuss in Chapter 2, Adal-

---

within German Aristocratic Society, 1050–1225," in Bisson, ed., *Cultures of Power*, pp. 36–55.

[36] Scholars no longer believe that the stirrup was introduced into the West in the eighth century, or that with its introduction came "the invention of feudalism." Bernard S. Bachrach, "Charles Martel, Mounted Shock Combat, the Stirrup, and Feudalism." Idem, "*Caballus et Caballarius* in Medieval Warfare," in Howell Chickering and Thomas H. Seiler, eds., *The Study of Chivalry*, pp. 183–98. For medieval horse breeding, see Matthew Bennett, "The Medieval Warhorse Reconsidered," in Church and Harvey, eds., *Medieval Knighthood V*, pp. 19–40.

[37] Kelly DeVries, *Medieval Military Technology*. For the very finely crafted swords, see Ian Peirce, "The Development of the Medieval Sword, c. 850–1300," in Harper-Bill and Harvey, *Ideals and Practice of Knighthood III*, pp. 139–58.

[38] Adalbero, "Carmen," lines 295–96, p. 22. Georges Duby, *The Three Orders*.

bero was not presenting an accurate assessment of eleventh-century society, it is important to note that he considered the functions of fighters and workers fundamentally distinct, and his formulation was new. In previous centuries the most prevalent categorical distinction applied to laymen had been between the free and the servile, with nobles and free peasants grouped together into a single category. Adalbero still did not put nobles into a distinct group, since he was less interested in social status than in function, but he did put the knights and nobles together by reason of their fighting, leaving both free and servile peasants together in his category of workers.

Castles

Linked with the appearance of knights was the development of castles. Fortifications, of course, had a long history, going back to the Bronze Age, and a number of French cities had had substantial walls since the early Middle Ages. The term *castrum* had for some time been used at least intermittently to mean a public center of defense or a fortified place.[39] But the stone keeps that began to spread across the major routes, hilltops, river crossings, and political frontiers of France around the year 1000 were more than fortifications. These castles combined two functions that had been separate in the early Middle Ages, the defensible fortress and the elegant palace—that is, both the place where men gathered in times of war and the private home for the family and attendants of a rich and powerful lord. They were not meant to be used only in times of fighting but to be the permanent residences of individual lords.[40]

Castles developed and spread through most of France at nearly the same time, in the final years of the tenth century and especially in the eleventh.[41] In England, by contrast, virtually all the castles postdate

[39] Monique Gramain, " 'Castrum,' structures féodales et peuplement en Biterrois au XIe siècle," in *Structures féodales et féodalisme dans l'Occident méditerranéen*, pp. 119–34.

[40] Joachim Bumke, *Courtly Culture*, pp. 103–19. Gabriel Fournier, *Le château dans la France médiévale*, p. 65. Palaces persisted as separate structures, especially for bishops, even after the emergence of castles.

[41] Xavier Barral I Altet, "Le paysage architectural de l'an mil," in Delort and Iogna-Prat, eds., *La France de l'an mil*, pp. 174–76. This is true even in southern France, long thought to have been slow in development of such institutions as compared to the north. See José-Maria Font Ruis, "Les modes de détention de châteaux dans la 'Vielle

Beaugency, on the Loire, is one of the oldest surviving castles. Other than the buttressing and some elegant window treatments located high up, this square stone keep still looks much the same as it did when the count of Anjou had it built at the end of the tenth century.

the 1066 Norman Conquest; indeed, William the Conqueror used the building of castles as a major tool in consolidating power over his new country.[42] In Germany, where the term *Burg,* in both medieval and modern usage, can mean earthenwork fortifications or even a town as well as a castle, the chronology is less clear, but there, too, stone castles seem to have become an important part of the landscape by the twelfth century. Thus, like Adalbero's new formulation of society's structures, the appearance of castles is an indication that the nobles, whose homes had earlier stressed elegance over defense, were increasingly seeing themselves as military leaders in the eleventh and twelfth centuries.

Castles as we are accustomed to picture them were a feature only of the High Middle Ages, the eleventh through thirteenth centuries. By the end of the fourteenth century the development of gunpowder and cannons had made castles vulnerable, since sustained cannon fire could take down even a tall castle wall. As a result squat, massive military forts began to be built by those who wanted defense, while elegant châteaux with large windows were erected by those who wanted a residence combining charm with a statement of wealth and status, recognizing that security no longer came with high walls and arrow slits.

It is striking that castles were built *not* during the most violent periods of the ninth and tenth centuries, when Vikings and Magyars were making their incursions, but rather during the eleventh century, when these invasions were past.[43] In part of course one needs a certain amount of time and breathing space to build a castle; one cannot spot the Viking sails coming up the river and then decide that some high walls might be useful. But to a certain extent castles were not meant to be frequent and active participants in violent battles—al-

---

Catalogne' et ses marches extérieures du début du IXe au XIe siècles," in *Les structures sociales de l'Aquitaine, du Languedoc, et de l'Espagne au premier âge féodal,* pp. 63–72; Richard Landes, *Relics, Apocalypse, and the Deceits of History,* pp. 25–28; and Charles Higounet, "Structures sociales, 'castra,' et castelnaux dans le sud-ouest aquitain (Xe–XIIIe siècles)," in *Structures féodales et féodalisme,* pp. 104–16.

[42] Orderic Vitalis pointed out this strategy at the beginning of the twelfth century, and his conclusions are supported by modern archaeology. Orderic Vitalis, *The Ecclesiastical History* 4, 2:218. Richard Eales, "Royal Power and Castles in Norman England," in Harper-Bill and Harvey, *Ideals and Practice of Knighthood III,* pp. 49–78. N. J. G. Pounds, *The Medieval Castle in England and Wales,* pp. 3–8.

[43] Poly and Bournazel, *The Feudal Transformation,* pp. 26–28.

though until the fourteenth century they could always function as such if necessary. Rather, they were symbols of power, authority, and even stability. In eleventh-century France, where the central government was much weaker than it was in England or Germany at the same time, the castellans were the givers of justice, the leaders in war, and the collectors of dues and taxes. A castle made that authority visible.[44] It is certainly significant that by the end of the eleventh century nobles began taking the names of their castles as parts of their own names. Even today, the massive walls of a ruined hilltop castle send a clear message ("Don't even *think* about it"), and to the warriors of the High Middle Ages, who themselves lived in castles, the message must have been even clearer. In practice, until the development of gunpowder, castles were so much harder to take than to defend that most were not attacked more than once a generation, if that, and some were not attacked at all.

In the eleventh century many castles were originally built of wood, especially in England, where the "motte and bailey" style was common, consisting of a tower and a steep mound, the "motte." In such castles the lower story of the tower was sunk into the mound, or the tower was built first and then dirt was heaped around it to make the upper stories harder to attack. The motte was generally surrounded by a dry ditch from which the dirt had come to build it. Surrounding this mound was the "bailey," the courtyard where cookhouse, stables, kennels, storerooms, and other structures were located. The entire complex would be encircled by a stockade.[45]

Wooden castles were cheaper and faster to build than stone castles, but they were also harder to defend successfully. In France stone castles first appeared around the year 1000, and by the twelfth century most castle building was in stone. The center of a stone castle, the first part to be built, was the keep, originally a big square three- or four-story tower, situated by preference on a natural rise or on a motte. Enormous amounts of money went into castle building and updating throughout the Middle Ages, and virtually no eleventh- or early twelfth-century castles survive as originally built. Square towers of

[44] Dominique Barthélemy, "Dominations châtelaines de l'an mil," in Delort and Iogna-Prat, eds., *La France de l'an mil*, pp. 101–13.
[45] M. W. Thompson, *The Rise of the Castle*, pp. 48–59. Fournier, *Le château*, pp. 65–80.

Perched on hilltops and other commanding locations, castles sent an intimidating message to those living nearby. Those who lived in their shadows could never forget the power exercised by the lord who ruled there and his knights. The castle of Najac has dominated its village and the adjacent valley since the twelfth century. The parish church, seen at the lower left, is approximately the same age as the castle.

undressed field stone built in the eleventh century were succeeded by round towers of smooth quarried stone in the twelfth century, and improvements and inventions in arcading and fireplaces led to extensive rebuilding. But even while busily remodeling and adding to their castles every generation or so, lords held onto their keeps. Many a castle in which the great hall, the outer walls, and the chapel are all of thirteenth-century construction still has its eleventh-century keep looming over it, a last powerful bastion of defense if the less grim later construction should fail.

The first French castles were built by counts, the most powerful regional lords, whose counties—and, in some cases, whose ancestors—

had been in place for over a century.[46] But others quickly began to build castles of their own, so that a few decades into the eleventh century lords of castles, called castellans, were beginning to be an important part of society. Even a count, if he built several castles (as did the count of Anjou), needed to put representatives into them. By the middle of the eleventh century the castellans were unquestionably a part of the nobility, even though their ancestry was not nearly as exalted as that of the counts, their lords—or former lords (many a count must have been startled when a supposedly loyal man developed an unexpected independent streak once he was behind high stone walls). Many castellans doubtless began as dependents of the counts; in other cases, where the counts' position was weaker, wealthy local landowners simply built their own castles on their own lands.[47]

Local historians of many different parts of France have marked a change in the political structures of their regions a generation or so into the eleventh century (the year 1030 is frequently cited as a turning point).[48] There seems to have been a rapid rise in the power of the castellans, who replaced both the counts and the viscounts in many cases as the chief judicial figures. Public, fiscal property that counts had once held in the king's name became merged into the patrimony of the wealthiest families. Part of the castellans' rise was due to their own strength and the strength of their castles, but in large part it was a symptom of the weakening of the counts' authority. In many French counties, within a roughly thirty- or forty-year period centered around the year 1000, individual comital families suffered dynastic crises that weakened them, and the castellans quickly took advantage of the opportunity to acquire power for themselves.[49]

[46] For an example of a count's castle-building program, see Bernard S. Bachrach, "The Angevin Strategy of Castle Building in the Reign of Fulk Nerra." See also Robert Hajdu, "Castles, Castellans, and the Structure of Politics in Poitou"; and Jim Bradbury, *The Medieval Siege*, pp. 60–66.

[47] Charles Higounet, "En Bordelais: Principes castellas tenentes," in Contamine, *La noblesse au moyen âge*, pp. 97–104. Idem, "Le groupe aristocratique en Aquitaine et en Gascogne (fin Xe–début XIIe siècle)," in *Les structures sociales*, pp. 221–29. Olivier Guillot, *Le comte d'Anjou et son entourage au XIe siècle*, pp. 325–51. Edouard Perroy, "Les Châteaux du Roannais du XIe au XIIIe siècle."

[48] In part our vision of the eleventh century as a period of rapid change is shaped by the chroniclers of that period, through whom much of our information on the earlier Middle Ages is filtered, and who saw their own age as one of transition. See Patrick J. Geary, *Phantoms of Remembrance*.

[49] Poly, *La Provence*, pp. 96–97. Stephen Weinberger, "Cours judiciaires, justice, et responsabilité sociale dans la Provence médiévale." Fournier, *Le château*, pp. 109–14.

The castle of Angers was originally built by the count of Anjou as his capital at the end of the tenth century. The castle was taken over by the king in the thirteenth century, at which time these massive round towers were built. Although built primarily for defense, the towers with their alternating rows of dark and light stones, echoing a similar effect in the walls of Constantinople, were also meant to be a display of wealth and status. The deeply cut ditch that surrounds the castle is now a garden.

Whether dependent on a count or not, whether large or small (and many eleventh-century castles were very small), castles needed a staff of warriors, and here is where the newly emergent knights found a position. These professional fighters, ever ready for war, lived in the castles under the direction of the castellans. Many chroniclers in both the eleventh and twelfth centuries drew connections between castle building and the raids of rapacious warriors against what they called the "wretched people" of the surrounding countryside; castles might be refuges for the populace in times of war, but in times of peace they could be refuges for idle warriors, apt to relieve their boredom with violence.

It is a mark both of the stabilizing effect of castles and of how violent French society still was that the Peace of God movement—an attempt by the bishops to persuade knights and nobles to swear not to harm the defenseless—appeared in France at precisely the same time as knights and castles. That is, society was at least momentarily calm enough, free enough from outside invasions, that the bishops thought it worth making the effort; and yet it was still a common enough event for farmers and merchants to be attacked unprovoked by well-armed knights, often as a part of a private war they were carrying on against other knights, that the bishops felt steps had to be taken.[50]

Beginning in the 980s in southern France, bishops, sometimes assisted by the local counts, began to hold councils to try to reestablish order. It is important not to think of this movement as a simple conflict between laymen and ecclesiastics, for at least a few powerful laymen, such as the duke of Aquitaine, were involved on the side of the bishops from the beginning.[51] Rather, the movement reflected the tension between those who considered themselves the guardians of stability, primarily but not exclusively bishops, and the newly powerful knights and castellans they thought were disrupting that stability.

The Peace of God movement spread northward in a society that was rapidly losing the remains of the old system of public justice. It involved a series of councils in which knights and nobles were persuaded to swear oaths to limit violence against and exactions from the unarmed and clerics. These oaths seem to have originated in forms that had been used for some time in southern France to reinforce the protection of persons and goods dependent on the church and to maintain the right of sanctuary in the churches. The Peace of God is not an indication of some "chivalric ideal"; warriors were not agreeing to follow any code of conduct they had previously accepted but were being persuaded to accept a new standard. The (partial) success of the Peace of God was an indication that knights and nobles

[50] Elisabeth Magnou-Nortier, "The Enemies of the Peace: Reflections on a Vocabulary, 500–1100," in Thomas Head and Richard Landes, eds., *The Peace of God*, pp. 58–59. Stephen D. White, "Feuding and Peace-Making in the Touraine around the Year 1100," pp. 202, 262–63.

[51] Jane Martindale, "Peace and War in Early Eleventh-Century Aquitaine," in Christopher Harper-Bill and Ruth Harvey, eds., *Medieval Knighthood IV*, pp. 147–76. André Debord, "The Castellan Revolution and the Peace of God in Aquitaine," in Head and Landes, *The Peace of God*, pp. 135–64.

were engaged in creating new structures of stability and order to replace those power structures which were going or gone.[52]

By the 1030s and 1040s, the French bishops felt they had made enough headway in persuading the powerful not to attack the helpless that they expanded their efforts by preaching the Truce of God, urging knights and nobles to agree not to kill even *each other* on certain days of the week. The Truce started by establishing Sunday as a day of peace and spread to cover several other days and certain seasons of the year (especially Advent and Lent). The Truce and the Peace of God eventually merged into a single peace movement. The peace councils so flourished that by the end of the eleventh century virtually every ecclesiastical council in France, even those led by the pope (such as the 1095 Council of Clermont, which launched the First Crusade), proclaimed the Peace of God.

The beginning of the movement marked a shift in underlying views of society, from an acceptance of war as the normal occupation of men to the equation of God's will with peace. Although these councils were probably not overwhelmingly successful in reducing the overall level of violence in society—after all, mercenary soldiers first appeared in France in any numbers in the second half of the eleventh century, at the same time the peace movement was at its height—they doubtless made some nobles think (at least) about what they were doing and even occasionally moderate their behavior.[53]

Nobles and Knights

The knights who appeared along with the development of castles, and who were preached against at Peace Councils almost from their first appearance, spent much of the eleventh and twelfth centuries trying to make themselves into nobles. It is not surprising that they should have emulated the lords they served, in their behavior, their

[52] Hans-Werner Goetz, "Protection of the Church, Defense of the Law, and Reform: On the Purposes and Character of the Peace of God, 989–1038," in Head and Landes, *The Peace of God*, pp. 259–61. Landes, *Relics, Apocalypse, and the Deceits of History*, pp. 28–37. Flori, *L'idéologie du glaive*, pp. 135–57. H. E. J. Cowdrey, "The Peace and Truce of God in the Eleventh Century." Jean-François Lemarignier, "Paix et réforme monastique en Flandre et en Normandie autour de l'année 1023," in *Droit privé*, pp. 443–61. For the oaths and their origins, see Elisabeth Magnou-Nortier, *La société laïque et l'église dans la province ecclésiastique de Narbonne*, p. 304.

[53] Georges Duby, "Guerre et société dans l'Europe féodale," pp. 449–82. Contamine, *War in the Middle Ages*, pp. 270–80.

clothing, even perhaps the architecture of the houses in which some lords set them up after they had grown too old to fight (probably in their thirties).

At the same time, while the knights were moving toward the nobles, nobles were moving toward the knights. Knights and nobles still did not constitute a single social group in the twelfth century,[54] but increasingly they adopted many of the same functions. The military function of knights, which had not been a specifically noble attribute in the early Middle Ages, was increasingly adopted as a noble prerogative during the twelfth century. Seals, which castellans started using in the mid- or late eleventh century, virtually always showed them on horseback, carrying a banner or sword. Suger, writing in the mid-twelfth century of the glorious youth of King Louis VI, called him a "marvellous swordsman and brave champion," who was always at the forefront of battle.[55]

By this time, the coming-of-age ceremony for young noblemen was called "knighting." Thus, whereas knights were originally not nobles, nobles could by the twelfth century be knights. The two meanings of "knight," a warrior who served a lord and a noble who had come of age, were expressed by the same Latin term, *miles*, in legal documents and by the same vernacular term, *chevalier*, in Old French. Even the epics and romances, though they called their noble heroes knights, did not in the twelfth century (any more than had the Latin sources of the eleventh century) imply by the word *chevalier* any necessary attributes beyond those of mounted warriors.[56]

But in the thirteenth century in France knights and nobles were fused through a definition of nobility which made their military functions primary and distinctive. Even kings took the title of "knight,"

---

[54] Bernard of Clairvaux, writing to the count of Troyes who joined the Templars in 1125, said that from a rich man he had become a poor man, and from a count a knight, thus putting knights into the same category as poor men, far below counts. Letter 31, *Opera* 7:85.

[55] Georges Duby, "The Diffusion of Cultural Patterns in Feudal Society," in *The Chivalrous Society*, pp. 171–77. Flori, *L'essor de la chevalerie*, pp. 223–35. Brigitte Bedos Rezak, "Medieval Seals and the Structure of Chivalric Society," in Chickering and Seiler, *The Study of Chivalry*, pp. 330–34. Lutz Fenske, "Adel und Rittertum im Spiegel früher heraldischer Formen und deren Entwicklung," in Josef Fleckenstein, ed., *Das ritterliche Turnier im Mittelalter*, pp. 75–160. Suger, *The Deeds of Louis the Fat* 2, p. 30.

[56] W. Mary Hackett, "Knights and Knighthood in *Girart de Roussillon*," in Christopher Harper-Bill and Ruth Harvey, eds., *The Ideals and Practice of Medieval Knighthood II*, pp. 40–45. Linda Paterson, "Knights and the Concept of Knighthood in the Twelfth-Century Occitan Epic."

---

although the word had earlier implied service.[57] For the first time, noble lords had their tombs decorated with images of themselves wearing knightly armor.[58] It is striking that it was only in the thirteenth century, when many people without political standing or noble birth could challenge the older aristocracy at least in terms of wealth, that the nobles felt it necessary to define themselves. Earlier, when the economic and social gap between nobles and everyone else had been much larger, there had been no need for such a definition.

According to the late thirteenth-century definition of "nobility" used, for example, at pretentious tournaments that limited attendance to those of impeccable credentials, one had to have been knighted and, preferably, to be able to prove that all one's grandfathers and great-grandfathers had been knighted as well. This formal knighting, which distinguished a nobleman from the late thirteenth century to the end of the Middle Ages, was a very elaborate, very expensive coming-of-age ceremony that celebrated the young man's mastery of military technique and might require a party that would go on for days. Certainly none of the original knights of the eleventh century, or even the young twelfth-century nobles receiving their first spurs and sword, had gone through anything comparable.

Ironically, this elaborate ceremony, the very expense of which was supposed to keep parvenus from participating, became in many cases too expensive for the nobles themselves. As a result, many men with noble blood ended up spending their whole lives as "squires." The term had originally applied only to someone (not an aristocrat himself) who assisted a noble or knight with his horse and armor, but by the thirteenth century it specified a boy training for knighthood, and finally it meant someone qualified by birth to become a knight who for various reasons had not yet gone through the ceremony.[59]

Because in the late Middle Ages the term "knight" was thus used to indicate wealth, honorable behavior, and noble bloodlines, it is not

---

[57] Georges Duby, "The Transformation of the Aristocracy: France at the Beginning of the Thirteenth Century," in *The Chivalrous Society*, pp. 178–85. Bumke, *Concept of Knighthood*, pp. 72–73. Giovanni Tabacco, "Su nobilità e cavalleria nel medioevo."

[58] Judith W. Hurtig, *The Armored Gisant before 1400*, pp. 2, 188–214.

[59] Matthew Bennett, "The Status of the Squire: The Northern Evidence," in Christopher Harper-Bill and Ruth Harvey, eds., *The Ideals and Practice of Medieval Knighthood*, pp. 1–11. Linda W. Paterson, "The Occitan Squire in the Twelfth and Thirteenth Centuries," in ibid., pp. 133–51. Barthélemy, *La société dans le comté de Vendôme*, pp. 942–47.

surprising that scholars long assumed that the word already had this meaning when it first became prevalent in the eleventh century. But it is important not to read history backward, or to think that a pattern that existed at one period must also have existed earlier, even three centuries earlier. Knights were originally very different from the lords they served, and to assume they had always been the same would be to minimize their generations-long campaign to rise into noble ranks.

Nobilitas, then, can best be understood for the High Middle Ages not as a concrete noun, meaning "the" nobility, but as a collection of attributes and personal gestures. "Nobility" was not something unequivocally assigned to certain members of society or defined unchangingly. It evolved, flourished, and took new directions over the centuries. Originally constituting a powerful sector of society so unequivocally set off from the rest that there was no need to create standards or even definitions of nobility, those who considered themselves noble perceived enough threat to their position by the late thirteenth century that they felt it necessary for the first time to try to delineate noble attributes. Interestingly, the critera used were military, even though fighting had not been an original part of noble self-definition.

Early medieval *nobilitas* had not been strictly equivalent to any other single attribute, such as freedom or service to the king, nor had it resided solely in descent from premedieval Roman senators or Germanic warlords. Rather, those who shared in *nobilitas* possessed a combination of wealth, power to command, and birth to parents (or at least one parent) also considered noble.

A turning point came around the end of the tenth and beginning of the eleventh centuries, when noble ranks began to expand. When dukes and counts built castles to defend their borders and staffed them with castellans—or as ambitious local strongmen built their own castles—the lords of these castles almost immediately came to be considered a part of the nobility. With the spread of castles came the first appearance of knights, armed men fighting on horseback, serving the counts and castellans but initially in no way their social equals.

Over the next two centuries, the knights and the nobles moved toward each other, taking on some of each others' attributes. Those with noble birth, wealth, and position also increasingly wanted to see themselves as great and glorious fighters; at the same time, the knights who served the nobles tried to emulate them and even marry into their ranks. Not until the thirteenth century, when a need was felt for a clear definition of nobility, were knighthood and nobility explicitly equated.

In the next chapter I put the nobles and knights of the High Middle Ages into their social and institutional context. Relations between different members of the aristocracy had to be worked out and institutionalized as the size of that group—and its definition—changed. Kings, on one hand, and increasingly wealthy townsmen, on the other, threatened noble position in the twelfth and thirteenth centuries. The new idea that a noble was a wealthy, glorious, and nobly born warrior on horseback, whom all must obey, was undermined even before it was fully formulated.

CHAPTER TWO

Nobles and Society

Knights and nobles of the High Middle Ages interacted not just with other aristocrats but with the society around them, a society that included kings, townsmen, and peasants. Although only a small proportion of the total population (probably 5 percent at most), the aristocracy was enormously influential. As landlords, lawgivers, powerful fighters, and royal agents, nobles had the power to command new revenues and the resources to spend, to hire, to buy, and to give away on a scale most people could barely imagine.

Throughout the High Middle Ages a shifting set of social structures helped shape the interactions between nobles and the rest of society—and among each other. These structures were never codified, however, and the people of the time who wrote about the functioning of society put into their descriptions as much of what they wanted to see as what they actually saw. Modern scholars therefore have to infer the underlying social structures and the unwritten and continuously changing norms that governed human interactions.

Recently a great deal of scholarly effort has gone into disproving certain very persistent myths about medieval social structures, which continue to appear everywhere from high school textbooks to *Time* magazine to scholarly monographs by those whose own area of specialization is not medieval social history. It seems wise, in view of this persistence, to begin by saying what medieval society was *not*. Most important, it was not neatly divided into "three orders," however appealing it may be to visualize a society made up of praying churchmen, fighting warriors, and working workers. People's duties, responsibilities, and horizons were of course limited by circumstance and situation, but not by membership in any predefined "order."

Interestingly enough, this appealing vision of tripartite society was created in the Middle Ages, in the early part of the eleventh century. It was first fully enunciated by Bishop Adalbero of Laon, who wanted to keep the monks, "those who pray," out of government, where he thought they were interfering with "those who fight." Ironically, Adalbero thought it entirely appropriate that *he*, a bishop, counsel the king.[1]

Adalbero's vision of society took some time to become popular. It was different from most earlier attempts to describe how society was structured; before the eleventh century, most commentators (with no greater claim to accuracy than Adalbero) had divided society into two groups, the free and the unfree, or sometimes into four: monks, priests, lords, and workers. It was also different from many of the constructs that followed. A theorist writing a century after Adalbero also divided society into three categories, but he put bishops, abbots, kings, and counts in the upper order; priests, townsmen, and knights (*milites*) in the middle; and peasants and serfs at the bottom. Suger, counselor of King Louis VI, used language that echoed Adalbero's, but his three groups, "those who prayed, those who toiled, and the poor," were in *addition* to the powerful and the warlike. Andreas Capellanus in the late twelfth century, categorizing society in order to suggest how love might be pursued between different groups, distinguished five: the upper nobility, the nobility, the middle class, peasants, and clergy.[2]

Adalbero's tripartite picture was catchy, however, and by the thirteenth century, more theorists were picking it up.[3] Its crowning moment occurred at the beginning of the fourteenth century, when King Philip IV, feeling he needed a more or less united France at his back in his quarrels with the pope, called the first Estates General, summoning representatives of French society to court according to their "es-

[1] Adalbero, "Carmen ad Rotbertum regum," lines 295–96, p. 22. Georges Duby, *The Three Orders*. Claude Carozzi, "Les fondements de la tripartition sociale chez Adalbéron de Laon." Jean Flori, *L'idéologie du glaive*, pp. 158–65.

[2] Giles Constable, "The Structure of Medieval Society according to the *Dictatores* of the Twelfth Century," p. 255. Suger, *The Deeds of Louis the Fat* 2, p. 29. Andreas Capellanus, *The Art of Courtly Love*.

[3] It was by no means generally accepted even at the end of the thirteenth century. Susan Reynolds, *Kingdoms and Communities in Western Europe*, pp. 316–17.

tates": churchmen, nobles, and everybody else. Adalbero's vision then, three centuries after it was first articulated, had become an organizing element of French royal government. Though not a particularly important element, the Estates General did persist until the Revolution of 1789. That the tripartite division of society was far from universal, however, is signaled by the medieval English Parliament. Much more important in government and nearly two generations older than the French Estates General, it was divided into only two houses, the Lords, which included *both* churchmen and nobles, and the Commons, the "everybody else" group, which, in spite of its name, was composed not of people we would consider "common" but rather of wealthy merchants and knights who were still not of sufficiently elevated status to be Lords.

In practice, the boundaries between what Adalbero would have liked to make into distinct orders were always porous. The leaders of the church and the leaders of secular society came from the same social group, for example, and the majority of monks also came from aristocratic ranks. The nobility thus overlapped with "those who pray," and with members of Adalbero's third category as well. The knights were not considered noble in Adalbero's time, or even a century later. Yet they were certainly not mere workers, and throughout the High Middle Ages they emulated and married people of noble blood. Moreover, even in the early eleventh century, "those who work" was not an especially accurate description of everyone who was not a noble or a churchman, and it became even less accurate in the twelfth and thirteenth centuries. Adalbero's schema left out what was by then a flourishing urban society of merchants and craftsmen who bought from and supplied the rural nobility. Merchants who had made their fortunes set themselves up in town to live as much like aristocrats as possible, sometimes marrying women from aristocratic backgrounds.

Clearly, society was much more complex than any simple model can show, and nobles had relations with all the other sectors. In this chapter, I begin by describing the king's role. Next, I discuss relations among nobles or between nobles and knights, concentrating on fiefholding relationships, often called "feudalism." Finally I outline some of the ways in which nobles interacted with both urban society and the peasantry, leaving their relations with the church for Chapter 5.

Nobles and the King

Kings were members of the nobility, able to confer power on other nobles and yet deriving their own power from the consent of their fellow nobles. The rule of kings, like the counties and duchies, had roots in the ninth century.[4] In the beginning and until the end of the twelfth century, the office of king was elective in France, and the electors were the most important nobles and bishops of the kingdom, or at least whichever of these men were present at the council where the new king was elected. The office, nevertheless, also rapidly became hereditary, and kings were careful to have their eldest sons formally elected during their own lifetimes.

From the eleventh through thirteenth centuries, the French kings became steadily stronger, with wider-ranging powers, thus threatening the position of the nobility.[5] The eleventh-century kings of France were fairly weak politically, but they had an important, almost sacred, ritual position, and no one tried to challenge them for the throne. Kingship itself was special even without practical political advantages: only kings were crowned, and they were imbued with Old Testament sacerdotal symbolism. Beginning with Robert II at the beginning of the eleventh century, the French believed their kings could even heal the skin disease scrofula by touch alone. In practical terms, nevertheless, kings had much less power than the great French dukes and counts—certainly collectively and in some cases individually. The eleventh-century kings had direct control of less territory, influenced elections in fewer monasteries and bishoprics, and were more openly ignored by the regional castellans than were the dukes of Normandy or Aquitaine or the counts of Anjou.[6]

In the twelfth and thirteenth centuries, however, the Capetian kings of France steadily increased their authority, in competition with

[4] Karl Ferdinand Werner, "Kingdom and Principality in Twelfth-Century France," in Timothy Reuter, ed. and trans., *The Medieval Nobility*, pp. 243–90.

[5] Jean Dunbabin, *France in the Making*, pp. 133–40, 162–69, 256–68. Gabrielle M. Spiegel, *Romancing the Past*, pp. 11–13.

[6] Geoffrey Koziol, *Begging Pardon and Favor*, pp. 109–73. Andrew W. Lewis, *Royal Succession in Capetian France*, pp. 122–23. Marc Bloch, *The Royal Touch*. Jean-Pierre Poly, "Le capétien thaumaturge: Genèse populaire d'un miracle royal," in Robert Delort and Dominique Iogna-Prat, eds., *La France de l'an mil*, pp. 282–308. Jean-Pierre Poly and Éric Bournazel, *The Feudal Transformation*, pp. 337–39. Jean-François Lemarignier, *Le gouvernement royal aux premiers temps capétiens.*

A king, wearing his crown and holding the scepter that represented his authority, was carved into one of the pillars of the church of Notre-Dame-en-Vaux at Châlons-sur-Marne. This particular king was most likely the biblical King David, but he is portrayed in twelfth-century garb.

"Strong of Body, Brave and Noble"

that of the nobility.[7] The kings had not given the dukes and counts their noble status and thus could not take it back, but by the thirteenth century the kings could ennoble those who served them, thus creating rivals for the longer-established aristocracy.[8] Although it was quite clear in the High Middle Ages that counties and duchies were hereditary, and the twelfth-century kings could not reassign counts as the ninth-century kings had done, during the twelfth century the king did persuade the counts and dukes that they were his vassals and thus owed him homage.

Not long after castellans began exercising the judicial functions that had once been exclusive to the counts, the kings and royal courts began absorbing more and more legal business. Moreover, the kings began to build the foundations of a formidable military apparatus independent of their counts' and dukes' military service. Rather ironically, at the same time as the nobles were increasingly defining themselves by their military function, kings were fighting many of their own wars with lowborn mercenaries. Thus the eleventh century in many ways might be considered the origin of the real local power of the French castellans, increasingly independent of the counts and dukes. But the eleventh century also began the growth in royal power, which in the twelfth and thirteenth centuries was centralized as a national government, a government whose functions threatened noble status and power.

Although the French dukes and counts gradually came under the sway of the king, in other countries their equivalents, the German princes and English barons, maintained much more autonomy. In England in 1215, the barons forced King John to sign Magna Carta, the great charter spelling out the principle that the king was not above the law, which historians much later identified as the "foundation of English liberties." Some have sought the origins of this principle in Anglo-Saxon England or even in the German forests before the Angles and Saxons crossed the channel to Britain. It seems much more likely, however, that its immediate inspiration was the developing canon law of the church, which spelled out due process for the ac-

---

[7] Elizabeth M. Hallam, *Capetian France*, pp. 111–203. For the growth of power of the French king around the year 1200, see John W. Baldwin, *The Government of Philip Augustus*. For an example of kings challenging the position of their powerful counts, see Michel Bur, *La formation du comté de Champagne*.

[8] Léopold Genicot, "La noblesse médiévale: Pans de lumière et zones obscures," p. 351.

cused and the principle that the ruler—even the pope—was subject to the law. After all, Stephen Langton, archbishop of Canterbury, helped draft Magna Carta and is the first of the great lords of England mentioned in it. But it was primarily the secular barons who, in subsequent centuries, provided a constant check on the power of the English kings, until James I in the early seventeenth century, well after the end of the Middle Ages, first enunciated the concept of the divine right of kings.

In Germany the great princes had more opportunities to develop their own power, for the king of Germany in the twelfth and thirteenth centuries was also Holy Roman Emperor and felt compelled to act as king of Italy, the other major portion of his Empire. The king's absence in Italy, together with the repeated outbreak of conflicts between emperor and pope during this period, gave the princes the latitude they needed for independent action. But the continued strength of these princes was not merely a result of a failure of kingship, for given the limitations of their circumstances, the German kings did their best to extend their jurisdiction and governing authority. Rather, the German princes, even more than the English barons, established independent power to balance that of the kings. They made their presence felt by expanding territorial authority from their own hereditary power centers, by means of political maneuvering, jurisdictional reform, and exploitation of the growing economy. The German kings, occupied with imperial duties that the princes and kings alike considered vital, encouraged German nobles, much more than either the French or English kings encouraged their nobles, to develop their own regional jurisdictions.[9]

The establishment of strong centralized royal government in France, then, cannot be seen as inevitable. And even there, where in the thirteenth century Louis IX won the affection of his subjects and in the fourteenth century his grandson Philip IV could count on the backing of Frenchmen even against the pope, the nobles were key political figures. No French king of the High or Late Middle Ages could govern without at least some measure of approval from his great lords, and if the kings developed a strong, bureaucratic state it was at least in part because the nobles let them.

[9] Benjamin Arnold, *Princes and Territories in Medieval Germany.*

Fief Holding and Feudalism

One of the most important developments in the relationship between nobles and knights—and with the king—was the rise of fief holding in the eleventh and twelfth centuries. To understand this key institution, it is necessary to clear away a lot of the underbrush associated with the word "feudalism," for this term, laden with unexamined and outdated assumptions, often seriously misleads those trying to understand the Middle Ages.

The word "feudalism" might at first glance appear valid, inasmuch as it comes from a genuine medieval Latin word, *feudum*. A *feudum*, usually translated as "fief," was a piece of property which one aristocrat, called the vassal, held for his lifetime from another, his lord, in return for loyal support. Fiefs were given in return for fidelity, not for a monetary rent, and fief holding involved only the aristocracy, not the great mass of society. Fief-holding arrangements were a development of the eleventh century, when it first became common for aristocrats to use grants of property to cement sworn alliances with each other, and of the twelfth century, when the format of the oaths and obligations entailed in a fief became increasingly standardized.

If fief holding in the High Middle Ages were all that was meant by "feudalism," the word might well be acceptable, despite the universality the -*ism* ending unfortunately implies about what was actually a very narrow phenomenon.[10] But over the last three centuries the word has been loaded with a multitude of other meanings. Scholars and the popular press alike have used the term in so many different ways—many of them mutually exclusive and even contradictory—that it is often impossible to carry out a productive discussion about the various institutions that might be described as "feudalism." Everyone who uses the term seems to have his or her own definition. Elizabeth Brown over twenty years ago concluded that the term "feudalism" had become virtually devoid of meaning and thus proposed that it be entirely dropped from scholarly discussions—an eminently sensible suggestion that has regrettably not yet been fully adopted.[11]

[10] The narrowness of the place fief holding occupied in overall medieval society and politics has most recently been stressed by Susan Reynolds, *Fiefs and Vassals*.

[11] Elizabeth A. R. Brown, "The Tyranny of a Construct."

Part of the problem is that "feudalism" is not a medieval term. It was created in the seventeenth century by historians to describe what I would prefer to call "fief holding," a system linking aristocrats together with each other via oaths of loyalty and conditional transfers of property. But all sorts of other meanings began to be attached to the word soon after it was coined. During the French Revolution, it was seized upon as a synonym for "old-fashioned" or "outmoded." Thus, when the ancien régime was dismantled during the summer of 1789, and such elements of privilege as noble exemption from royal taxes, or exclusive hunting preserves, and the selling of judicial office were eliminated, the delegates to the National Assembly announced that they were getting rid of "feudalism." None of these privileges had anything to do with the fiefs the people who coined the word "feudalism" had thought they were describing. Indeed, none of the privileges abolished in August 1789 were even medieval; all had developed in subsequent centuries. Yet this equation of "feudalism" with special privileges for a small sector of society has persisted. When the popular press calls developing countries of the twentieth century "feudal," this is usually what is meant.

But the biggest difficulties with the word "feudalism" derive from its adoption by Karl Marx in the nineteenth century. To its original, seventeenth-century meaning of a form of social institution linking aristocrats together (an institution that began in the High Middle Ages) and its eighteenth-century meaning of legal privilege (which, in fact, developed in the postmedieval period), Marx added a third meaning: economic exploitation of peasants (of a sort that began in the late Roman Empire). His view of economic forces was bound up with a particular vision of Western history, in which the exploitation of slaves in antiquity was directly replaced in the Middle Ages by the exploitation of serfs. For him, "feudalism" was a counterpart to "slavery," even though he considered the subjugation of serfs somewhat of an improvement over slavery. For Marx, "feudalism" extended from the end of antiquity until the French Revolution, when it was replaced by exploitation of the urban proletariat under "capitalism."

Marx was certainly no medieval historian. Medievalists who consider themselves Marxists have adopted his concern for the poor and oppressed but not his tidy vision of serfs being exploited in a uniform way for twelve hundred years, from the sixth century to the eighteenth.[12] Nevertheless, Marx's use of the word put an end to any possibility that "feudalism" might be usefully employed to describe the complex and dynamic social patterns which actually characterized the Middle Ages.

One might have hoped that after a word had been used in such highly discrepant social, legal, and economic senses (to say nothing of its application to institutions that developed a millennium or more apart), it could be jettisoned as no longer useful. Instead, in the twentieth century there have been repeated attempts to retain the term while adding even more layers of meaning to it. "Feudalism" has sometimes taken on political significance, describing a system in which power is decentralized, held by many different people acting essentially independently, so that the wealthy became the de facto political leaders. More weakly but even more pervasively, "feudal" is sometimes used as a synonym for "noble," so that every castle becomes a "feudal" castle, the Crusades become an exercise in "feudal" warfare, and monasteries that buried their noble patrons become "feudal" churches. In the extreme version, "feudal" is simply a synonym for "medieval," on the assumption that we need a single word (*other* than "medieval") to describe a society that included both fief holding and landlord-peasant relationships. Thus, we read of "feudal times" or "feudal society."[13]

Clearly, if the term can mean a form of political organization, a model of economic exploitation, a type of social institution, legal privileges, or even, very vaguely, "the way things were back then," its continued use can only obscure meaning. Many medievalists, especially in the United States, have dropped the term entirely, leaving it to scholars of the French Revolution or Marxist thought (since at least they seem to know what they mean by it), while trying to remind them that the characteristics of the ancien régime were not those of medieval society. French scholars, while recognizing the problem,

[12] For example, the Marxist historian G. E. M. de Ste. Croix resists characterizing serfdom as "feudalism." *The Class Struggle in the Ancient Greek World*, pp. 267–69. Chris Wickham has proposed a modified Marxist definition of "feudalism" as a mode of production in which tenants, not necessarily serfs, paid rents to a monopolistic landowner class. "The Other Transition."

[13] This is the sense in which it is used by Poly and Bournazel in an otherwise thoughtful work, *The Feudal Transformation*, pp. 1–3, 351–57. Susan Reynolds has sought to replace the stereotype of medieval "feudalism" with the concept of "community." *Kingdoms and Communities*.

have tried to cling to the term, using "féodalité" (usually) in the narrow sense of fief holding and "féodalisme" to mean everything else.[14] But the "everything else" remains problematic, and English does not even have the luxury of two terms.

The only unifying feature of this diverse usage is that "feudalism" has virtually always been used pejoratively. It is *bad* that some people have special privileges, that landlords exploit workers, that power is decentralized, or whatever. Hidden in every description of medieval society as an age of feudalism is an a priori moral judgment that the Middle Ages were not as good as modern times. Believing, then, that the term is a clear hindrance to genuine understanding and analysis of the past, I avoid "feudalism" in my discussion. (The adjective "feudal," however, seems unavoidable. In using it, I refer specifically to fiefs.)

With these obfuscations cleared away, it is now possible to examine the medieval social pattern of fief holding. Certainly, it was an element of aristocratic society in the High Middle Ages, and certainly, it must be stressed again, it was a very narrow phenomenon. Not even all the elite were involved in it. Indeed, while fiefs became increasingly common during the twelfth and thirteenth centuries, French nobles continued to own a great deal of land outright, property they held in fief from no one. These "allods" were made up of land which, it was sometimes said, the nobles held only from God. The practice of swearing oneself to the service of a political leader was much older than fiefs and continued in the High Middle Ages with or without them. Originally fief holding was quite ad hoc. When it first appeared it usually involved neighbors, such as two castellans or a castellan and a knight, and it might be used to resolve a quarrel or formalize an alliance.[15] At first, it did not involve the kings; rather, it was a series of relations between aristocrats, in which one lord might be in a position of social or political power over his vassal, but when a different fief

[14] This is the distinction made, for example, by Dominique Barthélemy, "Dominations châtelains de l'an mil," in Delort and Iogna-Prat, eds., *La France de l'an mil*, pp. 101–13. See also Pierre Toubert, "Les féodalités méditerranéen: Un problème d'histoire comparée," in *Structures féodales et féodalisme dans l'Occident méditerranéen*, pp. 1–14.

[15] Pierre Bonnassie, "Les conventions féodales dans la Catalogne du XIe siècle," in *Les structures sociales de l'Aquitaine, du Languedoc, et de l'Espagne au premier âge féodal*, pp. 187–208. Dominique Barthélemy, *La société dans le comté de Vendôme*, pp. 615–18.

was involved the same lord and vassal might switch positions, the lord becoming the vassal and vice versa.

Vassal homage and fiefs began to appear in the records fairly abruptly in the early decades of the eleventh century in France. This was a period of major social transition, when the counts in many parts of France were threatened by the rise of the new castellans, knights first appeared in large numbers, the last of the old judicial courts based on Carolingian models disappeared, the Peace of God was formed to try to deal with endemic violence, and banal lordship (a new form of castellan authority over peasants) began to spread. Marc Bloch, noting these transformations two generations ago, said they marked the beginning of a "second feudal age."[16] Even though it is now clear that the period before the eleventh century, Bloch's "first age," was not in any definable sense "feudal," scholars in the last fifty years have been in remarkable agreement that the early eleventh century marked a real turning point in French social and political history.[17]

Laymen in the late tenth and early eleventh centuries kept very few written records. Fief-holding relationships between them, thus, would not have been recorded, and the precise origins of such a relationship must therefore remain unknown. The earliest known description of feudal obligations, the *forma fidelitatis*, was given by Bishop Fulbert of Chartres around 1020.[18] The bishop had been asked to describe the duties of lord and vassal for the duke of Aquitaine. Clearly the fidelity under discussion here was more than the loyalty kings had been demanding of their subjects for centuries. That the duke had to ask and the bishop had to research his answer indicates that fief holding was not a commonly recognized system in early eleventh-century French society.

[16] Marc Bloch, *Feudal Society*, pp. 59–71.

[17] Modern models of a turning point in the generation centered on the year 1000 grow especially from the work of Georges Duby, *La société aux XIe et XIIe siècles dans la région mâconnaise*, and Jean-François Lemarignier, "Political and Monastic Structures in France at the End of the Tenth and Beginning of the Eleventh Century." For the historiography, see Dominique Barthélemy, "La mutation féodale a-t-elle eu lieu?" Although overly enthusiastic emphasis on the decisiveness of the break has led, in reaction, to greater emphasis on continuities, T. N. Bisson has recently defended the idea of a radical transformation. "The 'Feudal Revolution.' "

[18] Fulbert of Chartres, Letter 51, in *The Letters and Poems*, pp. 91–93. See also David Bates, *Normandy before 1066*, p. 52.

In his answer Fulbert assumed that *fidelitas* was an alliance set up between two aristocrats. The lord granted a fief, a piece of land, to his vassal. The vassal, though he paid no rent for this fief, accepted certain duties and responsibilities, as did the lord in granting it. Fulbert emphasized the negative side of these obligations: the vassal swore not to harm his lord or to act against his interests. In addition, Fulbert noted that the vassal should aid his lord, both physically and with good counsel, and that the lord in turn should swear to be faithful to his vassal. In swearing to help and not hinder his lord, a vassal went from being at least a potential—and sometimes a very real—threat to the lord's interest to being his supporter.

At one time scholars tried to find in Charlemagne's court—if not, indeed, in the Roman clientage system or the war bands of the Germanic tribes—some form of "protofeudalism." (The danger of using such a term to describe Carolingian governmental institutions, of course, is in implying that their only interest or importance was in leading to the rise of fiefs.)[19] Indeed, the view that fief holding originated in the ninth century may at least in part derive from twelfth-century epic poems about Charlemagne and his vassals, in which twelfth-century institutions—including fief holding—were unabashedly transferred to a period three centuries earlier.

Although it was in fact new in the eleventh century, certain elements of vassalage did have similarities to and doubtless roots in earlier social and political structures. Carolingian kings of the ninth and tenth centuries had insisted on the fidelity of their powerful counts, just as Capetian and Plantagenet kings of the end of the twelfth century insisted on the fidelity of their powerful vassals.[20] Even some of the terms used to describe fief holding in the High Middle Ages were the same terms used—although in a different sense—in the ninth century. For example, in the High Middle Ages a fief was sometimes called a *beneficium,* a word used in the ninth century to describe the temporary grant of an office (such as that of count) by the king to a great noble. The difference was that a *beneficium* was assumed to be temporary, something the king normally took back after a few years, whereas a fief was a lifetime grant with a strong presupposition of heritability. Similarly, the ninth-century kings used the term *vassus* for

[19] For examples of older works that found "feudalism" in Charlemagne's court (if not before), see Carl Stephenson, *Feudalism,* and F. L. Ganshof, *Feudalism.*
[20] Heinrich Fichtenau, *Living in the Tenth Century,* pp. 152–56.

their close attendants and retainers, a word very similar to the eleventh-century *vassalus,* even though a ninth-century *vassus* could simply be a boy, with none of the responsibilities of the later vassal.[21]

This carryover of terminology misled scholars until a series of close regional studies began to be published in the past decades. After a large number of regional specialists concluded that "feudalism" was "late" in reaching their regions, scholars realized that in no region did fief holding exist prior to the eleventh century, and the old model of ninth-century fief holding had to be revamped.[22] It is interesting that studies from the south of France have been particularly influential, inasmuch as previous generations of scholars assumed that the Mediterranean littoral was much less "feudalized" than areas farther north.[23] The initial spread of fief holding there, which took place between about 1020 and 1060, seems to have come out of a period of endemic warfare among the newly powerful castellans and between these castellans and the counts, wars fought by *milites.* By the end of the century, fief holding seems to have gained fairly broad acceptance and become widespread. Even in regions that were spared the intense civil wars that marked southern (especially southwestern) France in the first half of the eleventh century, fief holding developed at approximately the same time.

At its fullest development, fief holding never became the tidy pyramid now often seen in high school textbooks. Again, this oversimplified vision does indeed have medieval origins, but it was a desired (and never realized) goal of the kings, not a description of how society was actually structured. By the end of the twelfth century, kings would have liked to see themselves at the apex of a pyramidal structure within which all members of the aristocracy were either directly dependent on them or dependent on lords who were dependent on the king.[24] This goal was, however, impossible to achieve in practice.

Of all western monarchs in the High Middle Ages, the English

[21] Reynolds, *Fiefs and Vassals,* pp. 84–105. Jean-Pierre Poly, *La Provence et la société féodale,* pp. 143–47. Poly and Bournazel, *Feudal Transformation,* pp. 48–49.

[22] Constance B. Bouchard, "The Origins of the French Nobility," p. 531, n. 91. Theodore Evergates, *Feudal Society in the Bailliage of Troyes under the Counts of Champagne,* p. 152.

[23] Pierre Bonnassie, *From Slavery to Feudalism in South-western Europe,* pp. 104–31. Hideyuki Katsura, "Serments, hommages, et fiefs dans la seigneurie des Guilhem de Montpellier."

[24] Poly and Bournazel, *Feudal Transformation,* pp. 202–10.

kings came the closest to establishing something like a feudal pyramid, although they had the advantage of starting with what was essentially a clean political slate in 1066. William the Conqueror's insistence that the men who accompanied him from Normandy hold their English lands from him in fief was an innovation, not the simple importation of an established French "feudal system." In Normandy, as elsewhere in France, fief holding was undeveloped and unsystematic at the time.[25] And even in England in the High Middle Ages, where the great barons did hold in fief from the king, anything that could be construed as a tidy pyramid broke down below them. In the eleventh century the knights and lesser landholders were not organized by any regular system of fiefs granted by the barons, and in the twelfth century many of these landholders became dependent on the king directly, rather than via the king's great vassals.[26] Moreover, even the king himself was not at the apex with regard to all his possessions: he was simultaneously king of England and, as duke of Normandy and, after the middle of the century, duke of Aquitaine and count of Anjou and Touraine, a vassal of the French king for those territories.[27]

The French and German monarchs had much more trouble than the English kings in persuading their great nobles to consider themselves the king's vassals. It is important to note that the increased power of these twelfth-century kings over their nobles was *not* built on a longstanding relationship of lord and vassal. Rather, the nobles gradually agreed to become the kings' vassals. The concept of a hierarchy of fiefs, with the king standing higher than any other lords, seems to have developed in France only in the first half of the twelfth century, and not until the end of the century did the king systematically inventory the fiefs held from him.[28]

More immediately successful were some of the great French dukes and counts, who bullied and threatened the castellans of their regions, starting in the second half of the twelfth century, into agreeing

[25] Emily Zack Tabuteau, *Transfers of Property in Eleventh-Century Norman Law*, pp. 51–65, 95–112. Bates, *Normandy before 1066*, pp. 122–24.

[26] Jean Scammell, "The Formation of the English Social Structure." For the complicated process by which tenurial patterns changed in England in the twenty years after 1066, see Robin Fleming, *Kings and Lords in Conquest England*, pp. 107–231.

[27] Ralph V. Turner, "The Problem of Survival for the Angevin 'Empire.'"

[28] Baldwin, *Government of Philip Augustus*, pp. 259–63. Reynolds, *Fiefs and Vassals*, pp. 115–18.

that they were in fact the vassals of these dukes and counts.[29] The duke of Burgundy, for example, managed in 1197 to persuade the count of Chalon that he held the castle of Auxonne in fief from him and would lose it if he dared pay homage to the count of Champagne.[30] The descriptions of a pyramidal society constructed by political theorists at the great courts in the late twelfth and thirteenth centuries were largely based on wishful thinking.

Fief holding was very much a personal relationship between aristocrats. A vassal received his fief in a ceremony known as "homage," from the Latin *homo*, because the vassal swore to be his lord's "man." (Women too could do homage, although it was rare; female homage was called "feminage.") By the twelfth century the form of this homage was fairly well established. The vassal knelt to make his oaths of fidelity, as a symbol of his subjection to his lord. He might offer his lord a symbolic object, such as his sword, or merely raise clasped hands to him. Then his lord put his own hands around the vassal's upraised hands, drew him up, and kissed him, to symbolize their ultimate equality.[31] Hence the form of homage established a delicate balance between two men who were at the same time social equals and political unequals, one of whom granted property in the fief-holding agreement and one of whom received it.

The delicacy of this balance can be seen most clearly in the fact that a knight or noble could, in essence, impel another to accept him as his vassal. If two men were fighting, say, over control of a castle, one of them—even the one who was losing—could supplicate the other with the request to become his vassal. Such a request was difficult to refuse if made humbly enough. This man would thus receive the castle in fief and gain unquestioned authority over it, in return for recognizing the other as its ultimate lord and giving promises to aid the man he had so recently been fighting. In the twelfth-century epic *Raoul de*

[29] John F. Benton, "Written Records and the Development of Systematic Feudal Relations," in *Culture, Power and Personality in Medieval France*, pp. 275–90. Evergates, *Feudal Society*, pp. 60–95. Thomas Bisson, "Feudalism in Twelfth-Century Catalonia," in *Structures féodales et féodalisme*, pp. 173–92. Reynolds, *Fiefs and Vassals*, pp. 260–76.

[30] Alexandre Teulet, ed., *Layettes du trésor des chartes*, 1:193–94, no. 470. For Count Stephen of Chalon and Auxonne, see Constance Brittain Bouchard, *Sword, Miter, and Cloister*, pp. 278, 314.

[31] One of the clearest descriptions of the ceremony is from the late 1120s, when the new count of Flanders received homage from his vassals. Galbert of Bruges, *The Murder of Charles the Good* 56, pp. 206–7. Ganshof, *Feudalism*, is still useful for its description of the homage ceremony and vassal obligations in the twelfth century.

Cambrai, a count on the verge of defeat tries this strategy, saying he will become Raoul's "vassal on whatever terms you like." In this case, Raoul is too furious to consider such an option, but it was certainly worth a try.[32]

The oaths of support and counsel which had been rather vague in Fulbert's eleventh-century formulation became more specific in subsequent generations. By the twelfth century, it was well understood that a vassal was required to fight for his lord for forty days a year, that he had to help ransom the lord if he were captured, and that he had to help pay the expenses of the wedding of the lord's eldest daughter and the knighting ceremony of his eldest son.[33] Military service was the least exploited aspect of vassal homage; many lords rode to war with their household knights or hired mercenaries, not their vassals.[34] Although by this time the kings had managed to persuade most of the great nobles that the latter were royal vassals, they found it awkward to be limited to forty days' military service a year from them. Quickly the kings began persuading their vassals to pay a fee (scutage) in place of the military service, using these fees to hire professional mercenaries who would fight for however many days a year one wanted as long as they were paid.[35]

In spite of the growing use of such fees, homage remained an intensely personal relationship. In the epic *Raoul de Cambrai,* whose plot turns on fiefs and homage, the honest Bernier initially remains true to Raoul, even though he "is more villainous than Judas," because Raoul is, after all, his feudal lord *(mesires)* to whom he has sworn fidelity. Not until Raoul murders his mother and strikes him until he bleeds does Bernier defy Raoul and his allegiance to him.[36]

In the twelfth century vassal homage was common enough that it became a symbol of the close emotional ties between man and woman and of the relations between God and man. An ideal lover would go down on his knees before the lady of his heart in exactly the

[32] *Raoul de Cambrai* 143, p. 177.

[33] An early version of homage seems to have required that the vassal pay for the marriage of a daughter and the *ransom* of a son. See Tabuteau, *Transfers of Property,* p. 56.

[34] Joachim Bumke, *The Concept of Knighthood in the Middle Ages,* pp. 40–41.

[35] In England scholars once assumed that the replacement of vassals' military service with fees marked a late development, a "bastard feudalism." For a thoughtful discussion of the difficulties of this term and of the early use of mercenaries, see J. M. W. Bean, *From Lord to Patron,* pp. 1–8.

[36] *Raoul de Cambrai* 113, p. 143.

same way a vassal would kneel to his lord. In the early thirteenth-century *Quest of the Holy Grail,* God explicitly tests Perceval to make sure he is his "true knight," completely loyal to the Lord, his "suzerain."[37] In the same period, praying by kneeling with one's hands clasped and upraised became the standard practice. What is now assumed to be the customary attitude of prayer was thus taken directly from the stance of the vassal during the homage ceremony. Earlier, people prayed either standing or lying prone with arms out-stretched; now one "offered" oneself to God as a vassal did to his lord.

The fief itself *(feudum)* made the vassalage agreement between lord and man concrete. It was not an absolutely necessary component of the fidelity of one noble to another,[38] but in most parts of France it performed a central role in homage agreements in the twelfth century. The lord gave the fief to the vassal to hold for his lifetime. Sometimes the fief was symbolized by a glove or something similar that the lord gave his new vassal. Although the lord retained ultimate ownership of this piece of property, he could not take it back or receive the income from it as long as the vassal remained true to his oaths. In some cases a vassal might grant some of his fief to a vassal of his own in fief. This vassal of a vassal was generally known as a *vavassour,* a French word also used in the chivalric romances for a member of the petty nobility.

A knight or noble could simultaneously be the vassal of more than one lord, receiving fiefs from and swearing oaths to each. The difficulty, of course, was that such a vassal would have divided allegiance if two of his lords went to war with each other. To attempt to deal with this problem, the concept of "liege homage" was devised, in which it was made clear that the lord to whom liege homage was given (the "liege lord") would take precedence if there were quarrels involving any other of a vassal's lords. A vassal would do liege homage for an especially important fief. In practice, lords attempted to woo liege vassals with appealing fiefs, and vassals happily promised multiple lords liege homage in return for those fiefs; so

[37] *The Quest of the Holy Grail,* p. 120.

[38] Elisabeth Magnou-Nortier has argued that while oaths of fidelity played a key part in the political order of Languedoc throughout the eleventh century, fiefs are not found in the documents there until the end of the century. "Fidelité et féodalité meridionales d'après les serments de fidelité (Xe–début XIIe siècle)," in *Les structures sociales,* pp. 115–35. More generally, see Reynolds, *Fiefs and Vassals,* pp. 118–23.

multiple liege homage quickly became the same problem multiple ordinary homage had originally been.

Fiefs were not, strictly speaking, hereditary. Because homage was a personal relationship, it had to be renewed every generation. That is, when either the lord or the vassal died, even though there was a strong presupposition that the deceased's heir would take up the responsibilities of lord or vassal, the ceremony had to be repeated. The ambiguity over the heritability of fiefs forms the starting point of *Raoul de Cambrai,* in which the emperor grants the county of Cambrai to someone other than the late count's infant son. Young Raoul tells this fictional emperor, "Everybody knows that a father's fief ought in all justice to pass to his son." Yet the emperor does not agree with what "everybody knows" and sets the plot in motion by trying to make it up to Raoul by giving him someone else's fief! Twelfth-century nobles knew that kings might do such a thing, but they certainly did not like it. The idealized description of a king's duties in "The Coronation of Louis" prominently includes the pointed comment that a good king would "not seize the fief of a young orphaned baron."[39]

By the late twelfth century, the real kings of both France and England would take a fief back temporarily if their vassal's heir was a woman or minor, saying that they were "taking care" of it and, in practice, deriving as much income from it as they could until they could no longer postpone granting it again in fief. But even here, the presupposition was that the fief would be granted again to a member of the same family as soon as a minor boy had reached the age to assume a vassal's duties, or as soon as a female heir had acquired a husband to discharge those duties.

Fief holding actually flourished for only two or three centuries during the High Middle Ages. By late medieval times it had declined to a minor element of the relations among nobles. The development in the fourteenth and fifteenth centuries of royal "orders" of knighthood, elaborate bodies designed to promote and reward loyal service to the sovereign, is an indication that the loyal service to one's lord which fief holding had entailed was no longer sufficient for kings trying to keep their great nobles in line.[40]

[39] *Raoul de Cambrai* 33–34, pp. 43–45. "The Coronation of Louis" 7, in *Guillaume d'Orange,* p. 65.
[40] D'Arcy Jonathan Dacre Boulton, *The Knights of the Crown,* pp. 1–26.

Nobles, Manorialism, and the Rural Economy

At least part of the land an aristocrat held in fief was likely to be agricultural land, on which peasant tenants, hired labor, and even members of the lord's own household grew food for him to sell at market or to serve on his own table. Although the knights of the romances and tales of adventure had very little contact with agriculture, in practice one of the nobility's most important functions was that of landowner and landlord in the rural economy (such lordship is called *seigneurie* or *seigneurie foncière* in modern French). Interestingly, however, the relationship of nobles to the non-nobles under their authority is probably the topic least studied by historians of the aristocracy.[41] Economic historians of the High Middle Ages have preferred to start with the peasants themselves, not with the men from whom they rented.[42] And yet on a daily basis nobles must have devoted far more time to their function as landlord than to their functions as warrior, lawgiver, or chivalric knight.

Nobles were in regular contact throughout the year with the peasants who rented from them and worked for them. Chivalric literature vilifies peasants and characterizes them as stupid and uncouth more often than it expresses sympathy or respect for them.[43] Nevertheless, the nobles needed the peasants. Most of the nobles' food was raised on their own lands, at least partially under their own supervision, and certainly the money that allowed them to buy silks, spices, and the latest armor came from agricultural rents—and they knew it. The rapid agrarian and commercial expansion of the High Middle Ages directly benefited the lords who owned a good deal of the land and controlled many of the mills, markets, and toll bridges. Ordinarily, nobles probably worried more about the agricultural cycle than about adventure. And yet the relationship between noble and peasant was not a simple one.

The modern English term "peasant" comes from the French *paysan*,

---

[41] Thomas N. Bisson, "Medieval Lordship."

[42] The best survey of the agricultural economy of medieval France in the last forty years remains Georges Duby, *Rural Economy and Country Life in the Medieval West*. Among recent works on peasants, Robert Fossier, *Peasant Life in the Medieval West*, focuses on France, and Werner Rösener, *Peasants in the Middle Ages*, discusses Germany.

[43] Linda W. Paterson, *The World of the Troubadours*, pp. 130–33. On the other hand, as Paul Freedman has pointed out, peasants' very poverty and humility could be described as the epitome of Christian virtue. "Sainteté et sauvagerie."

meaning simply a person of the countryside. More specifically, the word means a farmer, especially a farmer whose labor provides the economic support for an aristocratic sector of society. The people who formed the peasant sector were a far more diverse group than the modern stereotype of downtrodden laborers with hoes. For one thing, by no means were all medieval peasants associated with aristocratic landlords; there were always plenty of peasant allodists, those who worked land they owned outright themselves. Moreover, most villages had no castle or manor house associated with them; so even if the local peasants had to pay rents and dues for their land, the castellan was not a daily presence in their lives.

Overall, there must have been a great deal of ambivalence among medieval peasants about the aristocracy. On the one hand, the nobles were admired and emulated and looked to for protection. On the other hand, they could be extremely dangerous. In the modern United States, most law enforcement officers are from working-class backgrounds, rather than from the wealthy segments of society, and yet society as a whole fears the poor rather than the rich. In the Middle Ages society feared the powerful as those most likely to do them harm or seize their goods, even though the only protectors they had were these same powerful men. In most cases, landlords would have been too sensible to harm their peasant tenants actively; after all, their own livelihoods depended on the peasants' energy and success. But such considerations would not have kept a lord from riding merrily through the barley fields of another lord's peasants. And if a peasant's own lord did turn against him, he was essentially helpless against overwhelming force.

Like the nobility, the peasantry constantly changed and developed over the centuries. The economic relationship between noble landlords and peasants dated back to the beginning of the Middle Ages and the final collapse of the Roman system of using large gangs of agricultural slaves to work the fields. Slaves, worked in chains under a harsh overseer, are not particularly efficient economically, and the system depended on a constant supply of new slaves to replace the ones who had been worked to death. Once the curtailment of the Roman wars of conquest cut off the main source of new slaves, the powerful lords of the fifth through seventh centuries stopped relying on slave labor in the fields. The spread of Christianity also played a role, although it was not opposed to slavery per se. After all,

This early thirteenth-century depiction of a knight on the facade of Amiens cathedral represents the virtue of courage, emphasized by the lion on his shield. Seated, he presents not a threat but fortitude against evil and readiness to defend the helpless.

the church had developed in the Roman Empire, the world's biggest slave society, and really expected the equality and brotherhood of all to be manifest only in the next world. Nevertheless, the church preached the virtue of freeing slaves and insisted that free Christians should not be enslaved.

Regardless of the precise balance of influences, at the beginning of the Middle Ages a new economic system developed between those who owned the land and those who worked it, a system now generally known as "manorialism." (It is important *not* to call this form of economic organization "feudalism.") The term "manorialism" has problems of its own, in particular its nonmedieval origins, but at least medievalists do essentially agree on what they mean when they use the term.

At its most basic level, manorialism, from the sixth century through the thirteenth, entailed the division of a landlord's property into two parts. One part, called the "demesne," produced the food for the lord's own household. The other part was divided up into small units, called *mansi* in Latin (*mansus* in the singular), which were rented to peasants. Each *mansus* theoretically constituted enough land to support one peasant family.[44] Since people will always work harder for themselves and their families than they will for a slave driver, early medieval peasants with their own plots of land would both support themselves and reproduce themselves, thus solving the perennial problems of slaveowners: feeding their slaves and acquiring new ones.

The lord would not work his demesne, the land that produced his family's food, with his own hands. In the first centuries of manorialism some of the labor might have been done by household slaves, but for the most part, the peasants to whom the lord had rented *mansi* came and worked on the lord's demesne lands as part of their rent. That is, in return for their own plots of land, the peasants would work for their noble landlord, usually one or two days a week. These "workdays" could be provided by the peasant tenant himself or by a son or representative. Thus, a noble had people to work his demesne lands and raise his food without having to feed them or pay them.

In some ways the relationship between peasant tenants and landlords under manorialism was very similar to the tenant-landlord relationship now familiar to anyone who has rented an apartment. One main difference, of course, was in the form the rents took. Today most landlords want cash. Early medieval landlords wanted labor. These labor dues, however, were usually supplemented by additional rents in cash, say a few pennies a year, and additional produce from the tenant's own *mansus*, say several bushels of wheat or two chickens a year.[45]

In one additional and very important way, however, manorial rents differed from the sorts of rents we now take for granted: they were

---

[44] Rösener, *Peasants in the Middle Ages*, pp. 16–19, 211–18. N. J. G. Pounds, *An Economic History of Medieval Europe*, pp. 51–54.

[45] Theodore John Rivers, "The Manorial System in the Light of 'Lex Baiuvariorum' I, 13."

perpetual, heritable, and unchanging. That is, if a person paid two chickens and a bushel of wheat each year and two workdays each week for his *mansus,* he would *always* pay that much, and his heirs would also pay the same amount. In practice, of course, it can never have worked out in precisely this way, for peasants died without heirs, moved away, or took up additional lands, and both peasants and landlords tried delicately to "remember" their rents as being either higher or lower than the other one thought. Since none or almost none of this agreement would ever have been put in writing, faulty memories must have caused problems even if both sides were trying to be scrupulously honest. But all sectors of society, lords and peasants alike, believed in the force of tradition, which meant that rents should not be raised and that a peasant whose ancestors had worked a particular plot for generations could not be displaced.

One occasionally reads that medieval peasants were "tied to the land" as though this were some great disadvantage. We could also say that the peasants could not be unwillingly removed from land, and that the land was thus more tied to them than vice versa. Even if a landlord sold or gave a piece of land to another person or to a church, or if he granted it in fief to a vassal, the peasants went with it, though they now paid their rents to their new landlord. Thus, whereas early medieval peasants were subject to exactions a modern tenant would find unacceptable, they also enjoyed a high measure of security. They might find themselves suddenly and arbitrarily shifted to the authority of a different lord, but they had the compensation of knowing that they and their descendants would remain on the land their ancestors had cultivated.

The manorial system was never universal. In some parts of France, especially in the south, it was relatively rare; many peasants owned their own land, and many great landowners worked their fields strictly with members of their household, instead of relying on labor dues.[46] Even in areas where manorialism was prevalent, there were always peasants who owned their own land outright. Additionally, a peasant who rented a *mansus* from the local lord might also own a field of his own, or might rent from several different lords. One family might end up with several different *mansi,* or a *mansus* might be subdivided among several families. Some lords had essentially no

[46] Poly, *La Provence,* pp. 99–106.

demesne lands and lived almost entirely from rents in coin and produce. But the basic manorial system, in which aristocrats owned much
of the agricultural land, part of which they rented to peasant tenants
and the rest of which they used to raise food with the work of peasants
who paid much of their rent in labor, was the major system of rural
economic organization from the sixth century until the thirteenth.

This manorial system had obvious advantages for the landlords,
who received both food for themselves and rents with which to buy
luxury goods. But, it has been argued, the organizing aspects of
manorialism also created advantages for the economy as a whole, including the peasants.[47] The landlords were more than greedy thugs;
they were also (not always intentionally) facilitators of economic development. Because they had the capital to invest, they could afford
such technological innovations as the new iron plows that began to
be used in the tenth and eleventh century. Peasants who were ex-
posed to such innovations while working the demesne land could
then decide if they were worth buying—or they could rent the lord's.
By producing more food than his family needed on the demesne
lands and by collecting produce from all his tenants, the lord could
generate a surplus to sell to the towns as these began to grow in the
eleventh century, thus providing a necessary factor in the developing
urban economy.

The biggest change to the manorial system in the High Middle Ages
was the rapid decline in the twelfth and thirteenth centuries in the importance of labor dues.[48] During this period landlords increasingly
"commuted" labor dues to cash payments, so that peasants no longer
worked on the lord's demesne but paid more of their rent in money.
This monetary payment might keep the memory of its original function, being called, for example, the "March raking" payment. The
landlord used this money rent to hire laborers to work the demesne.

Both sides originally considered this new arrangement advanta-
geous. The peasants preferred to devote all their labor to their own
fields, and the landlords found that hired laborers, who were paid
only if they worked, were more reliable than peasants who were
grudgingly performing labor dues when they would rather have

[47] Georges Duby, *The Early Growth of the European Economy*. Ronald G. Witt, "The
Landlord and the Economic Revival of the Middle Ages in Northern Europe."
[48] Rösener, *Peasants in the Middle Ages*, pp. 218–22. Pounds, *An Economic History*,
p. 209–11.

been home tilling their own plots. The need for hired labor also created opportunities for young peasants without land but with a willingness to work to earn money. This was the period in which Europe's peasant population grew rapidly—doubling, by some estimates—and landlords no longer had to insist on the fulfillment of labor dues to have their fields cultivated. But money rents, like rents for the previous five centuries, were fixed and did not increase along with inflation. This situation was fine with the peasants, who found their rents decreasing in real terms every year, as prices steadily edged upward in the twelfth and thirteenth centuries, but was not so fine for the landlords, who discovered their rents would buy less and less, especially as the hired laborers demanded higher and higher wages.

By the mid-thirteenth century many landlords had stopped commuting labor dues to rents, and some even tried, without notable success, to change them back. But by this point the manorial system, with its close relationship between lands rented to peasants and peasants working the lord's demesne land, was disintegrating. At the end of the Middle Ages nobles were still the major landowners, but they might have only a small "home farm" where their ancestors had once had vast demesne lands. By this time, the aristocracy had become distanced from the agricultural cycle; instead of worrying about hired labor or labor dues, nobles were content to live on their rents. But during much of the Middle Ages the produce raised in the fields around them had been a vital concern of theirs. Some of it was sold to buy the goods they wanted, and the rest of it was, after all, their own food.

Serfdom

Another element of the lord-peasant relationship in the first half of the Middle Ages was the system of serfdom. A serf was someone who was legally unfree, usually a peasant, and although not all peasants were ever serfs, a great many of them were in the early Middle Ages. It is important to note that while serfdom, a legal condition, was certainly embedded within the economic organization of manorialism, it was not an essential or defining element. That is, the economic functioning of manorialism was essentially the same whether those paying labor dues and other rents were serfs or free peasants. As I have pointed out, before the eleventh century one of the most important distinctions was between the free and the unfree. One could certainly be a peasant tenant without servitude (just as people who rent their homes today are not in a position of personal servitude), but it certainly mattered to the peasants themselves whether they were servile or free.[49]

The modern word "serf" comes from the Latin word *servus*, the same term used by the Romans for a slave. And yet it should be stressed that medieval serfdom was very different from the slavery of antiquity (or, for that matter, the slavery of the antebellum American South). A slave is subject to his or her master's *arbitrary* will and must obey all orders. A slave can also be bought and sold like an animal. Under the Roman Empire, one could beat a slave to death with no more reprimand than one would receive now for doing the same to a vicious dog. A serf, on the other hand, was recognized as fully human and, in the medieval West, as part of the Christian community. He or she could not be sold or arbitrarily killed. Although a serf's obligations might be very heavy or degrading, they were set and known, and the lord could not decide to increase them on a whim.

In France agricultural slavery had for the most part disappeared by the sixth century, replaced by manorialism. Since no new slaves were coming in, when slaves were freed or ran away they were not replaced. Slavery probably persisted longest in domestic work; there were still occasional references to household slaves in the eighth century, and they might, as I have noted, help out on the demesne. But by far the most common form of servitude was serfdom, not slavery.[50]

The essence of serfdom was a personal, dependent relationship to one's "lord of the body," a dependency into which one was born. This hereditary subjection of one person to another meant that the serf's will was not free. It should be noted that a serf's lord of the body, the master to whom his birth subjected him, might or might not be the landlord from whom he rented. Some early medieval serfs were the descendants of slaves; others were the descendants of free peas-

[49] Karl Bosl, "Freiheit und Unfreiheit."
[50] Hans-Werner Goetz, "Serfdom and the Beginnings of a 'Seigneurial System' in the Carolingian Period." Poly and Bournazel, *Feudal Transformation*, pp. 119–21.

ants who had been maneuvered by circumstances and landlords into servitude during the late Roman Empire.[51]

While the distinction between slavery and serfdom made sense theoretically, in practice the picture was always very confused. Beginning in the thirteenth century, there were attempts to draw up definitive statements of the attributes of serfdom, but these were made centuries after the advent of serfdom, indeed, well after serfdom was even prevalent. The picture obtained from an analysis of early medieval sources is that people could recognize serfs when they saw them, and certain general attributes applied to most serfs, but like early medieval nobility, early medieval serfdom existed without any unambiguous definition.

There were no special rents or dues that one owed to the lord of one's body just for being a serf, although servile status often entailed juridic liabilities. If a serf's lord of the body was also his landlord, the serf might end up owing higher rents than his free neighbors for comparably sized *mansi*, but not universally so. There were great variations within servile status, depending in part on how one had become a serf: that is, whether one was the descendant of a slave or of a free man who had commended himself to a lord as his serf in return for the land he needed to live. In different parts of Europe, servile status was treated somewhat differently, although churchmen routinely agreed that a serf, not having control of his own will, could not become a priest. Nobles were more likely than members of other sectors of society to be lords of the body, but free peasants could also own serfs—whom they might make perform their workdays for them—and there are even examples of serfs having their own serfs.[52]

In many areas serfs owed a head tax. This fee of one or two pennies brought annually to the lord on one's head was of minor economic significance but enormous symbolic significance, especially if, as in many areas, the serf had to come on his knees with a rope around his neck. Lords of the body often regulated their serfs' inheritance and usually demanded that their permission be asked—and often a fee

[51] For the late Roman transition from a society with both agricultural slaves and free peasants into a society of peasant serfs, see Ste. Croix, *Class Struggle*, pp. 205–59.

[52] Goetz, "Serfdom," pp. 37–38. See also Fichtenau, *Living in the Tenth Century*, pp. 359–78.

paid—if one of their serfs wanted to marry a free peasant or someone else's serf.[53] The lords were concerned that the dependency serfdom entailed, being hereditary, might become attached to a different lord or disappear altogether. (There is no truth to the common belief that a serf's lord had "first-night rights" to a young servile bride, a myth popularized in the nineteenth century by an overexcited Victorian mind.)[54]

Just as there were peasants who were not part of the manorial system, so there were early medieval peasants who were not serfs. In fact, recent scholarship has discovered that many of the free men who came to royal or comital courts in the Carolingian period and fought in Carolingian wars were not nobles, as was once assumed, but rather men who spent much of their time working the land. Free peasants were especially common in frontier areas, such as Catalonia, where pioneers settled land in the tenth century that had recently been under Muslim domination.[55]

Serfdom, thus never a tidy or universal system, was also essentially gone in France in the High Middle Ages. After having been part of medieval society for five centuries, it died out very rapidly in northern France at the end of the eleventh and beginning of the twelfth centuries. The terms *servus* and *ancilla* (the latter meaning "handmaiden," often used as a feminine form of *servus*) disappeared from French documents in the first decades of the twelfth century. After this, a peasant would be called simply *homo* or *femina*, man or woman.[56] The head taxes and the fees for marrying someone else's serf also vanished.

The disappearance of serfdom in the late eleventh century might seem surprising, because examples from some areas suggest that serfdom was becoming more prevalent early in the same century as local

[53] For such servile liabilities, see William Chester Jordan, *From Servitude to Freedom*, pp. 20–26; and Barthélemy, *La société dans le comté de Vendôme*, pp. 474–83.

[54] Alain Boureau, *Le droit de cuissage*. This book is a discussion of how the "first-night" myth developed in popular culture, without any scholarly support, and how it has always been used to describe a past from which "modernity" had fortunately freed itself.

[55] Paul Freedman, *The Origins of Peasant Servitude in Medieval Catalonia*, pp. 56–88. Poly and Bournazel, *Feudal Transformation*, pp. 126–27.

[56] The disappearance of serfdom in France at the beginning of the twelfth century was first noted in regional studies and is now generally accepted. See, for example, Duby, *La société mâconnaise*, pp. 201–12; Evergates, *Feudal Society*, pp. 16–20, 137–44; and Barthélemy, *La société dans le comté de Vendôme*, pp. 502–4.

lords consolidated their power.[57] The end of serfdom owes a great deal to the beginnings of an urban economy in this period and especially to the initiative of the serfs themselves. No longer willing to put up with degrading servile status, they found ways out of it. Some ran away to the newly expanding cities; some quietly passed for free, hoping no one would remember. A family of serfs that became quite wealthy in the rapidly-urbanizing region of Flanders in the 1120s had apparently been able simply to pass for free, and when members of the family murdered the count of Flanders, it was said that they did so because they feared revelation of their servile status.[58] Less spectacularly but certainly more frequently, serfs bought their way out of servitude. A lord who had been getting little of economic value from the payment of a few head pennies a year was generally delighted to free his serfs for a large lump-sum payment.

It should be noted, however, that even though serfdom disappeared in northern France, it persisted, to a greater or lesser extent, in England, the southern French frontier, and Germany. In England, where the royal courts were open in the twelfth century to any freeman, an excellent way to win one's case was to prove that one's opponent was actually a serf and therefore unfit to bring suit. In Catalonia peasants who had been free since settling there in the ninth or tenth century were subjected to serfdom for the first time at the very beginning of the thirteenth century; unless they could redeem themselves with cash, many peasants were unable to maintain their freedom against lords who, under the guise of "protecting" them, enforced the strictures that recently revitalized Roman law had put on slaves. In Germany serfdom persisted most strikingly among the *ministeriales*, the "serf-knights," men who kept throughout the thirteenth and fourteenth centuries the dependent status that knights originally had had in France, and who in fact were more dependent than French knights had ever been. Even while becoming powerful and wealthy, the de

[57] Although some scholars have suggested that a serfdom fairly close to Roman slavery persisted through the tenth century, and that after a sharp break at the beginning of the eleventh century a new form of serfdom was imposed for another century, Dominique Barthélemy has recently argued convincingly that the serfdom that died out at the beginning of the twelfth century was an institution that had been changing steadily but gradually for five centuries or more, not something new. "Qu'est-ce que le servage, en France, au XIe siècle?"

[58] Galbert of Bruges, *The Murder of Charles the Good* 7–8, pp. 96–102. Suger, *The Deeds of Louis the Fat* 30, p. 138.

facto nobility of their region, these *ministeriales* continued to be subject "in the body" to their lords, whose permission they needed to contract marriage.[59]

Banal Lordship

The ending of serfdom in France in the eleventh century was easier than it would have been earlier because the distinction between free and unfree peasants was already blurring. As noted above, people at this time were beginning to think of the major division within secular society as that between fighters and laborers, not between servile and free, and this grouping together of all peasants gave the serfs the opportunity to try to emulate the free peasants. One of the clearest indications that the boundary was being blurred was the emergence of banal lordship.

Banal lordship was a new form of authority exercised by the castellans in the eleventh century. It developed during the period when the power of the counts was weakening, castles were spreading, and fief holding was becoming common. Banal lordship included both the judicial and political powers counts had exercised until the end of the tenth century, such as judging criminals and leading the defense of the area against enemies, and also economic monopolies. Thus a banal lord would judge local peasants in his own court, charge them "customary dues" (in essence little more than protection money), and require them to pay tolls on his bridges and grind their grain only in his mill.[60]

Earlier, being a landlord had given a noble the economic right to collect rents and dues from his tenants, but not any right to command. Only counts and judges had these political and judicial powers in the early Middle Ages. With the disintegration of the counts' power in the decades around the year 1000, as noted in Chapter 1, the newly powerful castellans also began to exercise the rights of *bannum,*

---

[59] Paul R. Hyams, *Kings, Lords, and Peasants in Medieval England*, pp. 162–200. Freedman, *The Origins of Peasant Servitude*, pp. 89–118. John B. Freed, "The Formation of the Salzburg Ministerialage in the Tenth and Eleventh Centuries." Idem, *Noble Bondsmen*. Karl Bosl, " 'Noble Unfreedom': The Rise of the *Ministeriales* in Germany," in Reuter, *Medieval Nobility*, pp. 291–311. Bumke, *Concept of Knighthood*, pp. 46–71, 85–86.

[60] Léopold Genicot, *Rural Communities in the Medieval West*, pp. 62–89. Dominique Barthélemy, *L'ordre seigneurial*, pp. 93–99, 140–43.

The castle of Chinon, rebuilt and added to constantly from the twelfth century through the fifteenth century, still dominates its town and the river below (the Vienne, a tributary of the Loire). The outer walls with their square buttressing are the oldest part of the castle. It was at Chinon that both kings Henry II and Richard of England died, and where, some 250 years later, Joan of Arc first met the dauphin.

or command, in their regions. As the large manors of the Carolingian period shrank or, with the disappearance of serfdom, became less profitable, enterprising lords could recoup their losses by becoming banal lords of much larger areas than those from which they had previously received income.[61]

The "customary dues" (*consuetudines* in Latin) that banal lords exacted more or less on demand, from both peasants and monasteries (sometimes also called the *taille*), could be a substantial addition to their income. It is striking that in spite of the technical sense of *consuetudo* as a due or tax to which banal lords were entitled, the word appears very frequently as *malae consuetudines*—that is, *bad* exactions—the same term used by the Peace of God at the end of the tenth

---

[61] Poly and Bournazel, *Feudal Transformation*, pp. 28–34, 260–61.

century to characterize what they opposed. The power to exact dues beyond rents, especially dues that could be levied almost at will, was an invitation to abuse. Not all nobles became banal lords, but a great many of those who controlled castles did, and they backed up their demands with their knights.[62]

What is particularly striking about the banal lords and the *consuetudines* they made the local people pay is that these were assessed not just on their own tenants and those bound to them by servitude but on *everyone* who lived within a particular area, including free peasant allodists who might never have paid anyone any sort of dues before.[63] This kind of regional authority was new. Earlier, the only comparable power had derived ultimately from the authority of the king, and although some of the castellans' power, such as their judicial rights, might be considered public, it would be harder to place mill monopolies in the same category. At any rate, the modern distinction between public and private would have made little sense to the powerful in the eleventh century. For the peasants, the most important results of the rise of banal lordship were, on the one hand, the necessity of paying dues to yet another lord and, on the other, a leveling of status among all the peasants, free and unfree alike, before the banal lords. It was this development, perhaps paradoxically, which made escape from servitude easier.

From the viewpoint of the nobles, the great advantage of banal lordship was access to a new source of income and authority. It also, interestingly, created a new distinction within the ranks of the aristocracy, between those who did have such rights (mostly dukes, counts, and castellans) and those who did not. In the twelfth century, when inflation and greater spending on luxury goods began to bite into the incomes of many nobles who were living on fixed rents, the banal lords were able to keep their income up by raising tolls and monopoly fees, since there were no traditional limits on these exactions.[64]

---

[62] Elisabeth Magnou-Nortier, "Les mauvaises coutumes en Auvergne, Bourgogne méridionale, Languedoc, et Provence au XIe siècle: Un moyen d'analyse sociale," in *Structures féodales et féodalisme*, pp. 135–63. Duby, *Rural Economy and Country Life*, pp. 187–90, 224–31. Freedman, *Origins of Peasant Servitude*, pp. 29–30.

[63] Previous generations of scholars sometimes characterized the early eleventh century rather melodramatically as a period of new (and doubtless "feudal") oppression of previously free and equal yeomen; on this point, see Reynolds, *Kingdoms and Communities*, p. 109.

[64] Jordan, *From Servitude to Freedom*, p. 30.

Nobles and Economic Expansion

Banal lordship was by no means the only way for aristocrats to profit from the rapidly growing agricultural economy of the eleventh and twelfth centuries. Indeed, another trend counterbalanced the temptation of banal lords to levy ever-heavier exactions on local peasants. Certain landlords began to offer low rents and charters of liberties to encourage peasants to move onto heretofore uncultivated land and clear it for crops. Bringing large tracts of wild land under the plow created opportunities for peasants and income for lords who had not previously received anything for such lands. The twelfth century witnessed widespread felling of forests and draining of swamps, a process now known as "internal colonization" because areas between previously settled areas were being colonized. It was during this period that many of the marshes of Flanders were reclaimed and ditches and dikes constructed.[65] Forest clearance had proceeded so far that when around 1140, when Abbot Suger was building a new basilica at St.-Denis, usually considered France's first Gothic church, it was considered miraculous when he found enough tall trees to cut for the beams.[66]

Landlords also encouraged external colonization—that is, peasants moving out of regions that had only scattered empty areas into regions with extensive stretches of unsettled territory. German princes benefited as peasants moved into the relatively unpopulated countryside of the Empire,[67] and indeed, German peasants often kept on going, heading east into such regions as Poland, where the villages containing their descendants centuries later made it impossible for the negotiators at the end of World War I to draw coherent boundaries on the basis of ethnic identity.

To encourage peasants to settle on their lands, landlords often offered such inducements as low rents—even a low rent was much bet-

---

[65] This internal colonization was carried out both by landlords with their peasants and by monks with their lay brothers; the Cistercian order in Burgundy, for example, was a leader in swamp drainage, even though houses of the order in some other parts of France, especially Provence, primarily took up land that had long been under the plow. Pounds, *An Economic History*, pp. 170–74. Constance Brittain Bouchard, *Holy Entrepreneurs*, pp. 97–106.

[66] Jean Gimpel, *The Medieval Machine*, pp. 76–77.

[67] Arnold, *Princes and Territories*, pp. 153–60. Rösener, *Peasants in the Middle Ages*, pp. 34–42. Pounds, *An Economic History*, pp. 175–80.

ter than getting nothing for unworked land—and charters of liberties.[68] By the second half of the twelfth century it was fairly common for a landlord to lay out what was called a "new town" (although modern historians would call it a village rather than a town), with a rectangular street plan, plots for the houses of all the new tenants, and written guarantees that the peasants who settled there would be relatively free of domination by either the lord or his bailiffs. They would have fairly low rents, no labor dues, and the right to do a fair amount of self-governing and self-policing.

Such offers, of course, gave many peasants who had been unhappy where they were the opportunity to leave and settle elsewhere. Since by this time peasants had mostly freed themselves of servile status, landlords could not force them to stay against their will, and their best method of hanging onto their tenants and their rents was to be sure that conditions were not too harsh for them, even though they doubtless preferred to make as few concessions as they could.

Landlords and tenants might engage in complicated economic interactions for their mutual benefit in clearing new areas or establishing new crops for the expanding commercial market. One of the most common forms was *complant*, in which lord and peasant shared the expense of establishing a new vineyard to supply the increased market for wine. The lord would provide the land, the tools, and the rootstocks, and the peasant would provide his labor during the several years it took to establish the vineyard and bring it into production. After the grapes began coming in, the peasant would continue to tend the vines, and he and the landlord would split the profits equally.[69] This system is but one of the clearest examples of the need for landlord and peasant to work together in a period of rural economic growth.

The nobles of the High Middle Ages lived in a period of rapid growth in the urban economy as well. As already noted, the expansion of the cities provided the principal market for the surplus produce of rural lords. And yet the French aristocracy felt very uneasy about the merchants and craftsmen of the cities, even while they needed them, both as a market for the food and raw materials pro-

---

[68] For such rural "liberties," see Reynolds, *Kingdoms and Communities*, pp. 130–36.
[69] Pounds, *An Economic History*, p. 202.

duced on their manors and as a source for the luxury goods they bought for themselves. Thus the expansion and multiplication of urban markets in the twelfth century represented both an opportunity and a threat for the rural aristocracy, as much of the money the lords acquired flowed back to the urban economy

The term "city," incidentally, should not be used for the Middle Ages simply in the sense of a large settlement; it was, strictly speaking, a town that had a bishop, and the most successful French market towns of the High Middle Ages had been bishops' cities since the late Roman Empire. It was the presence of a permanent market, more than the number of inhabitants, which distinguished a city or town from a village. Although there was certainly buying and selling at the local village level, a town was a crossroads with continual commercial activity, in which buyers, sellers, and goods from some distance away all came together. Because of this commerce, towns might have food even when the countryside did not. Galbert of Bruges, describing an early twelfth-century famine in the Flemish countryside, said that many tried to reach the cities and towns "where they could buy bread."[70]

The romances and epics that French aristocrats enjoyed mention very few townspeople, and never as heroes. Those who do appear are treated with contempt or at least with marked distrust. A common motif is the contrast between a noble's liberal generosity and a merchant's crafty avarice.[71] While of course *being* rich was itself admirable in noble eyes, the way the wealth was acquired mattered considerably.

Northern French lords, however, seem to have been more conservative on this topic than their counterparts in southern Europe. Italian nobles—and, for that matter, bishops—were enthusiastic participants in the market economy from the twelfth century onward. The chronicler Otto of Freising, visiting Italy with his nephew, the German emperor, in the 1150s, was both impressed by and contemptuous toward the Italian knights grown wealthy from commerce. In Provence by the beginning of the twelfth century all the cities had acquired resident families of urban knights, not at all averse to commercial activi-

[70] Galbert of Bruges, *The Murder of Charles the Good* 2, p. 86.
[71] Peter S. Noble, "Knights and Burgesses in the Feudal Epic," in Christopher Harper-Bill and Ruth Harvey, eds., *The Ideals and Practice of Medieval Knighthood*, pp. 104–10.

ties.[72] But north of the Mediterranean the aristocracy considered it demeaning to acquire wealth through commerce, and even wealthy merchants, instead of being satisfied with their position, emulated knightly attributes.[73] The traditional land rents, agriculture, and of course, plunder were considered much more appropriate resources for members of the nobility.

One reason for noble suspicion of the cities was that they existed somewhat outside the system of manorialism and lordship found in the countryside. Nobles might own land within city walls, but at the beginning of the twelfth century in France (even earlier in Italy), cities set about trying to make themselves self-governing, rather than having to rely on the local secular lords for judicial services. Whereas nobles' wealth came, for the most part, from the rents and produce of agricultural land, urban wealth came primarily from craftsmanship and commerce. Medieval cities were so successful as commercial centers that historians used to describe them in a Marxist sense (more picturesquely than accurately) as "islands of capitalism" in a "sea of feudalism."[74]

Twelfth-century townsmen wanted self-rule even more than did the peasants in newly founded villages with charters of liberties for their associations. These townsmen commonly organized what was called a "commune," a republican form of government, although generally only wealthy male residents could be voting citizens in it.[75] Declaring themselves self-governing was usually not enough; townsmen, like peasant villagers, had to have some preexisting authority confirm their commune (in exchange, of course, for an appropriate financial consideration), and that authority was usually the local count or most powerful banal lord. In Burgundy, for example, in the 1150s the count of Nevers supported the townspeople of Vézelay in their ultimately unsuccessful attempt to establish a self-governing commune by breaking away from the banal lordship of the abbots of Vézelay.[76]

[72] Otto of Freising, *The Deeds of Frederick Barbarossa* 2.13, p. 128. Poly, *La Provence*, pp. 297–310.
[73] For examples, see H. Miyamatsu, "Les premiers bourgeois d'Angers aux XI et XIIe siècles."
[74] This rather quaint image has been refuted most recently by R. H. Hilton, *English and French Towns in Feudal Society*.
[75] Reynolds, *Kingdoms and Communities*, pp. 155–218. Pounds, *An Economic History*, pp. 225–28. Barthélemy, *L'ordre seigneurial*, pp. 116–19.
[76] Hugh of Poitiers, *The Vézelay Chronicle*, pp. 173–74.

The other person besides a secular lord to whom townspeople might have applied for recognition was the bishop, if theirs was an episcopal city, but French bishops were generally very reluctant to grant communes. (In Italy, by contrast, where the bishops enthusiastically joined in the commercial economy, they were not nearly so reluctant.) By the twelfth century French bishops had considered the cities in which their cathedrals were located *their* cities for seven hundred years, and they had enough trouble with the local counts, who also considered them *their* cities, without wanting to grant self-government to still another urban group.[77] They evidently had good reason for caution. An early twelfth-century bishop of Laon in northern France (bishop there a century after Adalbero) originally agreed to a commune, but then had a change of heart, which set off several days of rioting and murder, including the murder of the bishop himself.[78]

The counts, on the other hand, often considered a commune in their city an ally against the bishop and were quite willing to grant charters of franchise for a fee and for reserved rights and dues. The counts of Champagne, for example, did enormously well from the fairs conducted by members of the communes in their region in the second half of the twelfth century, collecting tolls and sales taxes, though also helping to police the fairs.[79] These counts showed how nobles who preferred to define themselves by their warrior courage and their courteous behavior—indeed, the court of Champagne was considered one of the chief centers of twelfth century courtliness could also be full participants in the economic growth of the High Middle Ages.

Far from being static, the society in which the nobility played a highly influential role evolved rapidly during the High Middle Ages. The difficulty medieval theorists had in defining the different "orders" of society in a way that would be generally accepted, or even plausible, a few generations later indicates how rapidly society was changing.

The French kings went from lords who had a recognized but sometimes vague semisacerdotal authority over the great counts and

---

[77] Constance Brittain Bouchard, *Spirituality and Administration*, pp. 85–86.
[78] Guibert of Nogent, *Memoirs* 3.7–11, pp. 144–73.
[79] Robert-Henri Bautier, "Les foires de Champagne."

dukes, but not much else, to leaders with substantial political and juridical authority. Townsmen and merchants, who had been a barely perceptible fraction of society in the early eleventh century, when Adalbero had managed to categorize all who did not pray or fight as "those who work," grew rapidly in numbers and wealth from the eleventh to the thirteenth century, to the point that the position of the wealthier ones could rival that of the lower aristocracy. Peasants, among whom a large number had been serfs and all of whom, servile or free, performed extensive labor dues, by the beginning of the thirteenth century were all free men and women, most of them free of labor dues as well, and landlords were hiring wage laborers to work their desmesnes. The increased amount of food these peasants produced made possible both the rapid expansion of towns and the development of a commercial economy that brought the nobles the luxury goods they wanted—or suddenly discovered they needed. Trade made possible the acquisition of goods their predecessors had never had, and also required cash outlays these predecessors had never had to make.

The nobility itself changed and developed during this period as well. As already noted in Chapter 1, nobles' self-definition gradually acquired a new militarism, at, ironically, the same time that kings were beginning to fight their own wars with lowborn mercenaries and the nobles' own serving knights were emulating them and marrying their daughters. Fief holding developed from a few oaths of fidelity into a relatively elaborate system of social and personal interaction among aristocrats, in which more and more of a lord's land would be considered not his personally but a fief held from someone else. Instead of simply collecting rents and dues from their tenants, the strongest or the most ambitious lords established monopolies of banal rights in their areas, agreed to authorize communes for a fee, and took an active role in clearing and settling new agricultural areas.

In this changing society, in which nobles' position was threatened from above by the kings and from below by merchants and knights, as well as by the ambitions of other nobles, most men and women relied above all on a group that had been there before kings, vassals, and agricultural expansion: the family. It is to the structure and function of noble families that I turn in the next chapter.

CHAPTER THREE

Noble Families and Family Life

Medieval nobles defined themselves by their families. Glorious ancestors were a key attribute of glorious aristocrats. Many of the decisions that modern society assumes are matters for the individual, such as choice of marriage partner, making a charitable donation, even buying and selling property, were carried out in the Middle Ages with the involvement and assistance of family members. Yet when discussing noble families it is important to keep in mind that these were not unchanging units, that the "family" varied in composition even for the same individuals at different times in their lives, and that however the nobles of the Middle Ages defined their families, it was never on the same basis as does modern society.

The Family and Family Consciousness

The term "family" must be used with some caution because of the multiple meanings attached to it. In modern usage, it usually means either the nuclear unit of father, mother, and children, or else a vague and rather unspecific collection of in-laws and more or less closely related people. Medieval Latin had no word for either of these meanings. People did indeed tend to live in nuclear units, but there was no single term to describe such a unit. The medieval Latin term *familia* meant not "family" but a household, including servants and attendants as well as actual relatives. A noble describing his relatives in unspecific terms might speak of his *consanguinei*, but these were people related to him strictly by blood, not his in-laws. For medieval nobles the important unit was the *stirps* or *gens,* a group of people related by blood, usually through the male line, existing in the dimension of time as well as space.[1] It is to this group that I normally apply the term "family."

The way that the medieval noble family perceived and structured itself evolved over time, and even in a single period there was no one standard of "family structure" which individual lineages tried to match. Because family structures must be inferred from many sorts of evidence, including families' own memoirs and genealogies, donations to monasteries, and patterns of naming and inheritance, modern scholars have not always agreed on how medieval nobles conceived of the family groups to which they belonged.

There has been particular disagreement among historians concerning the extent to which noble families were patrilineal over the course of the Middle Ages. There is no doubt that in the High Middle Ages, the eleventh through thirteenth centuries, nobles preferred to identify themselves in terms of the male line of descent.[2] What historians debate is whether this was a new development in the eleventh century, or whether nobles had always identified themselves patrilineally.[3] The question is of course complicated by the lack of any fixed or broadly accepted kinship standard, external to individual families, which nobles purposely followed and which itself underwent change. It seems most likely that nobles, even in the early Middle Ages, gave the most significance to the men from whom they descended and inherited. In the turbulence of the ninth and tenth centuries, however, it was often very difficult to establish the male-line

---

[1] Constance B. Bouchard, "The Structure of a Twelfth-Century French Family," pp. 41–43. Charlotte A. Newman, *The Anglo-Norman Nobility in the Reign of Henry I,* pp. 35–59. Dominique Barthélemy, *La société dans le comté de Vendôme,* pp. 517–18. Sally McKee, "Households in Fourteenth-Century Venetian Crete," pp. 27–28. Anita Guerreau-Jalabert, "Sur les structures de parenté dans l'Europe médiévale," pp. 1030–31. David Herlihy, *Medieval Households,* pp. 2–4.

[2] T. N. Bisson, "Nobility and Family in Medieval France," pp. 602–5. Karl Schmid, "Zur Problematik von Familie, Sippe und Geschlecht, Haus und Dynastie beim mittelalterlichen Adel."

[3] See the discussion of the issues by John B. Freed, "Reflections on the German Nobility," pp. 560–64. Régine Le Jan has recently argued that the transition from a large, amorphous kindred to a lineage took place in the ninth century, not the eleventh. *Famille et pouvoir dans le monde franc,* pp. 414–27.

dynasties they would have preferred, since fathers often had no surviving sons, or at least no sons who went on to have sons of their
own.[4]

I should note that even though some scholars (including me) argue
that male-line family consciousness had been the norm for at least
several centuries before the year 1000, there can be no doubt that primogeniture, privileging the eldest son over all other sons (and certainly daughters), became the norm only in the eleventh and twelfth
centuries. Even then, it was not an inflexible rule that the eldest son
inherited nearly everything and his brothers little or nothing.[5] The
"Life" of Herluin, a knight who became a monk in the early eleventh
century, says that the duke of Normandy assigned all his father's inheritance to him rather than to his younger brothers because he was
more "eminent in true nobility," not because he was the eldest.[6]
William the Conqueror's eldest son succeeded him as duke of Normandy, but his second son succeeded him as king of England. Nevertheless, the expectation that all sons might earlier have had, of at least
sharing in the family's patrilineal inheritance, was severely restricted
in the High Middle Ages.

As one follows the history of nobles from the early Middle Ages
into the eleventh century, it becomes easier to understand how
they perceived their families because they defined them much
more explicitly. In many cases, family gifts to local monasteries,
which became much more common in the eleventh century than they
had been earlier, seem to have encouraged identification with one's
ancestors. Gifts had always been made for the souls of the donor's
relatives, and as noble families began making repeated gifts over the
generations to the same religious houses and, indeed, were often
buried together at a particular monastery, their relationship with the

[4] For the debate, see Constance B. Bouchard, "Family Structure and Family Consciousness among the Aristocracy in the Ninth to Eleventh Centuries"; idem, "The
Bosonids"; K. Leyser, "The German Aristocracy from the Ninth to the Early Twelfth
Century"; and Benjamin Arnold, *Princes and Territories in Medieval Germany*, pp.
135–51.

[5] Barthélemy, *La société dans le comté de Vendôme*, pp. 527–35. Ralph V. Turner, "The
Problem of Survival for the Angevin 'Empire,'" pp. 83–84. Amy Livingstone, "Kith
and Kin."

[6] Gilbert Crispin, "The Life of Herluin," in Sally N. Vaughn, *The Abbey of Bec and
the Anglo-Norman State*, p. 71.

monastery itself became a tool for making family identification more explicit.[7]

One of the clearest signs of increasing male-line family consciousness was the gradual adoption of the *cognomen,* or second name (*cognomina* in the plural). Since the collapse of the Roman Empire a person had normally had only one name, but in the late eleventh century men whose fathers had witnessed charters simply as, for example, "Milo," might instead be inscribed as "Milo of Noyers." This phenomenon developed among the nobility well before the rest of society; peasants did not usually appear with last names until the fourteenth century.

In some cases, the *cognomen* might have its origins in a nickname; the lords of Brancion in the eleventh and twelfth centuries were all routinely called "Grossus." Most commonly it was a loconym, associated with the name of the family castle. When the castle became the key locus around which the newly powerful castellan families of the eleventh century organized themselves, the castle name became the clearest way to identify an individual. It should be stressed, however, that the *cognomen* was not, strictly speaking, a family name, even though relatives might all share the same one. Within a twelfth-century household, everyone from the serving knights up to the lord of the castle might take the same *cognomen,* whether they were related or not. Alternatively, a family member who moved to a different castle would generally change his *cognomen* to reflect his new home.[8]

Cognomina became prevalent at the same time as the number of given names in use declined. In the ninth century, an enormous number of names had been in common usage, but by the end of the eleventh century the number had shrunk markedly.[9] Thus the *cognomen,* as well as identifying a man with his castle and his relatives,

---

[7] Le Jan, *Famille et pouvoir,* pp. 45–52. For Italian parallels, see Cinzio Violante, "Quelques caractéristiques des structures familiales en Lombardie, Emilie, et Toscane aux XIe et XII siècles," in Georges Duby and Jacques Le Goff, eds., *Famille et parenté dans l'Occident médiéval,* pp. 93–94.

[8] Barthélemy, *La société dans le comté de Vendôme,* pp. 629–42. Joachim Bumke, *Courtly Culture,* p. 103. David Bates, *Normandy before 1066,* pp. 113–14. Bouchard, "Structure of a Twelfth-Century Family," pp. 44–47.

[9] George T. Beech, "Les noms de personne poitevins du 9e au 12e siècle." Jean-Pierre Poly and Eric Bournazel, *The Feudal Transformation,* pp. 90–91. Karl Schmid,

was also important in distinguishing him from (for example) all the other men named Hugh. Earlier, although it was possible to be named for one's relatives, as kings were with some regularity, it was also common to take only one syllable of a parental name or to combine syllables from the names of several relatives. For example, among the children born to the noble couple Theoderic and Aldana at the end of the eighth century were two named Theodino and Albana.[10] Families might go several generations without repeating a name, and this practice has proved intensely frustrating to modern scholars trying to establish family trees on the basis of name similarities. But from the eleventh century onward, aristocratic children were normally named for their relatives, their lords, or even such famous literary characters as Roland. This naming for people other than one's relatives, of course, poses different problems for the intrepid genealogist.

The spread of castles that were passed down from father to son—both the castles themselves and the castles' names—was accompanied, as discussed in Chapter 2, by the spread of fief holding. Although far from universal, this institution did stress the importance of a single designated male heir, able to take up the vassal duties his father had exercised before him. Generally it was the eldest son who was most likely to be of age when his father died. In this way as well, the *cognomen* came to be associated with the male line.

Even with the adoption of the *cognomen*, however, the given name remained more important for a noble of the High Middle Ages, and it was generally chosen specifically to identify the child with relatives.[11] Although there were no "rules" for parents to follow in choosing names, certain patterns may be discerned. Boys especially were named for their male-line relatives; the name of the paternal grandfather was the most obvious choice when naming a first son. The sec-

---

"'De regia stirpe Waiblingensium': Remarques sur la conscience de soi des Staufen," in Duby and Le Goff, *Famille et parenté*, pp. 53–54.

[10] Bouchard, "Family Structure and Family Consciousness," p. 655. Le Jan, *Famille et pouvoir*, pp. 193–200. For German parallels, see Reinhard Wenskus, *Sächsischer Stammesadel und fränkischer Reichsadel*, pp. 42–48.

[11] Karl Ferdinand Werner, "Liens de parenté et noms de personne: Un problème historique et méthodologique," in Duby and Le Goff, *Famille et parenté*, pp. 13–18, 25–34. Wilhelm Störmer, *Früher Adel*, pp. 29–69. Jean Dunbabin, "What's in a Name?"

ond son might be named for the father himself if his name was different from *his* father's.

One could thus end up with a family tree in which two names alternate for the lord of the castle, because each father named his eldest son for his own father. Or if father and son had the same name, then a single name might be given to each firstborn heir for generations, the name becoming so important to the family's sense of identity that a younger son might be renamed if his elder brother died. This happened to Duke William VIII of Aquitaine, who lived in the second half of the eleventh century. He was the younger brother of both William VI and William VII and like William VII, had originally had a different name (in his case Gui) before taking both the duchy and the name William. The lords of Montpellier, routinely named William as well, did not want to take chances with renaming; the Lord William who died in 1178 named *both* his eldest sons William.[12]

Because the people of the High Middle Ages did not regularly use numbers to distinguish different secular lords with the same name (most numbers attached to names, such as William VIII of Aquitaine, are modern), families had to find other ways to distinguish the generations. There was no consistent method of doing so. For example, two powerful families in which heirs were normally named William, the twelfth-century counts of Nevers and the aforementioned lords of Montpellier, followed quite different procedures. In the first case, individuals were distinguished by their descendants based on where they were buried, as in "William buried at Bethlehem," and in the second case by the names of their mothers, as in "William son of Sybil."[13]

If a son were destined for the church, parents might name him for an uncle already in the church. Thus one can sometimes observe what are essentially parallel ecclesiastical and secular dynasties, only on the ecclesiastical side the position and the name descended uncle to nephew, rather than father to son. Whether naming a boy or a girl, in most cases parents chose a name that had belonged to someone they

[12] Alexandre Teulet, ed., *Layettes du trésor des chartes*, 1:100–102, no. 257.
[13] Constance Brittain Bouchard, *Sword, Miter, and Cloister*, pp. 340–51. *Liber instrumentorum memorialium: Cartulaire des Guillems de Montpellier.*

had known themselves, generally no ancestor further removed than their own grandparents or uncles and aunts.[14]

New male names, however, could and did enter a lineage. If the eldest son died without heirs and the second son was not renamed, his might become the primary name for subsequent generations. If a man married a woman whose father was much more powerful than he was, then he might name even his first son and almost certainly his second for one of her relatives, rather than for his. In many areas, a powerful castellan's serving knights might all name a child for him, asking him to be godfather.[15] Although some scholars have attempted to draw family trees based on name similarities within a region, such sharing of names between a lord and those who served him makes all such attempts suspect.[16]

The family unit was in constant flux as births, deaths, and marriages took place, and only occasionally did it consist of individuals all sharing the same purpose. Indeed, because most noble wealth was inherited and brothers had to compete for the same inheritance, they often considered one another enemies. Even fathers and sons were at least potential rivals. Sons worried that their fathers would disperse the patrimony in pious gifts. Indeed, many young heirs in the eleventh and twelfth centuries immediately tried to reclaim what their fathers had given to monasteries on their deathbeds. Fathers, for their part, saw their sons as possible rebels. The Carolingian kings, for example, had routinely discouraged their sons from marrying while they were still alive themselves, because such marriages would make the sons into established figures with powerful allies in their in-laws.[17] Even in the twelfth century, a son often did not marry until his father died, unless he married an heiress with substantial property of her own.

Membership in the family varied both over the generations and in the relatively short term, as new family members were born. Here

[14] Constance B. Bouchard, "The Geographical, Social, and Ecclesiastical Origins of the Bishops of Auxerre and Sens in the Central Middle Ages," pp. 290–91. Idem, "Patterns of Women's Names in Royal Lineages," p. 4.

[15] The practice of a godparent naming a child for himself or herself first became prevalent in the late Carolingian period. Joseph H. Lynch, *Godparents and Kinship in Early Medieval Europe*, pp. 172–73.

[16] E. Warlop, *The Flemish Nobility before 1300*, 1:43–44. Constance B. Bouchard, "The Origins of the French Nobility," pp. 505–8.

[17] Sylvia Konecny, *Die Frauen des karolingeschen Köngishauses*, pp. 112–13, 139–42, 158–59.

the position of women is especially interesting, because they went during their lifetimes from membership in the family into which they were born to membership (or at least association) in the family into which they married. Because the *gens* or *stirps* was male oriented, a wife always remained something of an outsider to her husband.[18]

This status can be seen most vividly in the names noblemen chose for their daughters; because the given name, even after the adoption of the *cognomen*, was such an important part of someone's identity, these names were never chosen lightly. It was common to name the first daughter for the husband's mother and very unusual to name her for her own mother. If a woman gave her name to any of her daughters, it might well be only the youngest of a sizable family. The relative infrequency with which daughters (as compared to sons) are found in the charters makes it more difficult to trace their names, but several sources provide insights into naming patterns. When Lord William of Montpellier made his testament in 1172 he mentioned all his children, and it is interesting to note that his eldest daughter was named Sybil for his own mother, his second daughter Willelma for his sister, and none of the five girls then living for his wife.[19] If a wife was so foreign to her husband's family that he was slow to name a daughter after her, then it is not surprising that her own relatives, for example, her mother, were almost never sources for the names of a couple's girls. The main exceptions were found when the wife came from a much more exalted background than her husband.

And yet wives underwent an important transformation in status during their lifetimes as married women, from being considered outsiders to the family by their husbands and in-laws, to being considered integral members of the family by their sons. A son, as already noted, frequently named his first daughter for his mother. Thus women's names often skipped a generation; a woman would not give her name to any of her daughters but might have several granddaughters, by several sons, all named for her.[20]

[18] Guerreau-Jalabert, "Sur les structures de parenté," p. 1031. Karl Schmid, "Heirat, Familienfolge, Geschlechtenbewusstein," in *Il matrimonio nella società altomedievale*, pp. 103–37.

[19] Teulet, ed., *Layettes du trésor des chartes*, 1:100–102, no. 257.

[20] Constance B. Bouchard, "The Migration of Women's Names in the Upper Nobility," pp. 1–2. Idem, "Family Structure and Family Consciousness," p. 641.

The path to adulthood was very different for noble boys and girls in the High Middle Ages, but their experiences were very similar for the first six or eight years of life. Noble mothers rarely nursed their own babies, instead choosing a suitable wet nurse with whom an infant would spend the first year or two. Once weaned, noble children would receive their early training from their mother, often learning a little reading and writing from her or from a tutor. Saint Margaret of Scotland, whose *Life* was written around 1110, was praised for her careful attention to her children's education. Hugh, bishop of Lincoln, recalled that when he was growing up near Grenoble, he had turned eight and just begun learning to read when his father, a castellan, decided to send him into the church.[21] Girls would normally receive training and education at home until marriage.

In an aristocratic household, a girl's education could be fairly extensive. Heloise, eventual lover of Peter Abelard, was given an "education in letters," that is, Latin, by her uncle, a cathedral canon. He was willing to pay to have a tutor—Abelard—come in to teach her. She had, according to Abelard, a "gift for letters" that was "rare in women" and which seems to have been as powerful an aphrodisiac for him as her beauty. Heloise's extensive education was unusual, but all wellborn women seem to have been given at least a rudimentary literacy.[22] Wealthy women who became nuns in their mature years already knew enough Latin upon entry to be able to say the psalter.

But many of an aristocratic woman's skills lay in other provinces than letters. The most specifically feminine skill was needlework. The distaff, used to spin wool into thread, had long been a symbol for women, and the fine ladies in the romances routinely spent their time on sewing and embroidery. In addition, a girl with a suitably courtly education knew how to sing and perhaps play an instrument.[23] But household management skills were doubtless the most important part of a noble girl's training.

Boys, in contrast, commonly left home somewhere between the ages

---

[21] For Saint Margaret, see André Vauchez, "Lay People's Sanctity in Western Europe," p. 30. Adam, *Magna Vita Sancti Hugonis*, 1:6.

[22] Peter Abelard, "Historia calamitatum," in *The Letters of Abelard and Heloise*, pp. 66–67.

[23] Bumke, *Courtly Culture*, pp. 339–41.

Well-to-do medieval women preferred to hire wet nurses for their children. Here a thirteenth-century noblewoman tests the breast of a woman she is considering hiring for this purpose, to be sure she will produce enough milk. Aldebrandus of Siena, *Régime du corps*. By permission of the British Library, Sloan 2435, fol. 28v, detail.

of six and eight, to spend the rest of their childhoods elsewhere. For the parents, an important decision was whether to have a particular son raised as a knight or noble or to send him into the church. Nobles, as we shall see in Chapter 5, constituted a very sizable proportion of the membership in the medieval church, and an estimated 20 percent of the nobly born males who reached adulthood were monks or priests. A great many of these men had been sent when they were children to the cathedral school for priestly training or else to the monastery. Young girls, it should be noted, rarely entered the church before the late Middle Ages; in the High Middle Ages, the majority of nuns were adult converts, many of them widows. But when girls did become nuns in early life, it was generally at about the same age, roughly six or eight, that their brothers were sent off to the church.[24]

[24] Penelope D. Johnson, *Equal in Monastic Profession*, pp. 15–18.

Even if a boy was destined for life in the world rather than the church, the family still frequently sent him away. A young man commonly received training in chivalry and knighthood at a castle other than his father's, sometimes at his father's lord's castle, where a count, for example, might gather the sons of many of the castellans of his region for training in the hope of ensuring their long-term loyalty. This pattern is reflected in many literary sources. The first of the twelfth-century *Lais* of Marie de France has its hero Guigemar, a great baron's son, sent for his training to a neighboring king "as soon as [his father] could bear to part with the boy"; this king dubbed him when he grew up. In *Raoul de Cambrai,* after the hero becomes seneschal of France, every great lord in the region sends him "his son, his protégé, or nephew or first cousin" for training.[25]

If not with his father's lord, a young man might receive his training at an uncle's castle. Here the wife's family became important, for a maternal uncle was generally preferred to a paternal uncle for knightly training, in part because one's father's brother was always a potential rival to one's father and his inheritance. When only the eldest son inherited the castle, moreover, his brothers might have no place of their own in which their nephews could be trained. Because most aristocratic marriages involved husbands appreciably older than their wives, both a young man's father and his paternal uncles might be dead by the time he reached maturity, while his more youthful maternal uncles were still flourishing. Maternal uncles in the epics and romances often have special ties to their nephews, closer, often, than the father-son bond. In *The Song of Roland,* the hero, Charlemagne's most beloved and trusted warrior, is his sister's son, and in *Raoul de Cambrai* the hero is the maternal nephew of Emperor Louis. In the tale of "Tristan and Isolde," Tristan's loyalty to his king is all the stronger because he is the king's sister's son—and it is this great loyalty that comes into conflict with his love for Isolde, the king's wife. "All my weapons are pledged to him," Tristan tells her, in a scene in which they try to suggest—knowing they are being spied on—that Tristan's faithfulness is beyond reproach.[26]

While maternal uncles command loyalty and respect, stepfathers are always suspicious figures in the stories. The traitor Ganelon in

[25] Marie de France, *The Lais* 1, p. 43. *Raoul de Cambrai* 26, p. 31.
[26] Beroul, *The Romance of Tristan* 2, p. 51. For the role of maternal uncles, see also John B. Freed, *Noble Bondsmen*, pp. 104–8.

Roland is the hero's stepfather, for example, and stepfathers must have generated at least some ambivalence in real life as well. Such a man was more than just a rival for the affections of a boy's mother; he was quite often a threat to the boy's inheritance. Because marrying a young widow had some of the same force as marrying an heiress, permitting the new husband to take authority over the lands she administered for her children, it is not surprising that, at least in the stories, stepfathers often hoped to get their stepsons out of the way.

Warrior training was a serious business. The skills boys acquired would be used for war once they became adults and were constantly refined in the practice battles of the tournaments. There is no question that the knights and nobles of France were superbly trained and equipped fighters. Even their enemies recognized that they were. But it must have been hard for boys who lacked adult musculature or the concentration to enjoy the constant repetition that was required to perfect their skills. The biographer Suger, praising King Louis VI, said that even at the age of twelve or thirteen, unlike most boys, he was not "playful," nor did he "neglect . . . practice with weapons." The implication, of course, was that other boys did.[27]

Although much of a young man's education would be in warfare and in courtly activities, he was also expected to learn a good deal more reading and writing than his mother had taught him as a child. There are indications that, starting in the eleventh century, many young aristocrats attended church schools, either the cathedral school itself, where future priests were trained, or another school run by priests attached to a house of canons. Thus, without intending to become a churchman or even being associated with a monastery, a young noble could receive at least some of the same education that might be given to a young monk.

Of course not all young aristocrats learned their letters. Herluin, founder of Bec in the eleventh century, had to learn the alphabet when he decided in his late thirties to become a monk. But even in his time some young nobles were literate, as is indicated by the example of Hugh, abbot of Cluny and Herluin's younger contemporary. Even though his castellan father had destined him for a life in the world, Hugh was sent to study at the cathedral school of Auxerre, where his great-uncle was bishop. It was while learning grammar and being in-

---

[27] Suger, *The Deeds of Louis the Fat* 1, p. 25.

troduced to theology that young Hugh decided to run away from home and become a monk.[28] Bernard of Clairvaux, two generations after Hugh, was brought up by his parents with the expectation that he would become a knight, but he was nevertheless given an excellent Latin education at the house of secular canons in Châtillon—an education that enabled him to become one of the greatest Latin stylists of the twelfth century.[29] Indeed, the many young knights who became members of Bernard's Cistercian order of monks in the twelfth century could not have become choir monks as easily as they did had there not been by that time a general pattern of education available for young members of the aristocracy, so that they had already acquired much of the Latin needed for the religious life prior to their conversions.

Noble parents valued education, even if it was sometimes difficult to find a good school before the development of universities at the end of the twelfth century. The wandering scholars of the early twelfth century, among whom Peter Abelard numbered himself, were welcomed as sources for often difficult-to-find intellectual training. Without access to a school or a scholar, parents had to use whatever was available. In the eleventh century, for example, Guibert of Nogent recalled bitterly that in his boyhood there had been no wandering scholars available and he had received his early education from an incompetent priest.[30] Even if such incompetents were the only teachers available, however, aristocratic parents still thought it important that their sons, even sons not intended for the church, receive some sort of classical education.

The groups in which knighthood training for young nobles often took place were important to the social cohesion of the nobility. In addition to learning warfare, reading and writing, and by the late twelfth century polite behavior and even how to dance or play an instrument, young men also forged personal bonds with others who would be their associates throughout adulthood. Medieval nobles went to war, or joined the Crusades, or entered monasteries in the company of those with whom they had trained.

---

[28] Gilbert Crispin, "The Life of Herluin," in Vaughn, *The Abbey of Bec*, p. 71. Gilo, "Vita Sancti Hugonis Abbatis" 1.2–3, in H. E. J. Cowdrey, ed., "Two Studies in Cluniac History," pp. 49–50.

[29] William of St.-Thierry, *Vita Prima Sancti Bernardi* 1.1, PL 185:228.

[30] Guibert de Nogent, *Memoirs* 1.4–5, pp. 13–19.

A young aristocrat's knightly training and his formal education ended when he came of age, most likely in his mid to late teens. The epic hero Raoul de Cambrai was fifteen when the emperor knighted him.[31] By the late twelfth century, young nobles like Raoul underwent a formal coming-of-age ceremony called dubbing or knighting, which, as I noted, became so elaborate and expensive that lords customarily demanded of their vassals a contribution toward the cost of an eldest son's knighting. The feasting, the games, the tournaments, and the displays of skill might go on for days.

Once knighted and ready to take their place in society, many young nobles discovered that society as yet had no place for them. As long as their fathers were still alive, they could not very well take over their ancestral castles, and sitting at home during their years of peak physical energy could not have been very appealing. One can imagine the frequent friction between fathers not at all ready to give up the prerogatives of lordship and superbly conditioned young fighting men who were feeling restless. The son of a serving knight, of course, would be in a perfect position to take up his duties, but the son of a castellan had fewer obvious options.

Someone of this age was known as a youth, a *juvenis* (*juvenes* in the plural).[32] "Youth" was not strictly speaking a matter of age, for one could continue as a youth well into one's forties before being able to settle down and take up the responsibilities of lordly rule. Younger sons, who might at best receive some property in fief from an elder brother, which would revert to their nephews on their deaths, might become permanent *juvenes* if their elder brother were not even this generous.

The *juvenes* of western Europe provided many of the warriors in local wars and probably the majority of the Crusaders. Marie de France's hero Guigemar immediately after his dubbing left for Flanders, "where one could always find war and strife, in search of renown."[33] The *juvenes* also provided most of the converts to the strict monastic orders, which wanted their new members to be not children but people old enough to know their own minds. *Juvenes* inclined nei-

[31] *Raoul de Cambrai* 18, p. 25. Jean Flori "Les origines de l'adoubement chevaleresque," p. 214.

[32] Georges Duby, "Youth in Aristocratic Society: Northwestern France in the Twelfth Century," in *The Chivalrous Society*, pp. 112–22. Jane K. Beitscher, " 'As the Twig Is Bent . . .' "

[33] Marie de France, *The Lais* 1, p. 43.

ther for crusading nor monasticism might spend these years going to tournaments. Or sometimes they just rode around in gangs, terrorizing the countryside, until reined in by the local bishop or by fathers whose patience had finally snapped. Probably the best-known *juvenis* of the twelfth century was William Marshal, a younger son who made his fortune on the tournament circuit and, at the end of his life, became regent of England.[34]

The Crusades

Crusading always occupied a somewhat ambiguous position in high medieval France. It was encouraged by popes and bishops and embraced eagerly both by pious lords (including Kings Louis VII and Philip II of France) and by bored *juvenes.* Yet crusading was also discouraged by parents fearful of losing their sons—and even sometimes by monks, who worried when their most reliable secular supporters left them for the East. The abbot of Cluny welcomed the the lord of Beaujeu home from the second Crusade by saying that everyone eager for "peace," including churchmen, the poor, farmers, orphans, and women, was delighted to have him there again to protect them.[35]

The First Crusade, launched in 1095, was to be the only militarily successful one, although of course no one realized this at the time. Having crosses sewn on their clothes and believing that they were following God's commands, French knights and nobles braved shipwreck, disease, starvation, and unfriendly Byzantines (who were supposed to be their allies) before finally arriving in the Holy Land. Here, almost to their own surprise, they conquered the city of Jerusalem, which the Muslims had held for four centuries, and established a Christian kingdom centered there. They shaped the ruling institutions of this kingdom very much on the model of French administration (or, more specifically, the administration of the parts of France from which they came), and they quickly started building castles that owed more to European than to Middle Eastern military technology.[36]

[34] William Marshal has been a popular figure with scholars. See, most recently, Georges Duby, *William Marshal;* and David Crouch, *William Marshal.*

[35] Peter the Venerable, Letter 173, *The Letters,* 1:410–13.

[36] Jean Richard, "La féodalité de l'Orient latin et le mouvement communal: Un état des questions," in *Structures féodales et féodalisme dans l'Occident méditerranéen,* pp. 651–65. For the military techniques developed during the Crusades, see R. Rogers, *Latin Siege Warfare in the Twelfth Century.*

A thirteenth-century pious knight prepares to leave on Crusade: he can be
recognized as a crusader by the crosses on his surcoat and banner. He is clad in chain
mail that includes sleeves, leggings, a helmet, and even gloves. By permission of The
British Library, MS Royal 2A XXII, fol. 220.

Krak des Chevaliers, still standing in modern Syria, is one of the best surviving examples of a high medieval French castle.

Although Crusaders continued to head east for the next three generations (including the lulls between the great expeditions that are now numbered), and although the Second Crusade in 1147 was led by the French and German kings and the Third Crusade in 1189 by the kings of France, England, and Germany, the history of the Latin Kingdom of Jerusalem describes a fairly steady decline throughout the twelfth century.[37] The city of Jerusalem fell in 1187 (spurring the ultimately unsuccessful Third Crusade). Even while the Kingdom persisted, there was an increasing realization back home that going on Crusade was a particularly dangerous way to seek salvation and that it was certainly not a path to wealth and power. Milo of Montlhéry, who returned from the First Crusade "broken by the stress" and "devoid of all bodily strength," was only one of a continuing series of men who came back ill if they came back at all. Count Baldwin of Hainaut never came home. "Whether he was killed or captured," wrote a monastic chronicler, "no one knows to this day."[38] Parents soon came to dread the sight of their sons leaving for the East. A trip to the Holy Land became decreasingly appealing to all but the truly fervent as it became increasingly clear that few of those who left on Crusade ever came back.

By the thirteenth century, in spite of desperate attempts to revive the crusading ethos, it was becoming clear that it was no longer viable. The Fourth Crusade of 1204 ended up sacking the Christian (though Greek Orthodox rather than Roman Catholic) capital of Byzantium. Emperor Frederick II went on Crusade in the 1220s under papal pressure, but he went while excommunicate (and was excommunicated *again* for doing so). When King Louis IX attempted to reach the Holy Land in the mid-thirteenth century, he got no closer than North Africa. At the end of the century, Pope Boniface VIII tried to preach a Crusade against some of his own cardinals whom he considered his enemies.

And yet, in the twelfth century at least, crusading was a reasonable alternative to Christians killing Christians. Accounts of the preaching

[37] For the disastrous Second Crusade, see Odo of Deuil, *De Profectione Ludovici VII in Orientem.*
[38] Suger, *The Deeds of Louis the Fat* 8, p. 40. Herman of Tournai, *The Restoration of the Monastery of Saint Martin of Tournai* 33, p. 47.

of the First Crusade (it does not really matter whether they actually record what was said in 1095 or reflect ideas of a few years later, after the Crusade had succeeded) stress that French knights now had an opportunity to use their warrior skills in ways compatible with Christianity. The monk Bernard of Clairvaux, who helped establish the Crusading Order of the Templars, which combined a monastic way of life (shared property, chastity, and discipline) with fighting the infidel, contrasted the life of the Templars with that of secular knights, for which he had little use. He said that in this new order knights could fight and die for Christ instead of fighting a secular enemy, where winning put them in danger of losing their souls and losing jeopardized body and soul together.[39]

Although they were a distinctly problematic alternative to killing Christians, the Crusades were an inspiration to the writers of epics and romances, who were able to have their Christian and chivalrous heroes fight Muslims, thus exercising their warrior skills while not endangering their souls. The epic hero William of Orange took the opportunity, while preparing for a battle against a Muslim, to give a hundred-line summary of the events of the Old and New Testaments and the chief tenets of the Christian faith. When his enemy, naturally surprised, asked him the purpose of this "tirade," William responded that he had just prayed to God "that he would me in his goodness sustain, that I might all your limbs from your body tear."[40] Thus Christian, chivalrous knights in the stories not only could fight without guilt but had at least a reasonable hope that God would intervene on their side.

The Muslims of twelfth- and thirteenth-century stories would not have seemed realistic to anyone who had actually met one—nor, probably, were they meant to. Rather, they were described, enthusiastically if theologically incorrectly as the moral equivalent of heretics or pagans. The author of the *Song of Roland* made such an equation explicit by having Charlemagne's Muslim enemies worship both Mohammed (as true Muslims do not) and the Roman pagan god Apollo. The author of "The Coronation of Louis" similarly referred to the

[39] Edward Peters, ed., *The First Crusade*, pp. 2–5. Marcus Bull, *Knightly Piety and the Lay Response to the First Crusade*. Bernard of Clairvaux, "De laude novae militiae," in *Opera*, 3:213–39; trans. Conrad Greenia, "In Praise of the New Knighthood," in *Treatises III*, pp. 127–67. Jean Flori, *L'essor de la chevalerie*, pp. 209–14. For the Templars, see, most recently, Malcolm Barber, *The New Knighthood*.

[40] "The Coronation of Louis" 22, in *Guillaume d'Orange*, pp. 83–85.

enemy of William of Orange, his Christian hero, interchangeably as a Turk, a pagan, a follower of Mohammed, and a giant "hideous to behold."[41] The addition of giants and monsters to Muslim armies in these stories put into doubt not only their religious orthodoxy but their humanity, making them eminently suitable targets for chivalrous Christian knights to slay.

The difficulty, as the writers realized themselves, was that the killing of inhuman beasts was not nearly as interesting as a fight between knights of comparable training. The writers tried to finesse their way out of this problem by composing Muslim armies of pagans, monsters, *and* knights indistinguishable from the French knights in every respect except their religion. In *Roland,* for example, the Muslim contingent against which the hero's outnumbered knights fight to a standstill includes at least several men about which the French say that they would have been excellent knights if only they had been Christians. Interestingly, while praising some of the Muslims with the term "worthy baron," the author also felt compelled to say of one of Roland's men, "No pagan is such a good knight."[42]

A recurring motif, along with the Muslim knight who would have been admired but for his religion, is the Muslim maiden beautiful and refined in everything except her religion. Here the answer was easier: the hero could persuade her to convert and marry her. The twelfth-century stories of William of Orange had him doing just that. The thirteenth-century romance "Aucassin and Nicolette" portrays Nicolette as a Saracen girl, bought as a slave, freed, and baptized. Parzival's father in the German version of his story tried to do the same thing, but the lady agreed to convert only *after* Parzival's father had left her; he returned to France and married Parzival's mother instead. In *The Song of Roland,* even though Charlemagne seems unlikely to marry the Muslim queen, he does take her home with him, rather than kill her or force her to convert as he did all the other Muslims; he prefers to convert her "through love."[43]

[41] *The Song of Roland,* line 8, p. 29. "The Coronation of Louis" 21, in *Guillaume d'Orange,* p. 82.

[42] *The Song of Roland,* lines 899, 960, 3248–53, pp. 57, 59, 132.

[43] "The Conquest of Orange" 61, in *Guillaume d'Orange,* pp. 194–95. *Aucassin and Nicolette,* p. 4. *The Song of Roland,* line 3674, p. 146. See also Sarah Kay, The *"Chansons de geste" in the Age of Romance,* pp. 30–31.

Noble Marriage

The quickest way for a young noble with a healthy father to change his status from *juvenis* to young lord was to find and marry an heiress (normally a Christian, of course, not a Muslim), a woman with a (dead) propertied father and no brothers. But in the twelfth century even eldest sons often had to wait until their fathers died to marry if no convenient heiresses presented themselves.

Younger sons might occasionally be lucky enough to find heiresses of their own, but more often they had to resign themselves to remaining single, living with their elder brother or, at best, being allowed a lifetime interest in some of the family patrimony. A fear that family possessions were being dissipated among too many heirs seems to have led, as I have noted, to the adoption of strict primogeniture in the late eleventh and twelfth centuries. One result, of course, was rebellion by younger brothers unwilling to accept being left with little property and few chances to marry. Robert I of Flanders gained his county in 1071 by killing his late elder brother's son in battle, and Lord Haimo of Bourbon in the early twelfth century disinherited his nephew, taking the lordship of Bourbon for himself after his elder brother died. The troubadour Bertran de Born, the eldest son, complained that his younger brothers would not "tolerate my rights."[44] In the thirteenth century, however, tensions were reduced as younger sons began to marry more frequently, for reasons that will be discussed later.

The choice of marriage partner throughout the Middle Ages (and for that matter in antiquity as well) was a matter of political maneuvering and expediency for the aristocracy. The interests of the families took precedence over the particular desires of the couple, who might barely have met each other before the wedding. One castellan, for example, married his daughter to the illegitimate son of King Philip I at the beginning of the twelfth century, thus satisfying both Philip, who had found that particular castle a thorn in his side for years, and the castellan himself, who could thus be assured that his family would not lose it.[45]

[44] Herman of Tournai, *The Restoration of Saint Martin of Tournai* 12–13, pp. 26–27. Suger, *The Deeds of Louis the Fat* 25, p. 109. Bertran de Born, *The Poems of the Troubadour Poet Bertran de Born* 2, p. 118.

[45] Suger, *The Deeds of Louis the Fat* 8, p. 40.

During the twelfth century, however, the modern concept of falling in love and getting married began to appear in the chivalric romances. Of course, in these romances people usually fall in love with people whom it was entirely appropriate for them to marry anyway. In *Raoul de Cambrai* Lord Guerri's daughter conveniently falls passionately in love with the man with whom her father needs to make peace in order to avoid a new outbreak of war. "If you marry me, generous, true-hearted knight, then the peace might last, and the war be put aside for ever," she tells him.[46] In actual practice, young people were considered much less capable of judging whom it was suitable to marry than were their older relatives (especially older male relatives), but at least after marriage it was considered appropriate to love one's spouse.

One of the key elements in the arrangement of a marriage was the transfer of property from one family to the other or from one or both families to the new couple. Early Germanic law had emphasized the bride price, the money the groom's family gave to the bride's relatives. Roman law, on the other hand, had stressed the importance of a dowry, the money and property a woman brought to her husband, which remained his when she died or even if he divorced her for adultery or another suitably heinous crime. While a dowry was not absolutely necessary under Roman law, it was the normal practice, and if there was a question whether a man had merely taken a woman as his concubine or actually married her (a question that might arise, for example, if a wealthy Roman contracted a liaison with a woman of substantially lower status), the payment of a dowry could indicate unequivocally that a real marriage had taken place.[47]

The Roman dowry system predominated along the Mediterranean in the Middle Ages, and in northern Europe the Germanic bride-price was more important, but in France in the High Middle Ages *both* were often found, although the dower, property a husband would fix on his wife for her lifetime if he predeceased her, came to replace the old Germanic bride-price.[48] Given the dual system of dowry and dower, negotiations over who was to pay what to whom and when could un-

---

[46] *Raoul de Cambrai* 254, p. 339.

[47] J. A. Crook, *Law and Life of Rome*, pp. 102–3.

[48] Barthélemy, *La société dans le comté de Vendôme*, pp. 543–49. For the transition from bride-price to dower, see Jo Ann McNamara and Suzanne Wemple. "The Power of Women through the Family in Medieval Europe," pp. 83–101.

derstandably occupy the male relatives of an espoused couple for months.

An example of such negotiations is found in the agreement reached in 1201 between the count of Boulogne and King Philip II of France. These two agreed that the count's daughter Mathilda would marry the king's young son within forty days of when she reached "marriageable age." The count announced that she would bring as her dowry one-third of the county of Boulogne, or one-half if her mother had died before the marriage took place, indicating that the count had fixed a sixth of his county on his wife as dower.[49] Here, as doubtless in most important marriages, the political and financial dealings took precedence over any notions of love derived from the romances.

As this example suggests, an aristocratic bride's dowry, the property that she brought to her husband, could be fairly substantial in France in this period. It essentially constituted her inheritance in advance, so that ordinarily she received nothing more when her father died—not that the sons-in-law of wealthy men refrained from trying. During her marriage, a noblewoman had a fair amount of control over her dowry property, but her authority was still commonly exercised through her husband, and she could certainly not alienate it without his consent.[50] In some cases, the husband might even control and receive income from his wife's dowry just as from his own property during her lifetime. Still, it was not his own property. It passed at once to a couple's children upon a woman's death, even if her husband were still alive, for under medieval law couples did not normally inherit anything from each other beyond the wife's life interest in her dower.

In some families, dowry property was treated as something special and separate which arrived with a wife and left again with a daughter as *her* dowry, serving as nothing more than a temporary source of extra family income, if that, in the meantime. When one young noble girl was made a nun by her parents at the house of St.-Jean-le-Grand of Autun, the entry gift her parents made, the sum total of all of their property that she would receive, was said explicitly to be "that land which her mother had received as her own marriage portion."[51] Since

---

[49] Teulet, ed., *Layettes du trésor des chartes*, 1:226–27, no. 613. For this marriage, see also John W. Baldwin, *The Government of Philip Augustus*, p. 270.

[50] Penny Schine Gold, *The Lady and the Virgin*, pp. 125–30.

[51] *Le cartulaire de Marcigny-sur-Loire*, p. 104, no. 175. See also Bouchard, *Sword, Miter, and Cloister*, p. 59.

the mother's family—and hence the mother's dowry—might be located some distance from the possessions of the male-line family, a dowry that came into the family with a marriage might be more useful as something to leave with a daughter, as dowry or nunnery entry gift, than as income-producing property.

The dower property a husband fixed on his wife functioned a little differently from the dowry—or, for that matter, the old Germanic bride-price—because it never actually left the (patrilinear) family. It was ceded not to the relatives of the woman joining her new family but to the woman herself. By the thirteenth century a prenuptial agreement might specify what part of a man's property a wife would be entitled to after his death; a third of his assets was common. In addition to fixing a dower on her, a noble might also make his wife a "morning gift" (*Morgengabe*) after their first night together; this would be substantially smaller.

Whereas the rest of a husband's property could be given away by testament or passed directly to his heirs, the dower was his wife's as long as she lived. A castellan's widow whose dower consisted of some land and a manor house might retreat there when her son took over the castle, maintaining her own autonomous household during her lifetime. In *Raoul de Cambrai*, the hero's widowed mother is advised to "keep house on her dowerland" after her husband dies, "for she will have no legal concerns with, or income from" anything else of his.[52]

When a widow died, the dower passed to the children she and her husband had produced. Again it should be noted that husband and wife did not inherit from each other in the sense of acquiring full control over any property, beyond small gifts made when both were alive. Children would inherit from both their parents, but neither spouse obtained full rights to the other's property (at most a life interest) when he or she died. The marriage contract drawn up in 1178 between the noble couple Rudolph and Adelaide spelled out the property she would bring to the marriage as a dowry, *in dotem,* and specified that as a dower or marriage gift, a *donatio propter nuptias,* he had fixed half his property on her. If the couple had children, the contract noted, this dower property would pass to them after the wife's death; otherwise, it would return to his close relatives.[53]

[52] *Raoul de Cambrai* 10, p. 17.
[53] Teulet, ed., *Layettes du trésor des chartes,* 1:119–20, no. 289.

Among the aristocracy, women generally married substantially younger than did men. Once a girl reached puberty, she was considered ready for marriage, and in some cases parents who had found an appropriate bridegroom might not even wait for that. Boys might sometimes marry equally early. Guibert of Nogent, whose autobiography tells of family life at the end of the eleventh century, records that his parents got married when his mother was perhaps eleven and his father only a few years older; not surprisingly, they were then unable to consummate their marriage for several years.[54] But for the most part men seem to have married substantially later, in their thirties or even forties, after they had inherited or made their fortunes. The romances are full of young wives married to old husbands—and inevitably more attracted to men their own age than to the men they were supposed to love.

Because noblewomen frequently married men perhaps twice their age—who had had more opportunities to die unmarried in tournament, war, Crusade, or from disease—there were substantially more noblewomen in the High Middle Ages looking for husbands than noblemen looking for wives. The imbalance was further magnified because boys entered the church in much greater numbers than girls. Men were therefore able to pick and choose their spouses much more easily than could women. As a result, men could reasonably hope to marry women of higher social standing than their own or, at worst, settle for wives of a comparable situation. The knight Aucassin in "Aucassin and Nicolette" is urged to seek the daughter of a count or even a king as a rational alternative to the girl he loves. Women, on the other hand, could at best hope to marry their social equals and often had to settle for husbands beneath them in status.[55]

Marriages were thus an excellent opportunity for social advancement among the male aristocracy. Sometimes a castellan might tie his knights to him more tightly by making them his sons-in-law as well as his sworn warriors and vassals. Because of such marriages, nobles who could boast of glorious noble ancestors also had ancestors whose nobility and glory were at best dubious. At the beginning of the twelfth century the king of England found the marriage he was trying

[54] Guibert of Nogent, *Memoirs* 1.12, pp. 34–39.
[55] Constance B. Bouchard, "Consanguinity and Noble Marriages in the Tenth and Eleventh Centuries," pp. 279, 286. *Aucassin and Nicolette*, p. 6. For Austrian parallels, see Freed, *Noble Bondsmen*, pp. 99–104.

to arrange for one of his daughters thwarted when it turned out that she was a distant cousin of the chosen bridegroom; both were descended from a certain forester whose name was not even remembered.[56]

Of course a knight like Aucussin could not really marry a king's daughter. But as knights married castellans' daughters, castellans married counts' daughters, counts dukes' daughters, and dukes kings' daughters, the entire aristocracy was tied together into a network of blood and alliance in which women formed a key connection.[57] By the thirteenth century, even while nobles were desperately trying to reestablish the rapidly shrinking gap between the aristocracy and everyone else, knights' daughters might indeed find it expedient to marry young men of the wealthy urban classes.

In choosing marriage partners, families thus had a complex task. They had to consider not only political, financial, and social advantage but also the possibility of incest. From the seventh or eighth century through the beginning of the thirteenth century, church councils declared "consanguineous"—that is, incestuous—any union of people who were related within seven degrees. Degrees were calculated by counting back to the common ancestor, so that a brother and sister were considered related within the first degree—it was one generation back to their common ancestors, their parents—and first cousins, who shared the same grandparents, were related within two degrees, and so on. Theoretically, therefore, one had to be more distantly related than sixth cousins in order to marry. This early medieval definition of incest was much broader than that used in Roman law or any definition used today.[58]

Given that members of the nobility were all very closely related anyway and that the number of one's ancestors doubles with every generation (each person has two parents, four grandparents, eight great-grandparents, and so on), it very quickly became almost impossible to find potential marriage partners of suitable social status to whom one was not related within the forbidden degrees. This may have been an additional reason, beyond a desire to preserve the fam-

[56] Anselm, Letter 4.84, PL 159:243. R. W. Southern, *The Making of the Middle Ages*, pp. 79–80.

[57] Bouchard, "Origins of the Nobility," p. 524.

[58] Bouchard, "Consanguinity and Noble Marriages," pp. 269–71. Jean Gaudemet, "Le legs du droit romain en matière matrimoniale," in *Il matrimonio nella società altomedievale*, pp. 139–79.

ily patrimony, why in the twelfth century only the eldest son might marry; it was hard enough to find a wife for one son, much less for all of them. Concern about consanguinity also helped ensure that the serving knights, who, lacking noble ancestry, were *not* related to the castellans, made attractive marriage partners for castellans' daughters.

It has sometimes been said that the church imposed the broad definition of consanguinity on noble families in order to "control" them, to force them to disperse their property.[59] This cynical view does not accord with the evidence, however. Most obviously, of course, there was no such monolithic entity as "the" church, and most church leaders were themselves the brothers and cousins of secular nobles, more favorably disposed to their interests than otherwise. Additionally and most important, if noble families were principally interested in preserving their property rather than seeing it dispersed through marriages with outsiders, they would not have worried overmuch whether the church was forbidding marriages between sixth cousins or between second cousins; to keep property truly in the family, marriages between the closest possible relatives, even brother and sister, would have been necessary. This level of incest has been forbidden in virtually all human cultures, Christian or not. As the anthropologists say, if you can't kill him you can't marry his sister.

In the tenth and eleventh centuries, medieval nobles seem to have accepted the church's view of consanguinity, or at least to have done their best to live within its strictures. Laymen were just as insistent as churchmen—at least when their own interests were not compromised—that marriages not take place within the forbidden degrees. The count of Anjou, furious with King Philip I for eloping with his wife at the end of the eleventh century, was delighted to find, in checking his family tree, that he was the king's third cousin and that the king had therefore committed incest as well as adultery.[60]

Those who tried to marry their relatives in defiance of the church found themselves preached against at councils and, as in the case of Kings Philip I and Robert II (who attempted but failed to stay mar-

---

[59] This is the view of Jack Goody, *The Development of the Family and Marriage in Europe*, pp. 39–47, 123–25. See also James A. Brundage, *Law, Sex, and Christian Society in Medieval Europe*, pp. 606–7.

[60] Violante, "Quelques caractéristiques des structures familiales," pp. 90–92. Ivo of Chartres, Letter 211, PL 162:215–16.

ried to his cousin at the beginning of the eleventh century), faced serious political and social consequences. Marriages were difficult enough to arrange without fearing that all one's careful planning might go for naught when one was forced to dissolve the union. Until the twelfth century, members of the great noble families generally married people no more closely related to them than fourth or fifth cousins—that is, related within five or six degrees (closer than a strict interpretation of the church's rule would allow, but apparently distant enough).[61]

The nobles' acceptance of the church's prohibition against marriages between relatives was probably an inevitable part of their contemporaneous acceptance of marriage as a sacrament. This was something new in the tenth and eleventh centuries. Marriages in the early Middle Ages had been arranged by family members, involved the transfer of property between the families, were celebrated at big parties, and culminated in the tucking of the new couple into bed together. Even after Western society became generally Christian, the role of priests in early medieval weddings was limited, usually no more than blessing the bed. But this role grew steadily. The Bible, after all, says that God joins a couple together. By the ninth century, bishops were interfering in royal politics in the interest of queens whose husbands had decided to divorce them, arguing that marriage was something sacred, a sacrament, and therefore could not easily be put aside.[62]

From there it was a relatively short step to emphasizing the sacrality of marriage at the time of the wedding itself.[63] Marriage in the

[61] Bouchard, "Consanguinity and Noble Marriages," pp. 284–86. Léopold Genicot, "La noblesse médiévale: Encore!" p. 181. Donald C. Jackman has argued that the great noble families who appear to have avoided marriages with those related less closely than six degrees might in fact have been more closely related to their spouses if all cognate lines were considered. *The Konradiner,* p. 139 n. 230. The difficulty with this argument is that neither they nor modern scholars were aware of any such closer ties; although some unrecognized blood relationships surely existed, if they were unrecognized, they cannot have influenced the choice of spouse. A similar point is raised by Le Jan in *Famille et pouvoir,* p. 322, but most of the family trees she cites to show marriages between close relatives were either from the ninth century (before the nobility became too concerned about consanguinity) or else have gaps, where one has to infer parentage.

[62] Jane Bishop, "Bishops as Marital Advisors in the Ninth Century," pp. 55–63. Suzanne Fonay Wemple, *Women in Frankish Society,* pp. 75–123.

[63] For the development of the idea of a wedding as a religious event, see John Boswell, *Same-Sex Unions in Premodern Europe,* pp. 162–217.

High Middle Ages was a sacrament, unequivocally defined as such in 1215, but interestingly, it was the only sacrament performed not by a priest but by the couple themselves. The oaths that the man and woman took to be true to each other, often symbolized by an exchange of rings, were the sacral center of a Christian marriage. By the twelfth century weddings were normally performed at the church door—even if not inside the church itself, although the wedding party would generally proceed inside afterward for a nuptial mass. (Modern Catholic marriages still have two separate parts, the exchange of oaths and the mass, even though the whole process has moved into the church.)

Marriage became the single largest topic in the developing canon law of the High Middle Ages.[64] The specialists in church law in the twelfth century defined two elements as constituting a valid marriage, the exchange of oaths and the subsequent consummation of the union, the *copula carnalis*. Even if performed without a priest, even if performed in secret, a marriage was still valid if it included these two elements. Once both had occurred neither party could marry anyone else while the other lived. The count of Hainaut in the early twelfth century had made separate promises to marry two separate women, but a church council ruled that he was married only to the first one, with whom he had copulated.[65] Even though secret marriages were valid, however, the couple had to do penance, for church lawyers argued that there should be witnesses to the oaths. The families, too, wanted public weddings that took place before family members and only after property transfers had been suitably negotiated. Here the views of the bishops and the leaders of secular society coincided on the correct form of marriage.

As a sacrament, a marriage was not supposed to end in divorce. By the late eleventh century, only annullments were possible, declarations that a valid marriage had not taken place and that therefore the couple was not married at all (this is still the position of modern Catholicism). Grounds for declaring the marriage invalid included incest, bigamy (one or both parties were already married to someone else), indications that the oaths had been exchanged under duress, or an inability on one side or the other to consummate the marriage. The

---

[64] Brundage, *Law, Sex, and Christian Society.*
[65] Herman of Tournai, *The Restoration of Saint Martin of Tournai* 33, p. 48.

The medieval sacrament of marriage consisted of the oaths sworn between the individuals, but it was universally agreed that it was best to have a priest bless the union. Here a priest takes the hands of a young couple in preparation for joining them in marriage. The illustration was done for a collection of laws concerning marriage. Biblioteca Ambrosiana, B 43 Inf. 203v. Property of the Ambrosian Library. All rights reserved. Reproduction is forbidden.

early twelfth-century English recluse Christina of Markyate was eventually able to have her marriage annulled—in spite of her parents' objections—because even though she performed the "sacrament" by exchanging vows, she steadfastly refused to give up her virginity. In one of the *Lais* of Marie de France, a man decided at the last minute that he did not want to marry the woman with whom he had just exchanged vows before the archbishop, and the archbishop cheerfully annulled the marriage the next morning when the union was not consummated.[66]

And yet, though it was generally accepted, the church's definition of marriage presented the nobility with many difficulties. By the twelfth century it was becoming impossible to find spouses of the right age, social standing, and political suitability to whom one was not already related. The problem was especially acute for the most powerful families, since they were so few. The solution that emerged was expedient if somewhat cynical. Rather than try fruitlessly to find people to whom they were not related, members of the great noble families instead knowingly married cousins (maybe not first cousins but sometimes second cousins and certainly third). Then, if they decided for other reasons to seek a divorce, they could announce, with nicely modulated shock and horror, that they had discovered their union was consanguineous, and thus have it quite legitimately dissolved. Some of the most famous cases were the annulments on the grounds of incest of the marriages of the French king Louis VII and the German emperor Frederick Barbarossa, both in the 1150s.

Fed up by the end of the twelfth century with having what was essentially divorce on demand available to any noble couple willing to spend sufficient time examining their family trees for a common ancestor anywhere in the last century or two, the church reexamined the Roman law definition of "forbidden degrees," much narrower than that of the early medieval church. The definition of consanguinity was changed in 1215, eliminating much of the hypocrisy. The Fourth Lateran Council in that year reduced the number of forbidden degrees from seven to four. (This was the same council that formally defined marriage as one of the seven sacraments.)[67]

The change in the number of forbidden degrees proved very welcome. Just as when the number of degrees forbidden had been seven the nobility had settled, with the bishops' tacit consent, on six as the "real" boundary, so in the thirteenth century the nobles decided that three degrees (second cousins) were the cutoff on acceptability. Thus a flock of marriages followed the 1215 ruling which would have been ruled incestuous a generation earlier.

[66] *The Life of Christina of Markyate.* For Christina, see also Christopher J. Holdsworth, "Christina of Markyate," pp. 185–204. Marie de France, *Lais* 3, p. 67.
[67] John W. Baldwin, *Masters, Princes, and Merchants,* 1:332–37. Georges Duby, *The Knight, the Lady, and the Priest,* p. 209.

At the same time, younger sons who might previously have stayed single began to find spouses, now that the search was a much easier proposition. Families were more willing to allow these younger sons to marry, doubtless in part because they had seen that the strict primogeniture of the preceding century or two had resulted in the extinction of a number of male-defined lineages, when the one son on whom all the family's dynastic hopes were founded failed to produce an heir.[68] In addition, the opening up of careers at court in the thirteenth century, especially for those with university training, meant that, at least among the castellans and the knights, male brothers and cousins now had other options than taking a part of the family's landed wealth.[69]

It is surely to this increase in the number of sons who married in each generation that one must tie the increase in the average size of the dowry in the thirteenth century. Although it has sometimes been said that there was a "marriage market" at this time and that the reason women were accompanied by larger and more attractive dowries must have been because it was increasingly hard for them to find husbands,[70] in fact this economic model does not work. All the evidence indicates rather that it was *easier* for aristocratic women to find husbands in the thirteenth century than it had been earlier. In the twelfth century, most girls but only a portion of the young men had been destined for marriage; a century later, more young men were expected to marry, at the same time as nunneries had become more common, providing the alternative to married life which had formerly been much more readily available to men. Thus the increased size of the dowry should be seen as a function of its changing role. Rather than merely the inheritance a family bestowed on a daughter and her future family, property she would most likely pass on to her own children, the thirteenth-century dowry was needed to help establish the couple themselves in a period when the male-line patrimony was being sliced more thinly to accommodate more marriages in each genera-

[68] For younger sons in the twelfth century, see Theodore Evergates, "Nobles and Knights in Twelfth-Century France," in Thomas N. Bisson, ed., *Cultures of Power*, pp. 17–28. Duby argues that aristocratic families had greater liquid wealth at the end of the twelfth century than they had had earlier, thus making multiple heirs more feasible. *The Knight, the Lady, and the Priest*, pp. 274–78.

[69] Freed found a similar pattern among the Austrian *ministeriales*. *Noble Bondsmen*, pp. 133–45.

[70] David Herlihy, "The Medieval Marriage Market."

tion.[71] Thus the dower and dowry, institutions with roots going back well over a millennium, continued to adapt and grow to meet the changing needs of noble families.

One can thus see several different models of marriage at work in the High Middle Ages.[72] There were at least three different versions of suitable marriage: the romantic one of the union of true lovers, the politically, socially, and economically expedient one of the union of allies, and the ecclesiastically correct one of sacramental marriage only with nonrelatives. Individual noble families trying to arrange marriages for their children had to deal on at least some level with all of these.

Life in the Castle

Once a couple was married, if the husband was the lord of a castle they also became the symbolic parents of all the people in that castle.[73] Indeed, before the thirteenth century there was rarely more than one married couple in a castle at a time, since the heir usually did not marry until his father died. There were also usually no women other than the lady herself, perhaps a few female attendants, and her daughters. Perhaps the lord's mother, aunt, or sisters might live with him as well. All the staff in the castle, from the kitchen to the stables to the battlements, were men.

The lady of the castle had the responsibility of overseeing all these people. Because women married substantially younger than men, often in their early teens, and because when a girl did marry she might at once become the lady of a castle, responsible for all its functions, girls had to be trained in castle management from the time they were big enough to tag along behind their mothers, from the kitchen to the treasury to the grain storage bins. As well as making sure there was enough food for everyone in the castle, a lady's duties might

[71] This point is also argued by Freed, *Noble Bondsmen*, pp. 146–50.

[72] The idea of different models of marriage is that of Georges Duby, *Medieval Marriage*; idem, *The Knight, the Lady, and the Priest*. He and I differ in that he does not consider the extent to which nobles initially accepted the church's restrictions on consanguinity, and his "noble marriage" model, which he contrasts with the chuch's model, does not distinguish between political concerns and concerns based on personal feeling.

[73] For a lively introduction to medieval castle life, see Joseph Gies and Frances Gies, *Life in a Medieval Castle*.

even, if her husband was away, include commanding the castle's defense. Juliana, an illegitimate daughter of King Henry I of England, defended her castle against the king when she and her husband tried to rebel and went so far as to try to shoot him with a crossbow during a parley in which she had feigned repentence as a dutiful daughter. The king, to punish her, had her jump off the castle wall into the moat with nothing on but a shift; she was pulled out wet and freezing but still impenitent.[74]

Most castles' ladies were not as active or warlike as Juliana, but they were still expected to be knowledgeable, skillful, and full of initiative. The lady carried the only set of the castle's keys on her belt, including the keys to the treasury and to the spice chest (nearly as valuable). When Christina of Markyate ran away from home to become a recluse, her last act was to give the keys to her younger sister. With the responsibility for the welfare of everyone within the walls, the lady was the busiest person in the castle.[75]

The whole castle's population, lord and lady included, originally lived like one big family, eating and sleeping in one large room. The present-day distinction between public and private space (for example, in such buildings as the American White House) would have made no more sense to a twelfth-century castellan than the distinction between public and private rights and income. Since the early Middle Ages, as is evident in such poems as *Beowulf*, aristocratic life had centered around a large hall, the center of a complex of ancillary buildings, a room where people ate, slept, entertained, and received justice. The original castles of the eleventh and early twelfth centuries kept this focus on the great hall, the center of castle life. Often the hall filled the entire second floor of the keep, the large square tower that was the center of a castle's defense, although it might also be contained in an adjoining structure.[76] Here in the hall trestle tables were set up for meals, and the castle staff stretched out to sleep at night. Individual private bedrooms were not customary, even in the homes of the mighty, until the end of the Middle Ages.

This retreat toward privacy evolved gradually. Originally the lord

[74] Orderic Vitalis, *The Ecclesiastical History* 12.10, 6:212–14.

[75] *The Life of Christina of Markyate*, p. 93. Constance Brittain Bouchard, *Life and Society in the West*, pp. 199–200. Georges Duby, "Women and Power," in Bisson, *Cultures of Power*, pp. 80–84.

[76] M. W. Thompson, *The Rise of the Castle*.

and lady's bed was in the middle of the hall, separated from everyone else only by curtains. During the course of the twelfth and thirteenth centuries, however, their bed was gradually moved, first to a dais at the end of the room, then to a great chamber reached by stairs from the end of the great hall. By the late Middle Ages, even the great chamber was no longer private enough for the lord and lady. They might eat here in great formality and relative isolation, but they slept in a smaller room beyond it, called the closet (a word which has since lost all its original importance, being now only a place to keep the clothes or the mop). The retreat of the bedroom—accompanied by increasing formality—continued in the postmedieval period, until in eighteenth-century France one's status at the royal court could be determined by how far down the long corridors to the royal bedchamber one was allowed to go.[77]

The most important activity to animate the great hall throughout the Middle Ages, the event around which chivalric activity revolved, was the feast.[78] Entertainment, gifts, fine clothing, and even tournaments were all aspects of feasts. The food served would be a combination of meat and vegetables produced by the lord's peasants with wild birds and animals caught in the hunt—the whole flavored with imported spices. Many an Arthurian romance begins with a banquet at which something unexpected happens—someone, say, whether Perceval or the Green Knight, rides his horse into the middle of the hall. The feast also symbolized the unity of all the castle's inhabitants, in that they ate together rather than having the lord retreat for special, private meals.

Such feasts, which might go on for hours, were an opportunity to display elegant table manners, joke and flirt (in a refined and courtly way, of course), and revel in conspicuous consumption. Unusual, even imaginary birds and beasts show up on platters in the romances, and even in real banquets hard-to-produce foods were a source of pride for the host, as were enthusiastically used expensive spices, fine and expensive tableware, and the host of servants that really personal dinner service required.

The feast was the emblem of the court, the place where the model of "courtly" behavior developed. But there is another key aspect of

---

[77] Mark Girouard, *Life in the English Country House.*
[78] Bumke, *Courtly Culture,* pp. 178–273.

the feast: it took place within someone's family home. The greatest display of wealth and social skill took place in the heart of a lord's family, where the guests became almost extensions of that family. It is not accidental that the High Middle Ages had a perfectly good word for the household, the *familia*, whereas it had none for the nuclear family.

And yet a noble's broader kin group, the "extended family" in modern usage, was enormously influential, its consensus more important for many decisions than the wishes of the individual. In difficult times, one needs a group to which to belong, and the medieval patrilineal kin was the preeminent group of that sort. Blood ties had been important far before feudal ties or the sense of belonging to a specific kingdom, and they did not lessen in importance in the High Middle Ages.

In fact, during the course of the eleventh and twelfth centuries aristocrats defined their kin more and more clearly and precisely, all taking a shared *cognomen*, often based on a family castle, as well as continuing the earlier practice of virtually always giving a child the Christian name of an older relative. Kinship was especially oriented around the male line of descent and, increasingly over this period, around the eldest son, as symbolizing in himself the entire family. But even while men thought of their families in this way, they always found themselves in constant competition with other male members of the same family; being related did not mean a shared purpose but rather, in many cases, rivalry for the same inheritance.

Young nobles' training in the High Middle Ages could not have helped foster family harmony. While both young men and young women were given at least the rudiments of an education, girls were primarily trained for marriage, whereas boys were trained for a military life. The result was the rowdy bands of *juvenes* with few immediate options for their youthful energies and warlike skills. Set loose in a society that increasingly frowned on Christians killing Christians— especially their own close relatives—they instead channeled much of their energy into the tolerated violence of tournament and Crusade. They did so, often, to the dismay of elders who wanted the young men out of the way for the moment but alive and intact to assume their duties when the time came.

The eventual goal, for parents and *juvenes* alike, was marriage and children of their own. As discussed further in the next chapter, in many twelfth-century romances the hero finishes his adventures by marrying the girl who has won his heart. In practice marriage became a way for astute social climbers to gain alliance with kin groups more exalted than their own. Marriage was also an occasion for family members to spend a great deal of time and energy trying to reach agreements over property transfers via dower and dowry, agreements that were much more concrete and thus more important than the feelings of the couple involved. Marriage was increasingly considered the exchange of sacramental oaths, but this meaning was overlaid on what had always been an economic and political arrangement among the aristocracy.

While young noblemen were waiting for a chance to marry and come into their inheritance and young noblewomen were hoping for an acceptable husband, the society of the twelfth century provided them with increasingly sophisticated ideals for behavior, in warfare and in love. It is to these rapidly evolving—and often contradictory— chivalric ideals that I turn in the next chapter.

CHAPTER FOUR

Nobility and Chivalry

What is chivalry? The term comes from the old French word *cheva-lerie*, itself derived from *caballarius*, a medieval Latin term meaning someone on horseback. The word "chivalry" was not a legal or technical term (which would have been rendered in Latin); rather it had literary roots in the vernacular of the twelfth century. As the word was used in French literature of the High Middle Ages, its meaning is somewhat imprecise; it could refer variously to a group of mounted aristocratic warriors or the behavior of such a group or the standard that members of the group would have liked to meet.[1] In this chapter, I principally use it to mean a literary model for behavior among the male aristocracy.

To use the word "chivalry" in this sense, however, for both the twelfth and thirteenth centuries is somewhat of an anachronism. Until the final decades of the twelfth century, the Old French term *chevalerie* was used specifically to describe the warrior attributes of armed men on horseback, with no moral or social overtones.[2] Polite and virtuous behavior by nobles and the knowledge of how to behave correctly were initially described by a completely different term, *cortoisie*. Because the meanings of "chivalry" and "courtesy" tended to coalesce in the late twelfth and early thirteenth centuries, it seems easiest to treat them together in this chapter, and to give one name to

---

[1] Howell Chickering, Introduction to Howell Chickering and Thomas H. Seiler, eds., *The Study of Chivalry*, p. 3. The most important recent book on the ideology of chivalry is by Jean Flori, *L'essor de la chevalerie*.

[2] Jean Flori, "La notion de chevalerie dans les chansons de geste du XIIe siècle."

all ideals for knightly behavior, even while noting the multiple origins of what we now imagine to be a single concept.

An understanding of twelfth-century chivalry is made substantially simpler when one realizes that there was no single standard (or "code") which people of the time always meant when they referred to chivalrous (or courteous) behavior, and that modern scholars need not, therefore, seek a comprehensive definition. For a long time scholars assumed that in the twelfth century—if not indeed in the eleventh—there was a unitary knightly class, composed both of the descendants of the serving knights of the year 1000 and of the descendants of the great nobles who had ruled western Europe for centuries, and that they shared a single code of conduct called chivalry.[3] As the concept of a unitary knightly class has been rejected, however, so has the need to discover some monolithic ideal with clear rules that all knights and nobles followed.

In fact, the idea of a fixed "code of chivalry" which medieval aristocrats all knew and tried to observe is a modern, not a medieval invention. Some idealized standard for aristocrats first appeared in literary works at the very beginning of the twelfth century (about a hundred years after the appearance of knights and castles) and had become a common motif by the last decades of that century, but there were no conscious attempts to create explicit *definitions* of chivalry until the second half of the thirteenth century. Chivalry, then, is best defined operationally for the High Middle Ages. In the following pages, I use "chivalry" to mean a form of behavior knights and nobles would have liked to imagine they followed, both based on and reflected in the epics and romances, a form of behavior which took armed and mounted combat as one of its key elements.

It is important *not* to read the late medieval version of chivalry back into the eleventh and twelfth centuries. One must avoid the assumption that chivalry was unchanging and that the details one can glean from the systematic treatises of the fourteenth and fifteenth centuries must also have applied earlier.[4] Similarly, one must be careful not to load too many meanings onto the word "chivalry." If one discovers that everything from eleventh-century castles to thirteenth-century tournaments to fifteenth-century coats of arms is being described as

---

[3] For the long popularity of these assumptions, see Joachim Bumke, *The Concept of Knighthood in the Middle Ages*, pp. 3–5.

[4] Maurice Keen, *Chivalry*, pp. 6–15.

an attribute of chivalry, one should perhaps reconsider the use of the term.

Epics and Romances

The principal sources for studying chivalry are literary. Even if one is interested in what chivalry was "really" like, one has to go beyond the usual historical sources—that is, charters, letters, legal rulings, and annals—to the epics and romances, works of fiction created in the twelfth and thirteenth centuries. Some preliminary comments are therefore necessary on the nature of these sources and how they may be read for what might be considered historical information.

Postclassical fictional literature, that is, vernacular works not intended to be accurate portrayals of events even if they might sometimes deal with important and real themes, was essentially a twelfth-century creation. What has become at the end of the twentieth century the subgenre of "fantasy," tales of medieval warriors fighting each other with a strong admixture of magic, marvel, and the supernatural, constituted in the twelfth century essentially all the fiction written. Of course, because the medieval authors put such things as the military techniques of their own time into their stories, they were closer to the contemporary reader's "reality" than are sword-and-sorcery fantasies to twentieth-century readers.

These stories were most commonly set in a fictionalized past—in the days of Arthur, for example, or Charlemagne—when the authors frequently comment, "men knew the ways of courtliness, unlike men today." Of course, these twelfth-century authors had no intention of giving an accurate picture of the past (as modern writers of historical fiction often try to do). They knew perfectly well that the swords, armor, and social conventions in their stories were products of their own time; in fact, the very earliest mentions of some newly introduced military techniques or weapons styles are in the romances. Rather, by creating an idealized "past" to which to compare the present, these authors were able to critique their own societies.

Virtually all twelfth-century literature was written as poetry, even though it is now commonly put into prose in translation. Modern literary scholars often draw distinctions between medieval epics (or *chansons de geste,* sometimes unfortunately characterized as "feudal epics") and medieval romances, between stories with the emphasis on battles and those with an emphasis on emotions and the relations between men and women. I myself do not see this as a particularly crucial distinction, because it was not one that the authors of the High Middle Ages seem to have considered important themselves. The forms were not clearly differentiated in content or style.[5] Indeed, there has been much modern debate about which artificial category some individual stories belong in.

Although modern scholars can note that the "epics" tended to be based on some memory of distant historical events, the authors of the works were careful literary creators, not just scribes recording an oral tradition. Often the authors of the romances included a conventionalized assertion that they were retelling an "old tale," even when they were quite clearly creating a new story.[6] Certainly different authors told their stories differently—as might the same author at different times—but they were not trying to make them fit into clear and predefined categories. Hence, I discuss together works that modern readers might consider either romances or epics.

Although these literary sources were not intended as descriptions of reality, a great deal of "real" information can be extracted from them if we read carefully. Certainly the works cannot be treated as straightforward descriptions of medieval society, but the authors' assumptions, which they expected their audiences to share, can tell us a great deal about the society for which these works were written. I have already been using chivalric literature in this way in previous chapters. Even though the medieval authors and their audience knew that the works were fictional, they dealt with issues and themes that were very real contemporary concerns. But one must of course keep in mind that while the behavior of real aristocrats influenced that of the heroes of the romances and vice versa, the two were never identical.

As an example of the kind of concrete information on high medieval society one can gain from literary sources, a close study of the language of fictional literature can tell us, say, whether someone a poet called a "knight" was always of noble blood (in fact, generally not), thus illuminating vernacular usage.[7] Or literary sources may

---

[5] Sarah Kay, The "Chansons de geste" in the Age of Romance, pp. 1–5. Even among the epics, at least two different meters were used. Joachim Bumke, Courtly Culture, p. 92. Aldo Scaglione calls romance a "hard-to-define genre." Knights at Court, p. 115.

[6] Evelyn Mullally, The Artist at Work, p. 5.

[7] Flori, "La notion de chevalerie."

give insights into how those involved might react to aristocratic marriage arrangements, already known to us from legal documents. Most important for the purposes of this chapter, careful reading can give us some idea of what the authors considered "chivalrous" behavior and the extent to which they assumed their audience was or was not behaving this way.

In reading medieval literature for information on chivalry—or, for that matter, in reading any literature—it is important not to take isolated scenes or statements out of the author's carefully constructed literary context. We ought to know better than to take something presented as striking or unusual in a story and treat it as the norm, to assume a suit of marvelous armor in a story, for example, was the kind of armor most twelfth-century knights wore, and yet many cultural historians made just these sorts of assumptions a century ago. More insidious and just as misleading is the more modern habit of routinely treating statements made by individual characters in a story as though they represented the author's own opinions or, even worse, the opinions of his age.[8]

The impulse to treat characters' statements as accurate depictions of a standard on which all twelfth-century people agreed seems based on the perhaps unconscious assumption that there actually *was* such a code of behavior and that it can be reconstructed from the many incidents in which fictional characters quoted from it. Certainly plenty of characters in the romances, including many of the villains, made statements about the correct form of behavior for a courteous knight, but extracted from their context and taken together, they present an extremely murky and contradictory picture. Of course, this is the point: there was no single chivalric ideal on which all twelfth-century authors (let alone their fictional characters) agreed.

The men who wrote medieval French romances, in which the heroes behaved chivalrously and the villains (at least sometimes) did not, seem to have known what they meant by chivalry or courtesy, but the details varied from author to author, and sometimes even for the same author. For example, Chrétien de Troyes spoke extensively of *cortoisie* in his late twelfth-century tales and indeed was one of the first to use the concepts of "chivalry" and "courtliness" as though

---

[8] Douglas Kelly argues for the necessity—and difficulty—of finding the author's voice, which may or may not be that of the characters. *The Art of Medieval French Romance*, pp. 4–7.

they were congruent; King Arthur's court, he said, was the center of both "courtesy and valour."[9] Chrétien has a worthy gentleman describe the "order of knighthood" to his hero Perceval in the "Story of the Grail." The gentleman includes mercy to defeated enemies, a polite silence rather than chatter, consolation to ladies who needed it, and piety and prayer. But this was by no means an exhaustive or definitive list, even in this story, of what a courteous knight was expected to do. The hero's own mother, slightly earlier, had told her son to honor ladies and accept gifts from them but not to go beyond a kiss, to associate with gentlemen and always learn their names, and to pray frequently.

Partly, these differences reflect the difference in male and female advice; indeed, Chrétien's worthy gentleman warns the hero against thinking and talking too much about what his mother had taught him. Additionally, a number of the attributes of *cortoisie* the author gives must be treated as plot devices, not freestanding descriptions of courtliness. For example, Perceval's eagerness to obey his mother in accepting gifts from ladies leads him to steal a lady's ring, and his polite silence—obeying the precept not to chatter—when he should instead speak out loses him the grail.[10] With such differences even in a single work by a single author, it is clear that attempts to define a clear standard for "chivalry" or "courtesy" before the late thirteenth century are misplaced.

In reading the romances, it is also important to note that different authors were often in competition with one another for the public's attention. Many a story starts with the statement that although others have told the following tale, only the present author (or sometimes a nonexistent earlier author he will now "quote") knows how to tell it aright.[11] In the same way, individual authors' descriptions of "correct" chivalric behavior have to be understood as part of their dialogue with other authors. When two authors stress two quite

[9] Chrétien de Troyes, "Cligés," in *Arthurian Romances*, p. 125.

[10] Chrétien de Troyes, "The Story of the Grail (Perceval)," in *Arthurian Romances*, pp. 387–90, 402, 420–21.

[11] Gottfried von Strassburg, writing his *Tristan* in German at the beginning of the thirteenth century, attributed the correct version to one "Thomas," a figure he seems to have created. "Prologue," p. 43. Constance B. Bouchard, "The Possible Non-existence of Thomas, Author of *Tristan and Isolde*." In the same way, Wolfram von Eschenbach attributed the inspiration of his version of *Parzival* to a mysterious Kyot. *Parzival* 9, p. 232.

different characteristics, the modern reader cannot just assume that both are elements of uniformly accepted twelfth-century chivalry. Instead, in stressing one particular element, an author is, by implication, if not indeed explicitly, rejecting other possible elements put forward by rival authors as the centerpieces of chivalry.

Origins of Chivalry

The disagreements between medieval authors, on what a correct ideal for knightly behavior might be, have understandably proved problematic for modern scholars who want a single simple answer. And yet over the course of the twelfth and thirteenth centuries both the authors of the literature and the nobles themselves seemed to be moving toward a vague consensus. Even if they disagreed fiercely on the details, thirteenth-century authors all portrayed nobles who were, at a minimum, brave in battle and polite at court. The "Good Knight," as a thirteenth-century romance writer put it, "upheld loyalty, prowess, and honor" and was "prized for his deeds of arms." [12]

During the eleventh century, as noted, military prowess was added to the list of noble attributes which already included wealth, power, and birth. In the twelfth century, all nobles would have agreed that their warrior training and skill in arms were important to their status. They gloried in their courage, loyalty, and raw strength. Whatever its other attributes, late twelfth- and thirteenth-century chivalry was a conglomerate of ideas and ideals that glorified and ennobled warfare. [13]

But there was more to "chivalry" by the end of the twelfth century than the virtues of the battlefield. Elegant behavior was expected, especially at noble courts, and indeed the modern word "courtesy" comes from the root "court," behavior suitable for those at aristocratic centers. [14] "Courtesy" became a conscious goal during the twelfth century for any knight or noble with pretensions. This combination of politeness, especially to women; gentle and refined speech; and such skills as dancing and singing and dressing well was widely

[12] "The Knight with the Sword," in *Three Arthurian Romances*, p. 87.

[13] John F. Benton, " 'Nostre Franceis n'unt talent de fuïr': The Song of Roland and the Enculturation of a Warrior Class," in *Culture, Power, and Personality in Medieval France*, pp. 152–55. Flori, "La notion de chevalerie."

[14] For courtliness, see Scaglione, *Knights at Court*.

encouraged. Modern readers of pseudomedieval fantasies want their heroes to be rough-and-tumble (even barbaric) fighters; twelfth-century readers of the romances wanted to hear how courteous they were.

By the end of the twelfth century, a chivalrous or courtly knight (at least in most of the romances) was supposed to be at the same time a gentle admirer of women, a loyal vassal of his lord, a devout and humble Christian, and a powerful and independent fighter who had killed a hundred foes. Hunting skills, such as knowing how to field-dress a hart or train a falcon, were also considered appropriate in a young aristocrat.[15] He was also probably expected to be polite, well spoken, and merciful to his enemies, to wear fine clothing, have good table manners, and know how to dance or play an instrument. In the early thirteenth-century prose *Lancelot of the Lake,* the Lady of the Lake tells Lancelot that knighthood was intended "to protect the weak and the peaceful" and to defend the church, and that a true knight would be courteous, gracious, compassionate, generous, harsh to malefactors, absolutely fair in judgment, and "more afraid of shame than of suffering death."[16]

Even aside from the fact that no one could possibly excel at all these virtues simultaneously—as the knights and the authors themselves realized perfectly well—there is the question of how all these different elements came to be considered parts of one ethos. For a long time scholars have wondered how the eleventh-century knights, whom the bishops of the Peace of God movement had desperately tried to keep from wantonly attacking peasants and the clergy, had by the late twelfth century evolved into knights who liked to see themselves portrayed in the romances as polite to all and helpful to the weak. How, scholars have asked, did warrior skills begin to involve an ethical dimension, and how did the warlike practices of the service knights of the eleventh century became the refined chivalric culture of the late twelfth-century nobility?

The answer is that late medieval chivalry was a combination of two separate elements, both the warlike abilities that the Old French

---

[15] Hunting was the first thing the young hero learned when he began his knighthood training in the romance "Caradoc," in *Three Arthurian Romances,* p. 8. For the skills required for hunting and the elaborate ceremony surrounding the sport, see John Cummins, *The Hound and the Hawk.*

[16] *Lancelot of the Lake,* p. 52.

chevalerie originally denoted *and* courtliness. Courtliness or courtesy, it should be stressed, did *not* grow directly out of a warrior ethos, even though it was grafted onto chivalric ideals by the late twelfth century. Rather, as has recently been convincingly argued by Stephen Jaeger, many of the elements that went into courtliness were in fact classical Roman virtues, learned by priests as part of their twelfth-century classical education.[17] Ethics, self-discipline, and refined social interactions, which had been prized by the Stoics, were prized in turn by medieval bishops with classical training, first at the tenth-century imperial court, where these virtues received a religious imprint before spreading to bishops and priests elsewhere.

Once this Christianized stoicism had become established as an ideal among the clerics, it found a ready conduit to influence the nobility. By the twelfth century, values from a combination of clerical and classical sources were taught to the young knights-in-training at medieval courts as part of their Christian education. The training young nobles received for ten or fifteen years, beginning in childhood, included many hours' study with priests as well as hours on the practice field. Thus a courtly culture with origins very different from the bravery and fighting skills that the knights had always admired was gradually grafted onto "chivalry." Combining as it did warlike honor, Roman Stoic virtue, court fashion, and Christian morality, it is no wonder that chivalry was inherently self-contradictory.

Its militarism, of course, is striking as an increasingly important part of noble self-definition, but it should be noted that chivalrous warfare was not, as has sometimes been suggested, a *tool* for bringing knights and nobles together. That is, nobles did not first create a chivalric ethos and then allow knights to share in it. Nor, as has also been argued, did nobles cynically manipulate knights into behaving "chivalrously" by promising them equal stature in return for loyal service. As chivalric ideals in France did not flow from below, from the service knights, they also did not flow from directly above, from the kings. The literature in which chivalric ideas were most fully developed was sponsored at several different great courts in France, especially that of Champagne.[18] Rather, both the slow integration of the

[17] C. Stephen Jaeger, *The Origins of Courtliness.*
[18] John F. Benton, "The Court of Champagne as a Literary Center," in *Culture, Power, and Personality in Medieval France,* pp. 3–43. In Germany, however, it was at the

knights into the aristocracy and the development of a sense that any admirable noble would be skilled in warfare as well as in courtesy developed together. Both were the result of the increasing enthusiasm with which nobles followed military careers, rather than either being the cause of the other.

If chivalry was not, then, the inevitable result of the rise to power of those trained in knighthood, why should it have developed when it did during the course of the twelfth century? Here of course answers must be speculative, but recently some scholars have argued that the ethos developed partly in response to the threats that nobles were experiencing to their position, both from kings above and from knights below, as noted in Chapter 2.[19] That is, the increasing sense that their position was not self-evidently important made the nobles more eager to define themselves by clear standards, especially standards of skill and conduct whose mastery would take many years. It is an indication of how little consensus they had themselves on what were the chief elements of noble behavior that the chivalric literature they sponsored and to which they eagerly listened presented a self-contradictory picture.

Ideal and Reality in Chivalry

Rather than try to find some ethical dimension inherent in war on horseback, scholars of chivalry have more recently focused on the issue of "ideal and reality," contending that a shared chivalrous code of conduct existed as an ideal in the romances, even while reality was quite different. After all, it is quite clear that what these scholars describe as a chivalric standard was created for, if not indeed by, a group of powerful men who frequently killed, extorted, and betrayed. Even contemporary biographies of twelfth-century figures might give a much more "chivalrous" picture of them than do other

---

royal court that such ideas first became fashionable. William Henry Jackson, "Knighthood and the Hohenstaufen Imperial Court under Frederick Barbarossa (1152–1190)," in Christopher Harper-Bill and Ruth Harvey, eds., *The Ideals and Practice of Medieval Knighthood III*, pp. 102–4. For German versions of chivalry, see also Jill P. McDonald, "Chivalric Education in Wolfram's *Parzival* and Gottfried's *Tristan*," in Chickering and Seiler, *Study of Chivalry*, pp. 473–85.

[19] See, most recently, Gabrielle M. Spiegel, *Romancing the Past*. She argues that the fullest reaction to this threat came in the support of vernacular prose history in thirteenth-century Flanders.

sources.[20] The argument, then, has been to what extent real nobles adopted chivalric ideals, or which tensions in real life made the chivalric ethos take the particular form it did.[21]

I myself believe that this discussion is misplaced. It is, after all, fairly obvious that the real life of real aristocrats was quite different from that of the heroes of epic and romance. What is not obvious is the underlying assumption that there was a single ideal to which reality may be compared.[22] It seems clear, by contrast, not only that there was no "real" code of behavior to which all knights and nobles adhered but also that there was no single "ideal" of chivalry. The "chivalric code" to which one frequently sees reference was no more "real" than the idea that knights and nobles routinely followed it. Even if knights and nobles had wanted to behave perfectly chivalrously on all occasions, there was no agreed-upon standard for such behavior. Scholars trying to extract a chivalric code from the romances of Chrétien de Troyes, for example, might take the attribute of loyalty from one tale, of mercy from another, of generosity from a third, and of gracious love for ladies from a fourth, in the assumption that one can put them all together to create Chrétien's ideal knight.[23] But this procedure does violence to the very variety Chrétien so artfully put in his characters.

It is especially important to stress that what chivalric literature reveals most clearly are a host of contradictions and opposing goals. It was truly impossible to be fully chivalrous, even for the glorious heroes of the romances. Thus it is vital to read the literature with the knowledge that the authors were quite deliberately indicating tensions and conflicts within even the most idealized vision of chivalry. If at different times the same author holds quite different behaviors up as models, one should not simply assume that all these behaviors or attributes may be reconciled into a single vision of chivalry, but

[20] Jim Bradbury, "Geoffrey V of Anjou, Count and Knight," in Harper-Bill and Harvey, *The Ideals and Practice of Knighthood III*, pp. 21–38.

[21] Tony Hunt, "The Emergence of the Knight in France and England." Bumke, *Concept of Knighthood*, p. 120. The Strawberry Hill conferences, whose proceedings have been edited by Christopher Harper-Bill and Ruth Harvey, all focus on a tension between ideal and reality.

[22] On this point, see also C. Stephen Jaeger, "Courtliness and Social Change," in Thomas N. Bisson, ed., *Cultures of Power*, pp. 287–309.

[23] This is the purpose of Z. P. Zaddy, "The Courtly Ethic in Chrétien de Troyes," in Harper-Bill and Harvey, *The Ideals and Practice of Knighthood III*, pp. 159–80.

should look for the author's indication—usually quite explicit—that there were deep contradictions here. The authors of the romances were not so much describing or even creating a single ideal to which their readers might or might not measure up, as critiquing the very idea that such an ideal was feasible.

Consider, for example, the tensions and conflicts on which the plots of so many romances turn, when the hero, trying to emulate two different sets of ideals, becomes caught in the contradictions between them. The whole plot of the very popular Tristan and Isolde story, retold many times in the Middle Ages, always revolves around the tension between the sworn loyalty of Tristan to his uncle, the king—in which the family connection only strengthens the loyalty he owes him as knight and vassal—and his equally idealized love for Isolde, the queen. In loving her, Tristan finally realizes in the French version of the story, he has "forgotten chivalry and the life of a knight at court."[24]

For Chrétien de Troyes, the most common tension was also that between love and honor, usually the honor associated with warlike deeds. In his "Erec and Enide," for example, the action derives from the problems Erec faces when his love for Enide, his new wife, keeps him from adventures. "Erec was so in love with her that he cared no more for arms, nor did he go to tournaments." This negligence continues to the point that Enide herself becomes miserable at how low her husband's honor has fallen. "Wretch," she says, "unhappy me! . . . The very best of knights . . . has completely abandoned all chivalry because of me." When Erec responds by going to face bandits and battle, taking his wife with him, he treats her very harshly, ordering her, for example, to remain silent no matter what and chiding her for defying these orders even when she saves his life. Here the hero is trying to distance himself from love in order to find honor again, knowing well the tension between the two. But Chrétien was certainly not advocating such treatment of women any more than he was advocating that knights stay home, enjoying their wives' company and forgetting adventure, for eventually a repentent Erec asks Enide to forgive him for the way he has treated her. This resolution is an attempt to reconcile the conflict between love and honor, but the reader is nevertheless left, as Chrétien certainly intended, wondering

[24] Beroul, *The Romance of Tristan* 11, p. 96.

how a man can be a renowned warrior when he has just told his wife he wants to live "entirely at [her] command."[25]

The conflict between love and honor is also one of the key tensions in Chrétien's "Knight of the Cart (Lancelot)." The scene with the cart, though trivial in terms of the plot, is key for Chrétien's themes, for he named the whole story after it. In setting up this scene, Chrétien announces that it was dishonorable for anyone to ride in a cart in the Arthurian days in which his story was supposed to be set, because only convicted criminals rode in them. Chrétien seems to have invented this particular detail, but it serves his purposes well, for he is then able to put Lancelot in a dilemma when the only transportation available to take him to rescue the queen he loves is a despicable cart.

If he rides in it, Lancelot thinks to himself, he will be dishonored, but if he does not he might not reach the queen. "Reason . . . told him to beware of getting in, and admonished and counselled him not to do anything for which he might incur disgrace . . . but Love . . . urged and commanded him to climb into the cart at once." He tries to compromise, eventually getting into the cart but only after initially hesitating for "two steps." This compromise pleases no one. For the rest of the poem, the people Lancelot meet seem already to know that he had been in the cart and mock him for it, while the queen, on the contrary, is bitterly disappointed that he hesitated at all and refuses to speak with him when he arrives to rescue her.[26] Here honor and love were even more irreconcilable than in "Erec and Enide," and Chrétien's eventual realization that he had gotten his hero so deeply into a dilemma that he could never get out may have been his reason for leaving the story unfinished.

But love and honor were not the only aspects of chivalry to work against each other. Honor itself could take conflicting forms. The whole plot of the *Song of Roland* turns on the conflict between reckless courage, which ends up destroying much of Charlemagne's army, and the wise summoning of help, which the hero initially rejects as

---

[25] Chrétien de Troyes, "Erec and Enide," in *Arthurian Romances*, pp. 67–68, 72–74, 83, 97. Liliane Dulac has recently argued that this story makes much more sense if one concentrates on its structure of dualities and contradictions than if one tries to see the characters as psychologically consistent. "Peut-on comprendre les relations entre Erec et Enide?"

[26] Chrétien de Troyes, "The Knight of the Cart (Lancelot)," in *Arthurian Romances*, pp. 211–12, 260–62. Chrétien was the first to introduce Lancelot into stories about Arthur, and many elements suggest he was inspired by "Tristan and Isolde."

dishonorable.[27] In the thirteenth-century French *Death of Arthur,* even though King Arthur realizes that his kingdom will be destroyed by the loss of Lancelot if he is punished for his adultery with the queen, "yet it was better that Lancelot should die than that a king's dishonor should not be avenged."[28] Honor also frequently came into conflict with religion. Fighting and killing, it was fairly clear by the twelfth century, were incompatible with being a good Christian. Here the authors had to do far less maneuvering to get their characters into situations where different aspects of courtly behavior would be in conflict; rather, they had to try to maneuver to get them into situations where they could plausibly be Christian warriors at all. And loyalty, while indisputably good in its own right, was a fertile source of such conflicts as loyalty versus honor, or loyalty to one's lord versus loyalty to one's family, the conflict at the heart of the epic *Raoul de Cambrai.*

Thus, it is ultimately both impossible and misguided to give an unambiguous definition of chivalry, because the stories on which such a definition would have to be based were all constructed on the assumption that different aspects of chivalry were in conflict with each other. The creators of the medieval vision of chivalry, the authors of the romances, far from describing a single clear ideal, wrote their stories to indicate that even the most chivalrous hero would be trapped between conflicting ideals.

Warfare and Chivalry

The chivalric knights of the epics and romances were all great fighters, specifically great fighters on horseback. They had fine armor, keen swords, and routinely killed formidable opponents without even raising a sweat. The French heroes in the *Song of Roland,* for example, regularly drove their swords from the top of an enemy's head, all the way through his body, and ended by splitting the saddle and sometimes even the horse in two. Lancelot,

---

[27] I here disagree with Stephen G. Nichols Jr., *Romanesque Signs,* pp. 148–203. He reduces the conflict in the story between wisdom and courage to a somewhat trivial dispute, where neither side yet appreciates the necessity of the martyr's death of the exemplary hero Roland. See esp. p. 170.

[28] *The Death of King Arthur,* p. 111.

in the French *Death of King Arthur* written a century after *Roland*, sliced an enemy through his helmet and head down to the shoulders.[29] Even if hopelessly outnumbered, as were Roland's knights, romantic heroes usually managed to hold out for a surprisingly long time, dispatching scores of foes though already mortally wounded.

It was not admirable, however, to fight the helpless. This was the idea that the bishops had been promoting since the Peace of God originated around the year 1000. By the middle decades of the twelfth century it had been integrated into the image aristocrats wanted to have of themselves. The writer Beroul said that Tristan was "too noble and too courtly" to kill some disgusting lepers, even though they were carrying off Isolde and would have raped her if Tristan had not arrived in time. Bernier, the hero of the second half of *Raoul de Cambrai*, refuses to kill an unarmed man, saying that if he did "it would always be held against me," even though, interestingly enough, earlier in the poem he had tried to kill Raoul when the latter was unarmed. In the thirteenth-century *Death of King Arthur*, Lancelot decides it would be "unchivalrous" to attack from horseback a man on foot who was trying to kill him, and he dismounts to avoid taking an unfair advantage.[30]

Needless to say, the long lists of glorious blows and courtly deeds found in epics and romances were not—and were not meant to be—descriptions of actual medieval warfare. Nearly every French family of any importance lost someone at the Siege of Acre (1191–1192) during the Third Crusade, most dying from disease and lack of food, but these kinds of deaths were not recorded in the stories. The heroes of romance did not become lost and mired in the mud, did not fight to stalemates, and were not surrounded by the large numbers of far-from-wellborn foot soldiers and retainers who constituted a significant part of every real medieval army. For example, armies always had large contingents of lowborn bowmen, even though chivalric heroes all insisted that the bow was a coward's weapon (an attitude that probably kept bows out of aristocratic hands far more effectively than the repeated efforts of church councils to ban them from war). After

---

[29] *The Song of Roland*, lines 1188–1337, pp. 67–71. *The Death of King Arthur*, p. 116.

[30] Beroul, *The Romance of Tristan* 4, p. 75. *Raoul de Cambrai* 115, 318, pp. 145, 441. *The Death of King Arthur*, p. 107.

all, skillful bowmen could help you win, and chivalry was all very well but not if you lost.[31]

French knights and nobles spent rather startling amounts on weapons and equipment, both because in a warlike society they needed to have the latest weapons, and because these weapons were important forms of display. All their equipment, of course, was made by hand, and anyone who has attempted any metalworking will appreciate how long it would take to make a single mail shirt (hauberk) out of rings, each passing through all adjoining rings and riveted together.[32] Helmet, lance, and shield were additional expenses. The sword, the knight's most essential weapon, was made by repeatedly heating, folding, and hammering the blade. The process in essence created carbon steel (much harder than ordinary iron) but was enormously time-consuming and demanded the costly skills of a professional. Any lord who could afford it also remodeled his entire castle at least once during his lifetime, to incorporate all the latest military designs.

Yet even the strong, brave fighters of the epic poems did not win all the time. Roland ends up dead, surrounded by the bodies of hundreds of the best French knights. The poem "Aliscans," in the William of Orange cycle, starts with a fight against Saracens which the Christians lose.[33] Death and defeat or, if one were a little less unfortunate, pain, blood, and crippling wounds, were so intrinsic to the experience of the warriors who enjoyed chivalric poetry that no war story would have been convincing without them.

Dubbing and Knighting

The nobles of the twelfth century who liked to imagine they were courteous were interested in making warfare honorable, even glam-

---

[31] Jim Bradbury, *The Medieval Archer*, pp. 1–3. The emperor Conrad in the romance by Jean Renart, *The Romance of the Rose or Guillaume de Dole,* said that he would not have used a bow to kill someone "for half the treasure of Rome" (p. 19). Being a "skilled archer" was however a suitable skill for a noble when hunting, as Beroul made clear in his description of Tristan. *The Romance of Tristan* 5, p. 76.

[32] Ian Peirce estimates that it would take a skilled craftsman at least several weeks to make just one hauberk. "The Knight, His Arms and Armour in the Eleventh and Twelfth Centuries," in Christopher Harper-Bill and Ruth Harvey, eds., *The Ideals and Practice of Medieval Knighthood*, p. 155. See also Philippe Contamine, *War in the Middle Ages*, pp. 184–88; and Bumke, *Courtly Culture*, pp. 155–68.

[33] "Aliscans" 1, in *Guillaume d'Orange*, p. 197.

The castle of Peyrepertuse, high in the Pyrenees, commands its surroundings from a dizzying height. The part of the castle seen here was built in the twelfth and early thirteenth centuries and held by the heretical Albigensians. After it was captured and made over to the French crown, an even higher part of the castle was added—from which spot this picture was taken. The stones for this newer, late thirteenth-century part of the castle all had to be winched or carried up by human power, because it was built on a peak too steep even for mules to climb.

orous, and one of the clearest indications of this desire can be seen in the development of the dubbing ritual. This coming-of-age ceremony, also called "knighting" (just to confuse the modern reader who is trying to distinguish knights from nobles), first appeared at the beginning of the twelfth century and became common by the middle of the century. Previously, in the early Middle Ages, as Jean Flori's work has shown, the ceremony of receiving weapons involved almost exclusively the kings and the upper echelons of society, and its symbolism was that of taking up an office.[34]

But by the twelfth century all young warriors of noble birth might hope to participate in a ceremony where they were given their first adult weapons. Usually the ritual was performed by someone who had raised or trained the young man. When in the epic *Raoul de Cambrai* the emperor recognizes that the hero has grown "big and strong," he gives him a legendary helmet, an invulnerable hauberk, a golden sword, and a warhorse. Raoul follows up his own knighting by dubbing his good friend Bernier "with the best arms he could obtain." Alternatively, one might seek to be knighted by the most eminent lord one could find. In Chrétien de Troyes's "Cligés," even the son of the Byzantine emperor wants to have the acclaimed King Arthur gird on his sword, "for I do not wish to be knighted by anyone else."[35]

This knighting or dubbing ceremony was, in spite of its name, strictly for nobles and not for the far more numerous service knights, who underwent their training and received their military equipment from their lords without any ceremony that left its mark in treatises or in literature. This initiation into adult warfare was not at first a criterion of either knighthood or nobility, even though it did become so by the thirteenth century. As a ceremony already restricted to nobles, dubbing might confirm but could not bestow special social status. It was a solemn moment, but its original importance lay in marking a young aristocratic man's passage into full adulthood, not into knighthood per se.[36]

The knighting ceremony had at first none of the elaboration it would acquire by the late Middle Ages. Even in Chrétien's romance

[34] Jean Flori, "Les origines de l'adoubement chevaleresque." Idem, *L'essor de la chevalerie*, pp. 9–115.
[35] *Raoul de Cambrai* 22–25, 29, pp. 27–29, 35. Chrétien de Troyes, "Cligés," in *Arthurian Romances*, p. 124.
[36] Bumke, *The Concept of Knighthood*, pp. 85–87. Flori, "La notion de chevalerie."

"The Story of the Grail" the hero is made a knight—has conferred on him "the order of knighthood," as the author puts it—by nothing more than having the worthy gentleman who has been teaching him how to fight fasten on a spur, gird on his sword, and give him a kiss.[37] But by the late thirteenth century, when the dubbing ceremony had become a criterion of a man's nobility, it was highly elaborate,[38] and late medieval treatises gave symbolic significance to every aspect of the ceremony. The bath, the night-long vigil, the new clothes, the spurs and sword, and the light blow from an older knight, were all explained as symbols of the new knight's devotion to justice and loyalty, his courteous treatment of women, and especially his cleanliness of soul and commitment to protecting the helpless and the church.[39]

What one has, then, is a ceremony that is fundamentally political and military, essentially a combination of being issued one's basic equipment with some sense of being given a charge, onto which were progressively attached the additional meanings that chivalry acquired. Religious elements especially were grafted onto to what had begun as a secular ritual. It was an attempt to make a training in the skills of killing people into something both Christian and socially acceptable.

One of the earliest attempts to Christianize the dubbing ceremony may be seen in the treatises of John of Salisbury, who wrote in the mid-twelfth century. He created a pseudohistorical picture of an idealized soldier of the time of classical Rome, who was given his symbolic military belt only upon swearing a "sacred oath" to serve God and the (Roman) republic. Members of John's "military order," thus sworn in, were expected to "venerate the priesthood, to avert injuries to the poor," and to remain loyal to each other and to their leaders.[40] What one can see in this treatise is an attempt to create a model—even if projected backward in time—that would allow a man to be both a good fighter and a good Christian. This is an interesting development, considering that only a generation earlier Bernard of Clairvaux had conceived his "New Militia" of the Templars as Christianizing fighting only by creating a complete alternative to the nor-

[37] Chrétien de Troyes, "The Story of the Grail," pp. 401–2.
[38] A detailed romantic account of the ritual of dubbing in the early thirteenth century is given in "Caradoc," pp. 10–11.
[39] Keen, *Chivalry*, pp. 64–82.
[40] John of Salisbury, *Policraticus* 6.7–8, pp. 114–17. See also Flori, *L'essor de la chevalerie*, pp. 280–89.

mal knightly life. Yet John of Salisbury's attempt was symptomatic of increasingly common attempts to reconcile chivalry and religion.

Christian Chivalry

The term *miles Christi,* a soldier of Christ, had been in intermittent use throughout the early Middle Ages, usually referring to a monk, someone who fought Christ's cause here on earth through his prayers. The knights, the *milites* of the eleventh and twelfth centuries, wanted to find a way that they too could be "knights of Christ." The problem was that there was a long tradition in the church of equating power and wealth—the attributes of nobility—with oppression and evil. But already in the tenth century churchmen were trying to create a model of the ideal warleader, one who did not have to give up his place in the world to be a saint but who used his strength to care for the weak—preferably bloodlessly.[41] The blessing of the sword and the oaths to defend widows, churches, and the poor which later became integral parts of the dubbing ceremony were attempts to Christianize a warrior's training.[42]

The difficulty was that by the twelfth century churchmen had said often enough, and loudly enough, that Christians were not supposed to kill Christians that even the knights and nobles had begun to take notice. In the French romance *The Death of King Arthur,* Sir Gawain recalls that he killed eighteen knights on his quest, but rather than glory in this accomplishment, he says, "Indeed, it did not come about through my chivalry but through my sin."[43] When one has just defined one's status militarily, it is of course impossible to turn one's back on the military life (unless of course one wants to become a monk—as a number of young knights indeed did). Even the bishops realized that it was unrealistic to expect warriors to beat their swords into plowshares. Part of the tension within chivalry was always the attempt to make the incompatible compatible.

But in the twelfth century both churchmen and the aristocrats

[41] Barbara H. Rosenwein, *Rhinoceros Bound,* pp. 66–72. Idem, "St. Odo's St. Martin." Odo, abbot of Cluny in the first half of the tenth century, wrote a life of Gerald of Aurillac in which he tried to make this noble into a model of saintliness within the secular life. "The Life of St. Gerald of Aurillac." See also Jean Flori, *L'idéologie du glaive,* pp. 108–12.

[42] Bumke, *The Concept of Knighthood,* pp. 89–91.

[43] *The Death of King Arthur,* p. 24.

themselves tried to devise ways to allow the nobility to fight regularly without doing something actually so sinful as to kill other Christians (or at least not very many of them). The church's answer was the Crusades, in which western knights were encouraged to kill Muslims instead of each other. The aristocracy's answer was tournaments. At least in the twelfth century, the church, backed by many romance writers, was able to present fighting (and even converting) infidels as a viable alternative for Christian knights who were trained in fighting but worried about their sins. The problem was that there were enormous disadvantages to crusading, even while there was still hope that a Christian kingdom really could be maintained in the East—something that was becoming more and more implausible in the late twelfth and thirteenth centuries. Crusading was expensive, dangerous, and extremely unpleasant. If all that was demanded was to fight without killing Christians, French nobles much preferred the tournament.

Tournaments

The tournament, which first appeared at the end of the eleventh century (almost exactly the same time as the First Crusade), was a chance for knights and nobles to use their warrior skills against each other with the purpose of capturing the other person rather than killing him. It was sport, it was spectacle, and it was also an opportunity for the best to win fame and fortune. In *The Death of King Arthur*, the king calls for a tournament at the beginning of the romance because there were hardly any "adventures" any more in his kingdom, but he "did not want his companions to cease wearing arms." From the first, tournaments were wildly popular among the aristocracy. In fact, they eventually offered a new occupation for younger sons with the requisite battle skills. A good fighter could make a respectable career on the tournament circuit, because every man he defeated would usually have to pay a substantial ransom to redeem his person, horse, and armor.[44]

Virtually all the romantic heroes—or at least the ones not involved

---

[44] Michel Parisse, "Le tournoi en France, des origines à la fin du XIIIe siècle," in Josef Fleckenstein, ed., *Das ritterliche Turnier im Mittelalter*, pp. 175–211. Helmut Nickel, "The Tournament: An Historical Sketch," in Chickering and Seiler, *The Study of Chivalry*, pp. 213–62. Keen, *Chivalry*, pp. 83–101. *The Death of King Arthur*, p. 24.

The archangel Michael, depicted as a twelfth-century knight, fights the devil on the facade of the church of Anzy-le-Duc, in Burgundy. The archangel wears a helmet with nosepiece and a long shirt of chain mail and carries a round shield. He is barefoot because angels and apostles were always depicted barefoot.

in actual wars—took part in tournaments. They loved jousting; an oath of great austerity was to give it up. As noted, Erec was considered seriously disturbed when he was no longer interested in the tournament. Real nobles also took part enthusiastically. Charles the Good, count of Flanders at the beginning of the twelfth century, was said by his biographer to have frequented tournaments with his knights, both for their training and for the glory of Flanders.[45] As noted, William Marshal, regent of England in 1216, started his rise to fame as a star on the tournament circuit.

It was something of a problem that the church did not consider tournaments fundamentally different from all-out battles. Even though their purpose was not actually to kill the enemy, people cer-

[45] Galbert of Bruges, *The Murder of Charles the Good* 4, pp. 91–92.

tainly could be and were killed in them—for instance, the count of Brabant, killed in a tournament in 1095,[46] or Prince Henry, heir to the English throne, killed in 1183. Additionally, Christian moralists felt that tournaments encouraged all the vices. At the 1130 Council of Clermont, the pope first condemned these "detestable" events where *milites* gathered to show their strength and courage, endangering their souls and risking death. All the participants in a tournament might be excommunicated and those killed in it refused burial in holy ground. In the thirteenth-century romance "Aucassin and Nicolette," the hero says he would rather be in hell than not have his true love, for there at least he could associate with "fair knights who are slain in the tourney."[47]

Disapproval by the church seems, however, to have had essentially no effect. The biographer of Charles the Good comments that "he redeemed with God many times by almsgiving" any taint of "worldliness" acquired at the tournaments. The son of the count of Champagne wrote in 1149 to Suger, abbot of St.-Denis, to ask his help in freeing a noble friend taken captive in a tournament, evidently with the full expectation that the abbot would help him rather than lecture him about the immorality of tournaments. A story was told in the 1180s of a knight surprised to discover that he had been the hero of a tournament when he thought he had spent the day in prayer at a hermitage; it turned out that the Lord had provided him a "substitute" to fight in his stead. The same idea became in the thirteenth century a miracle story of the Virgin, who triumphantly took part in a tournament in the guise of a knight who was spending the day in prayer to her. Such stories certainly suggest a will to believe that God approved of tournaments. By the fourteenth century the church gave up its opposition entirely.[48]

Today's vision of the tournament (as depicted in movies), in which two knights charge at each other in the lists, lances held at the ready, is a late medieval version. The twelfth-century tournament was a

[46] Herman of Tournai, *The Restoration of the Monastery of Saint Martin of Tournai* 17, pp. 34–35.

[47] Council II of Clermont, canon 9, in J.-D. Mansi, ed., *Sacrorum conciliorum nova et amplissima collectio*, vol. 21, col. 439. *Aucassin and Nicolette*, p. 6.

[48] Galbert of Bruges, *The Murder of Charles the Good* 4, p. 92. Suger, Letter 72, RHGF 15:511. Walter Map, *De nugis curialium* 1.20, pp. 59–61. "The Knight Who Prayed Whilst Our Lady Tourneyed in His Stead," in *Aucassin and Nicolette*, pp. 207–10. Keen, *Chivalry*, pp. 94–97.

much more chaotic affair. It included individual combat, certainly; two knights would try to unhorse each other with their lances, and then usually leap up and swing at each other with their swords. The battle scenes in *The Song of Roland*, in which two knights issue challenges and ride at each other, one defeating the other before turning to the next enemy, seem to owe more to tournaments than to actual experience on the battlefield. But a key element of the early tournament was the *mêlée*, a battle involving large numbers of knights fighting on different teams. These teams were given arbitrary nicknames, such as the Inners and the Outers. Under such conditions, the distinction between a tournament and battle could become blurred. The mêlée was not restricted to the lists; it could take off cross-country and go on all day. At one twelfth-century tournament, the count of Flanders's men arrived but said they were there only to watch. Then, when everyone else was exhausted at the end of the day, they quickly saddled up and took a large number of prisoners, which everyone agreed was an excellent trick.[49]

Only at the very close of the Middle Ages, in the fourteenth and especially fifteenth centuries, did the tournament became a more formalized affair. By that time, the skills required of the participants were in essence stylized anachronisms, derived from battlefield practices centuries out of date. For the most part individual jousts replaced the mêlée. Tournament armor by the fifteenth century was heavy plate, not the supple chain mail used in the twelfth century. Plate mail had been developed originally to withstand musket fire. It is thus rather ironic that knightly jousting, which no longer represented actual battlefield tactics, should carry on this outmoded form of combat in the armor made for weapons that were never allowed at tournaments. Late medieval tournament armor was so heavy that participants often had to be hoisted onto their horses by cranes and tied into place because of the damage that would result simply from falling off. The horses, which had earlier been light and swift, probably part Arabian—Muslim Spain was considered the source of the best twelfth-century steeds—now were bred massive enough to carry heavily armored riders. With unhorsing, the earlier criterion for win-

[49] One of the most detailed descriptions of an early thirteenth-century tournament is given in the romance by Jean Renart, *The Romance of the Rose or Guillaume de Dole,* pp. 55–57. For the count of Flanders's trick, see David Crouch, *William Marshal,* p. 178.

A mid-twelfth-century knight rides off to battle on an energetic warhorse. His stirrups and high saddle will help keep him from sliding off when he thrusts his lance at another knight. Copyright Leiden © Universiteitsbibliotheek. MS B.P.L. 20, fol. 60R. Reproduced with permission.

ning, no longer possible, winners of jousts were now judged on style and skill (more like modern figure skating than modern combat sports).

Heraldry, an elaborate system of symbols on shields and coats of arms, grew out of the tournaments. Men wearing helmets that covered their faces needed to tell friend from foe, both in the mêlée and in actual battles, and the adoption of distinctive insignia on shields made identification possible. (Indeed, military forces have always used some sort of symbol to identify themselves, although actual uniforms came into use only in the seventeenth century.)

The earliest known use of insignia on shields is from the first half of the twelfth century. Chrétien de Troyes, creating an idealized picture of a tournament in the second half of the century, put eagles, dragons, leopards, pheasants, and lions on the participants' shields.[50] By the thirteenth century, heralds at the tournaments knew the main figures on the tournament circuit by their shields. Heraldry quickly developed an elaborate system of symbols, colors, and rules, including the terms under which one could or could not add new details to one's coat of arms. By the late Middle Ages, hereditary claim to elaborate coats of arms was one of the ways in which nobles with long ancestry desperately tried to symbolize their superiority over upstarts.[51]

The presence of highborn women in the audience was important at all tournaments. (There is no record of women actually participating in the lists themselves.) The men seem to have been convinced that the best way to win a woman's admiration was to acquit themselves well in the fighting. The romances are full of girls and women watching eagerly from windows and arguing with each other over their champions. Chrétien de Troyes's Lancelot tries, with only moderate success, to keep his eyes faithfully upon his lady while he fights. An acknowledged lover might receive some item of his lady's clothing to carry as a token into a tournament battle, most commonly a sleeve (in the twelfth century sleeves were detachable, not permanently sewn to the garment). In *The Death of King Arthur,* written a generation after Chrétien's version, Lancelot greatly angers Guinevere when, instead of a plume, he wears a young girl's sleeve on his helmet as a favor to her. Parzival's father similarly carries his queen's shift, which she then wears again in bed, complete with the holes and slashes it has acquired, glorying in her lover's victories.[52]

The tournament was thus a form of recreation, a spectator sport, a means of attracting the admiration of one's peers and of the ladies, and a way to keep one's skills sharp. But it could also have a judicial element. Even while the church was decrying tournaments, it was still common in the twelfth century to use a battle between champi-

[50] Chrétien de Troyes, "The Knight of the Cart," p. 278.

[51] Adrian Ailes, "The Knight, Heraldry, and Armour: The Role of Recognition and the Origins of Heraldry," in Christopher Harper-Bill, and Ruth Harvey, eds., *Medieval Knighthood IV*, pp. 1–21. Keen, *Chivalry*, pp. 125–42. For English parallels, see David Crouch, *The Image of the Aristocracy in Britain*, pp. 226–40.

[52] Chrétien de Troyes, "The Knight of the Cart," pp. 252–53. *The Death of King Arthur*, p. 30. Wolfram von Eschenbach, *Parzival*, p. 61. For another example of a sleeve worn in a tournament, see "Caradoc," p. 26.

ons as a way to determine guilt or innocence in "trial by battle." God, it was believed, would show where the guilt lay by giving victory to the champion of the right. Such a method was evoked, for example, in the *The Song of Roland* to cement the guilt of the traitor Ganelon. Even without a formal trial by battle, there was a sense that those in the right ought to win. In *Raoul de Cambrai,* the author explains that the king was unsuccessful in his fight "for he was in the wrong—justice was not on his side."[53]

The difficulty with trial by battle, as everyone in fact knew even at the time, was that the wrong man might win. Even in the romances the "right" person did not always win; in *Roland* Ganelon almost had to be freed because no one dared face his formidable champion. The church hierarchy, indeed, withdrew all support of trials by ordeal, including trial by battle, in the thirteenth century. But in spite of the doubts raised both in literature and in real judicial discussions, there was a sense throughout the late Middle Ages that he who won must have right and probably God on his side, not just his strength and his sword. As the knights put it in *The Death of King Arthur,* explaining why they would not act as champions for someone accused of murder, "They would have been dishonest if they had knowingly offered to defend an unjust cause," and even if they won, "everyone at court would know [they] had erred against justice and loyalty."[54]

Nobles and Love

At the same time as the knights and nobles of the twelfth century were increasingly defining themselves by their military function and trying to live what they considered an elegant and courtly life, they were putting a much greater emphasis on love between men and women. Of course, men and women have doubtless been falling in love with each other since the Stone Age, and the Christian tradition with which the medieval West was imbued included many biblical statements that assumed husbands and wives would love each other. Letters from husbands to wives in the early Middle Ages often in-

[53] Robert Bartlett, *Trial by Fire and Water,* pp. 113–26. *The Song of Roland* lines 3850–3933, pp. 152–54. *Raoul de Cambrai* 263, p. 353. See also Matthew Strickland, *War and Chivalry,* pp. 58–60.
[54] *The Death of King Arthur,* p. 98.

cluded expressions of affection. But the literary sources of the High Middle Ages suggest that love took on a new importance then.[55]

The principal sources for information on at least the idealized role of love in the twelfth century are the same romances and epics that give us information on other aspects of chivalry, together with an additional literary source, the troubadour poems. In contrast to the epics and romances, these poems, which had their origins in the Occitan culture of southern France, were short expressions of sentiment and ideas, usually related to love.[56] Such love poems were extremely popular; Jean Renart put a number of them into his early thirteenth-century romance *Guillaume de Dole* and had his knights and ladies compete in singing them as they strolled through the woods.[57]

The new emphasis on love was very much a literary phenomenon. Much of it was based quite consciously on Roman sources, especially Ovid's *On Love*. Ovid was known all through the early Middle Ages because he had been, under the Roman Empire, adopted into the school curriculum which was then continued in the medieval West. His love poems were officially studied for their use of language rather than for their content, but the latter proved popular as well, and young monks might surreptitiously try their hand at writing imitation Ovid.[58]

The love described in the romances, troubadour poems, and imitations of Ovid became one of the courtly games that young aristocrats could play. Any knight described in a poem as chivalrous and courtly would have attributes that suited him well to this game. In the twelfth-century romances the assumption was made for the first time that falling in love would be a *reason* for young aristocratic people to marry, rather than something that might happen once a couple was married.

In practice, of course, as noted in Chapter 3, it was highly unlikely that parents would allow their sons and daughters to wander about

---

[55] John Boswell points out that in the twelfth century, as in no other period until extremely recently, romantic love was such a prominent part of popular culture that society could be said to be obsessed by it. *Same-Sex Unions in Premodern Europe*, pp. xix–xx.

[56] On Occitan society see, most recently, Linda W. Paterson, *The World of the Troubadours*.

[57] Jean Renart, *The Romance of the Rose or Guillaume de Dole*, pp. 22–23.

[58] John W. Baldwin, *The Language of Sex*, pp. 20–25. Peter L. Allen, *The Art of Love*, pp. 46–58.

having adventures until they fell in love, but all the sources indicate that, at least after they were married, husband and wife were expected to love each other and be true to each other. Men might be allowed more license than women, but even in their case both the church and nobles themselves thought it most suitable that such license be practiced only before marriage or after a wife had died. Even in the *Lais* of Marie de France, with their celebration of adulterous love, a lord's knights urge him to give up his concubine, for "it would be a grievous loss if he did not have a child by his wife on account of his concubine."[59] King Henry I of England, who had over twenty illegitimate children but only one legitimate son, in fact suffered such a grievous loss when that son drowned; he should, it was generally said at the time, have kept his energies at home.

Looking good, dressing well, and having good manners were all described in the romances as sure ways for the unattached to win the attention of the opposite sex. Every romance is full of handsome young men who attract the women's eyes, and lovely young women to whom the heroes are immediately attracted. In this, twelfth-century fiction is scarcely different from modern fiction—or the dreams of modern adolescents. Poets tended to use stock descriptions of beauty. The lovely heroine is most commonly blond and fair skinned, but the poets were usually too modest to describe their bodies. Alternatively, ugly women are villainnesses. When Perceval sees a dark-skinned, hunchbacked woman with yellow teeth riding toward him, both he and the audience know at once that this woman does not wish him well.[60] A beautiful woman might be cruel—at least until the hero's winning ways make her kind—but it was hard for the romance writers to have an ugly woman be good.

A key part of beauty was sartorial elegance.[61] Both men and women at court prided themselves on their clothing, made of expensive fabric. Silk, imported at vast expense from a China they knew only by rumor, was enormously popular. The poets filled their romances with details of the fine hair and clothing of their heroes and heroines, marks of their status and taste. The account of Gawain's adventures in the thirteenth-century romance "The Knight with the Sword" be-

[59] Marie de France, *Lais* 3, p. 65.
[60] Bumke, *Courtly Culture*, p. 325. Mullally, *Artist at Work*, p. 20. Chrétien de Troyes, "The Story of the Grail," p. 438.
[61] Bumke, *Courtly Culture*, pp. 131–52.

gins by calling the hero "elegantly attired" and giving full descriptions of his cloak, shirt, breeches, and hose.[62] In an age before the invention of chemical dyes, vivid colors were rare, expensive, and highly prized. In the High Middle Ages, young men were clean-shaven, but they let their hair grow to shoulder length and, according to critics, curled it out of vanity with an iron. A short beard was considered suitable for a middle-aged man; a long beard was reserved for the old.

But good looks were not enough; one must know how to behave in polite company. In the allegorical *Romance of the Rose,* written in the first part of the thirteenth century, the God of Love gives the hero a long list of "commandments," bidding him give up slander and any other base activity, be well spoken and modest, honor all ladies, dress beautifully, wash thoroughly—not forgetting the fingernails—exercise regularly, and be generous. A troubadour poem written to honor the late son of King Henry II in the 1180s similarly recalls the prince as "generous and well spoken, and a good horseman, handsome, and humble in conferring great honors." Some of the knights on the Second Crusade spent much money on fine clothes, which, the Crusade chronicler said sadly, should better have been spent on military equipment.[63] The authors of the romances, doubtless more didactic than descriptive, have their heroes and heroines dress and behave fashionably, and the opposite sex is always captivated. Of course, the "fashion" of every poem was different; part of being up to date in any court circle must have been following the latest fashions in clothing and style, which can function to separate those in the know from everybody else only by changing constantly.

A striking element of love in the romances was the rather self-conscious pain it entailed. Marie de France, writing at the end of the twelfth century, has her hero and his chosen lady realize that they love each other when they both spend a sleepless night tortured by love. When Chrétien de Troyes has a couple fall in love, neither realizing that the other feels the same, the symptoms are indistinguishable from seasickness. The *Romance of the Rose* has the God of Love warn the hero of the "deep misery" he will experience: "No one has suf-

[62] "The Knight with the Sword," p. 87.
[63] Guillaume de Lorris and Jean de Meun, *The Romance of the Rose* 2, pp. 59–61. Bertran de Born, *The Poems of the Troubadour Bertran de Born* 15, p. 218. Odo of Deuil, *De Profectione Ludovici VII in Orientem* 5, p. 95.

fered who has not tried Love."[64] The only way to assuage this pain, according to the romances, was to find solace in the arms of the beloved—a remedy that gave added incentive to the literary pursuit of love.

One element of the game of love which runs through all the romances and troubadour poems is the idea that young chivalric men should serve their ladies as if they had been their lords. The beautiful young ladies did more than attract the handsome heroes by their good looks: they also inspired them. Increases in courage and fighting skills were routinely attributed to the love of a beautiful woman. Some of our earliest visual representations of the homage ceremony are illustrations showing a man doing "homage" to a woman, in a self-conscious imitation of vassalage. Poets loved to play with the language of fealty, using the same terms in which a vassal offered his loyalty to his lord for a young man to offer his loyal love to a lady whose heart he wanted to win. The knight would kneel before his lady in an attitude of deferential service, then try to win her by his courtly behavior. In Marie de France's "Equitan," the hero, a king, asks the lady of his heart to accept his "surrender" and treat him as her "vassal," even though she is in fact the wife of his own vassal.[65]

Alternatively—and often in the same poem—poets would use the language of religious worship, so that heroes were said to "adore" their ladies and adjured each other not with a saint's name but in the name of the one they loved. Many poems suggest a strong moral component was necessary to be worthy of love. Chrétien de Troyes deliberately uses religious language—sin, penance, and absolution— to describe Lancelot's devotion to the queen.[66] It must have been refreshing to wellborn women of the twelfth century when their would-be suitors realized that a display of good manners and an offer to obey were an effective way to win a woman's heart.

Part of the irony in this, of which the poets and doubtless their audiences were fully aware, was that women were *not* the lords of men. Although Christianity had preached from the beginning that men and women were equal in the eyes of God, there was a strong misog-

[64] Marie de France, *Lais* 1, p. 48. Chrétien de Troyes, "Cligés," p. 129. Guillaume de Lorris and Jean de Meun, *The Romance of the Rose* 2, pp. 63, 72.
[65] Bumke, *The Concept of Knighthood*, pp. 82–83. Marie de France, *Lais* 2, p. 58.
[66] Chrétien de Troyes, "The Knight of the Cart," p. 262. See also C. Stephen Jaeger, *The Envy of Angels*, pp. 319–22.

ynist streak in many churchmen, a fear that women, who had in Eve originally brought sin into the world, could easily be the cause of men's downfall again. And in ordinary society even aristocratic women had very few rights. Their marriages, especially their dowers and dowries, were arranged by their male relatives, not themselves, although a widow might have a little more autonomy. Even in the early thirteenth-century romance *Guillaume de Dole,* in which the emperor falls passionately in love with the heroine merely from descriptions of her charms, he still clears his wooing with her brother before he begins. Real aristocratic women do not seem to have been able to alienate even their own hereditary property without their husbands' participation; and they could bring suit in a court of law in their own name only in unusual circumstances.[67]

Probably in recognition of this irony, the poets who advocated abject service by knights to the ladies at the same time made fun of it. Lancelot, Chrétien de Troyes's very courtly hero, is satirized as an overly obeisant lover when he kisses the hairs that have been caught in Guinevere's comb, presses them to his breast, nearly faints with delight to have them, and treats them like a holy relic. Another of Chrétien's heroes, Alexander, becomes similarly excited when he discovers his beloved has worked some of her own hair into the stitching on his shirt; he embraces the shirt and kisses it "a hundred thousand times." The narrator comments, "Love easily makes the wise man a fool, finding such pleasure and delight in a strand of hair."[68] One could enjoy the game of love, Chrétien is saying, but it was always dangerously easy to become ridiculous.

And in many cases the poets criticized women even as they were advocating their service. Certainly if the heroes of the poems hoped to manipulate the ladies by their offered service, they were usually sadly disappointed, for the heroines routinely showed an independent, even saucy streak. Women were too fickle or too hypocritical, the poets sometimes said, unwilling to recognize a good man's love. The thirteenth-century author of "The Knight with the Sword" has his lovely heroine wantonly leave the knight she has just married for a total stranger, then comments that any woman in the world might

[67] Penny Schine Gold, *The Lady and the Virgin,* pp. 121–31. Constance Brittain Bouchard, *Holy Entrepreneurs,* pp. 161–63. Jean Renart, *The Romance of the Rose or Guillaume de Dole,* p. 60.
[68] Chrétien de Troyes, "The Knight of the Cart," pp. 224–26; "Cligés," p. 142.

In this illustration from a manuscript of the Lancelot story, Lancelot and Queen Guinevere speak and flirt surreptitiously while his friend stands guard. The Pierpont Morgan Library, New York, M 805, fol. 67 (detail).

do the same, "even if she were the lover and the wife of the very best knight from here to India."[69] Thus there was a fundamental contradiction in what the poets were advocating: on the one hand, women must be worshiped and obeyed, and on the other hand, they were not worth it. Much of this attitude seems to have come from unhappy personal experiences in the poets' own lives. "*She* does not love me," many a poet said in essence, "in spite of my worship for her, and therefore women are untrustworthy."

Courtly Love

The discussion of the complex and changing attitudes toward love in the twelfth century and of the enjoyment poets—and doubtless real men and women—had playing with these ideas has long been obscured by the blanket use of the term "courtly love," a term, note,

[69] "The Knight with the Sword," p. 101.

that is a modern invention. That is, medieval authors certainly spoke of "courtesy" and "courtliness," and they spoke of "love," but they never spoke of any clearly defined entity, much less an entity with fixed and accepted rules, known as "courtly love."[70]

Nevertheless, modern scholars sometimes assume that there was a single ritualized way for men to behave toward women in the High Middle Ages (especially women to whom they were not married), and that this behavior was considered an important part of chivalry.[71] Even though very few scholars would maintain that medieval noblemen routinely behaved according to "ideals of courtly love," many still take it for granted that there was in fact an ideal to which they all aspired or at least on whose features they all agreed. There have even been debates over where the ideal originated, with late eleventh-century southern France the chief candidate, and how this ideal spread northward, with the credit usually given to Eleanor of Aquitaine and her daughters.[72]

I would argue, however, that there was no clear "ideal of courtly love" in the High Middle Ages. As in the case of chivalry, comparing and conflating a number of different literary works only results in a single picture if one begins with the determination to find such a picture. Rather, the attributes that are now assumed to have gone into courtly love were again highly disparate, with different authors stressing different ones—indeed, quite consciously presenting ideas that contradicted the ideas of other authors. Specifically, as the following discussion will make clear, there was no agreement in this pe-

---

[70] The modern model of "courtly love" was essentially created by C. S. Lewis, *The Allegory of Love*, pp. 1–43. The eminently sensible suggestion of D. W. Robertson that the term be jettisoned has never been adopted. "The Concept of Courtly Love as an Impediment to the Understanding of Medieval Texts," pp. 1–18. Its hold is still regrettably strong on the scholarly imagination. Even as good a historian as Georges Duby allowed himself to accept its existence as a proven fact; then (oddly) he combined a literary *topos* from Occitan poetry (pining for the unattainable lady) with social structures from northern France to discuss its "origins." Duby, "The Courtly Model." The same idea is elaborated by R. Howard Bloch, *Medieval Misogyny and the Invention of Western Romantic Love*, pp. 165–97.

[71] Don A. Monson, "The Troubadour's Lady Reconsidered Again." See also Baldwin, *Language of Sex*, pp. xvi, xxii; he argues persuasively that concentration on reified "courtly love" has made scholars miss the twelfth and thirteenth centuries' multiple approaches to discussions of love and sexuality.

[72] Jane Martindale, " 'Cavalaria et Orgueil': Duke William IX of Aquitaine and the Historian," in Christopher Harper-Bill and Ruth Harvey, eds., *The Ideals and Practice of Medieval Knighthood II*, pp. 87–116. John F. Benton, "The Evidence of Andreas Capellanus Re-examined Again," in *Culture, Power, and Personality*, pp. 81–88.

riod on the value of a ritualized extramarital love, and the consistent inability of modern scholars to agree whether "courtly love" was supposed to remain a chaste yearning from afar or involve real physicality is a further indication how far from any single standard was its depiction even in the romances.[73]

Nonetheless, there are some elements in the modern notion of "courtly love" which are important for understanding medieval aristocratic culture. It is quite clear that part of a young noble's training by the twelfth century involved teaching him to speak pleasantly, even flirtatiously to women without actually carrying them off by force. Aristocrats at this time, as I have said, were usually raised away from home, in a lord or uncle's castle, along with a group of other young aristocrats. The lady of the castle served both as a symbolic mother for the boys (though given the frequent age disparities in noble marriages she would in many cases not have been substantially older than they were), and also as a symbolic lady on whom they could practice courteous behavior, such as writing poems to her. Some of the romances, such as the German *Parzival* of the beginning of the thirteenth century, assume that a noble would continue to treat the lady under whom he had been trained as his special lady, and a troubadour poem of the late twelfth century celebrates the arrival of a new viscountess in the Limousin by urging all the aristocrats of the region to be both polite and valorous in order to be worthy to be her "lover."[74]

It is scarcely surprising that while a young noble was coming into adolescence, when the only lady of his station with whom he had contact was the wife of his uncle or lord, he was encouraged in no uncertain terms to love chastely. But once he had finished his training and was out finding ladies of his own, there seems to have been very little yearning from afar. Indeed, it is difficult for those modern scholars who see chaste and refined love as emblematic of the twelfth cen-

---

[73] Jean Flori, whose work on the vocabulary of "chivalry" has done so much to demonstrate that there was no single twelfth-century ideal standard, is still oddly quick to assume that a chaste "courtly love" did exist, to which one can contrast the more sensuous love found in the *Lais* of Marie de France. "Amour et société aristocratique au XIIe siècle." Interestingly, Bloch takes these *Lais* as archetypal expressions of "courtly love," illustrating how use of such terms can hamper understanding or even communication. *Medieval Misogyny*, p. 166.

[74] Wolfram von Eschenbach, *Parzival*, pp. 46–59. Bertran de Born, *The Poems* 4, p. 132.

tury to explain the stories in which soon after falling in love the principals hop into bed together. The knights on their heroic quests in such stories repeatedly meet stunningly beautiful and wellborn ladies who immediately lust for the heroes' bodies. When in a heroic romance the knight stops for the night at a castle where the lord has a lovely daughter, one can be fairly sure she will try to slip into the knight's bed before morning. Even a cursory reading of the romances indicates that distant yearnings were no universal ideal in the twelfth century.

The extremely popular stories of Lancelot and Guinevere or Tristan and Isolde were in fact stories of adultery, in which the characters—and of course the authors—knew perfectly well that they were sinning, and their sin in a Christian sense was compounded in each case by the lover's betrayal of his sworn loyalty to his king. It was Lancelot's sin that kept him from the grail in the thirteenth-century "Prose Lancelot." In Chrétien de Troyes's "Cligés," the heroine is determined not to become an adulteress, sharing her body between her husband and her lover: "I could never agree to lead the life Isolde led." Even Marie de France, whose *Lais* turned on sympathetically portrayed adulterous love, pronounced, "Evil can easily rebound on him who seeks another's misfortune," telling of a couple who planned to murder the woman's husband and ended up dead themselves.[75]

These romances, of course, were not descriptions of reality and were not intended to be. The authors were giving their hearers and readers what they wanted in a good story, not presenting an accurate depiction of social norms. No one in the twelfth century considered realistic the common romantic picture of noble girls avidly pursuing unwilling heroic knights (whose eyes were doubtless fixed resolutely on higher goals), any more than modern readers find accurate social commentary in the equally stylized conventions of hard-boiled detective novels, where voluptuous clients or suspects routinely try to seduce the tough private eye.

Additionally, and even more important for understanding the role of love in twelfth-century culture, once the young hero of the ro-

[75] *The Quest of the Holy Grail*, p. 86. Chrétien de Troyes, "Cligés," p. 161. Marie de France, *Lais* 2, p. 60. On the Tristan stories, see Joan M. Ferrante, *The Conflict of Love and Honor;* she sees such a conflict as unique to the Tristan legend, whereas it is in fact endemic in medieval romance.

mances had cleared away the excessively lusty young ladies, he often *did* marry one, one he loved with all his heart. Part of Tristan's and Lancelot's tragedy was that they could not marry their ladies. Both the French Perceval and the German Parzival, on the other hand, fell in love with a beautiful young queen—who did climb into his bed when they first met but whom he embraced only chastely—and they were betrothed (in the French version) or married (in the German version) as soon as he had saved her people.[76] So the description of love to which nobles of the High Middle Ages listened might in many cases have adulterous elements, but love was certainly not something that took place only outside of marriage.

Andreas Capellanus

Even the medieval book that has caused the most confusion on the topic of love, Andreas Capellanus's *Art of Courtly Love,* as the title is usually translated, consists largely of a series of dialogues in which men try, with notable lack of success, to talk various women into yielding physically to them.[77] (A better translation of the title would be simply *On Love,* reflecting Ovid's influence.) Andreas was a late twelfth-century chaplain, perhaps at the court of Champagne, who would be totally obscure today were it not for his eccentric and highly popular treatise. The hoped-for result for Andreas's men was always the same, going to bed with the women they chose, even though their desire was generally foiled. Andreas, in his narrative voice, encourages a lordly man interested in the embraces of a peasant girl just to proceed, whether or not she is interested. A highborn woman, on the other hand, needs gentle persuasion, usually based on delicate logical principles. For example, a man trying to win the favors of a chaste married woman might try to persuade her that true love is not possible between a married couple.[78]

It is this argument, which Andreas offers for the cynical use of someone whose eye has been caught by a married woman—and indeed which he says was supported by the decision of the completely

---

[76] Chrétien de Troyes, "The Story of the Grail," pp. 405–17. Wolfram von Eschenbach, *Parzival,* pp. 104–10.

[77] Andreas Capellanus, *The Art of Courtly Love.* John F. Benton, "Clio and Venus: A Historical View of Medieval Love," in *Culture, Power, and Personality,* pp. 110–15.

[78] Andreas Capellanus, *The Art of Courtly Love* 1.6, 1.9, pp. 100, 150.

imaginary Love Courts of the countess of Champagne[79] —which some scholars have mistakenly expanded into an indication that all twelfth-century aristocrats believed love existed only outside of marriage. (Here, as in many other places in his work, Andreas appears to have picked up a motif from Ovid.) It is well to recall, however, that by no means all the romances involve adulterous love. Moreover, Andreas's would-be adulterers achieve scant success with this sly argument.

Although Andreas is sometimes read as a simple advocate for adultery, he is also on the contrary sometimes read as advocating a pure, nonphysical love. This conclusion, too, can be reached only by taking some of the would-be lovers' comments out of context. For example, a lord of the high nobility wooing a lady of the same station tells her that he wants only a "pure love," omitting the "final consolation," and this statement has sometimes been presented in modern scholarship as the ideal of courtly love. If one looks at this comment in context, however, it is clear that the highborn lover's aims are in fact far from pure: he protests that all he wants is first a kiss, then an embrace, then maybe a little nude touching and exploration, *but* nothing more! His lady sees through this transparent pretense at once and rejects his attempt to make her remove her clothing, suggesting that she at least puts no credence in any such ideal "purity."[80]

The chief difficulty with seeing Andreas Capellanus's work as a description of love among the aristocracy is that it was written at least in part as a sophisticated satire on both his society and recent intellectual trends. That is, it was not written as a handbook for nobles to consult before a big date, or as a description of normal aristocratic behavior, but rather as a commentary on the then-current vogue for scholastic argumentation and categorization, as well as on the romances that were becoming popular in his time. Arguing both for love, as Andreas did in the first two-thirds of his book, and against it, in the last third, has confused many scholars, who have tended to maintain either that he really did believe in everything he said in the first part, but was required somehow as a churchman to repudiate it,

---

[79] For the imaginary nature of these "courts," see Benton, "The Court of Champagne," in *Culture, Power, and Personality,* pp. 33–34; and Rüdiger Schnell, *Andreas Capellanus,* pp. 81–85.

[80] Andreas Capellanus, *The Art of Courtly Love* 1.6, pp. 122–23. See also Paolo Cherchi, *Andreas and the Ambiguity of Courtly Love,* pp. 31–32.

or (less commonly) that he really was against love but had been commissioned to write a work on it. It has even been suggested that the love Andreas advocated in the first two-thirds of his work was somehow different from the love he repudiated in the final third.[81] This division in his work, however, makes much more sense as a parody of the scholastic method of argumentation, in which the philosopher or legal scholar was required to provide arguments both for and against a proposition.[82]

In general, the ladies emerge with the upper hand in Andreas's set pieces; they see through all the sophistries of their would-be seducers and turn them deftly away. But also running through the book's sly humor is a rather bitter streak of misogyny, revealed in suggestions that women were foolish not to prefer the embraces of priests—such as Andreas was himself—to those of knights. In the final third of the book, Andreas tells the reader that anyone who actually follows his suggestions on how to seduce a woman will lose his soul, though even here he may be satirizing the moralistic literature of his time. Whatever one makes of this cranky, contradictory, and occasionally screamingly funny book, one cannot take it as the description of an unambivalent, routinely accepted standard of "courtly love."[83]

It should now be clear that the ideals for noble behavior which developed and crystallized in the twelfth century were far from rigid or even unambiguous. Yet certainly the aristocracy, both the nobles whose families had long been accustomed to command and the knights who wanted to emulate the nobles to the point of joining them, increasingly defined themselves by reference to such ideals. Certainly neither "chivalry" nor "courtliness," much less "courtly love" (the latter a modern term without even the advantage of a twelfth-century equivalent), was a clear code with well-understood rules, which nobles could simply learn and then follow. And yet, as nobles found their monopoly on wealth and power threatened in the High Middle Ages by the kings on the one hand and by townsmen on

[81] For a survey of these views, see Douglas Kelly, "Courtly Love in Perspective," and Toril Moi, "Desire in Language," pp. 13–15.

[82] Schnell, *Andreas Capellanus*, pp. 14, 127–30. Baldwin, *Language of Sex*, pp. 16–25. Bumke, *Courtly Culture*, pp. 361–62. Even Andreas's model, Ovid, wrote both *Ars amatoria* and *Remedia amoris*. See Allen, *Art of Love*, p. 13.

[83] Don A. Monson, "Andreas Capellanus and the Problem of Irony."

the other, as castellans realized that the marriage alliances they created with their knights meant that at least some of their grandchildren would not be born to noble fathers, they increasingly set out to define themselves by their behavior. The knights who so wished to join them could hope that similar behavior might help.

The difficulty was that there was no external codified standard of behavior which either knights or nobles could follow, and the epics and romances, which tried in part to create such an ideal, never could agree on all the key elements. Indeed, the authors whose heroes faced conflicts between loyalty to family and loyalty to feudal lord (as in *Raoul de Cambrai*) or between love and honor (as in several of the works of Chrétien de Troyes), seemed determined to demonstrate that a single, ideal, perfect, noble knight not only did not exist but was not even logically possible. And yet at the same time as they denied the possibility of such an ideal, they created a compelling illusion of one, though their vision of the constituents of the ideal varied greatly over the course of the twelfth century.

The most consistent element of the picture of the idealized and knightly noble was military prowess of a highly skilled and technically demanding kind, and this is exactly what "chivalry" originally meant: strength and skill in mounted combat, courage in battle, loyalty to one's companions. This ideal was understandable, even attainable, as nobles increasingly defined themselves by their ability to fight, using the costly and elaborate equipment and skills of the mounted knight. The growing importance of dubbing into knighthood, not originally a particularly widespread ceremony, signals the growing importance of this military role: receiving arms, the symbol of militarism, was by the late thirteenth century taken as a sign of nobility itself. Yet nobles had been attaching more and more importance to their military position for two centuries by that point. Louis VI became a beloved and widely honored king of France in the first half of the twelfth century in large part by personally leading his men into battle. Castles spread in the eleventh and twelfth centuries not just as centers of defense or as strongholds to awe the people of the countryside, although they certainly were that. They functioned as the center of noble courts, as had the palaces of former times, and much of the nobles' wealth in the twelfth century went into incorporating the latest military technology into these structures. Above all, castles defined the men who controlled them as war leaders.

But by the late twelfth century the military concept of "chivalry" was becoming blended with elements that had very different roots. The most important of these was what was called in the literature "courtliness," a standard of behavior that included general politeness, concern for the helpless, and overall good grooming and personal hygiene—in short, the antithesis of the hardened battlefield warrior. Being able to discourse wittily, dance, and play an instrument certainly helped. This ideal, taught to young aristocrats at courts as part of their education, thus became inextricably welded onto what had once been a battlefield ethic. The notion of being especially polite to ladies and enjoying a game of flirtation, of imagining being able to fall in love, in or out of marriage, with someone besides the politically suitable spouse chosen by parents, was part of this courtliness. (To call this flirtation game "courtly love," however, makes it sound both as though it were a category of its own and, quite mistakenly, as though there was even the vaguest consensus on how such a game should be played.)

By the thirteenth century, the term "chivalry" had absorbed the meanings in "courtliness," making it a very difficult amalgam. The mix was made even stranger by the hope, shared by the nobles themselves and the churchmen, that some element of Christianity could be introduced into whatever definition of "chivalry" was in use. Options varied wildly. Some, like Bernard of Clairvaux, saw no way a man could be both a good Christian and a knight unless one joined the Military Orders in the Holy Land and used one's sklls only against non-Christians, becoming quite literally a *miles Christi*, a "knight of Christ." The strength of the Crusade ethos suggests that a number of nobles agreed, at least intermittently and at some level, that it was hard to be a Christian if one frequently killed other Christians. And yet there was a desperate effort by the nobles, reflected in the literature, to allow aristocrats to fight as they had been trained against other men like themselves, and still somehow manage to keep it all Christian.

Scholars have long noted how difficult it is to create a single definition of "chivalry," and for a period the answer was to speak of different chivalric "models," to say, for example, that the church defined chivalry one way, the knights themselves another way, and the ladies a third.[84] Yet the picture is even more complicated than that, for there

---

[84] This was the approach of Sidney Painter, *French Chivalry*.

never *were* any clear and distinct "models." The epics and romances, which should have been able to portray monolithic ideals if anyone was thinking in those terms, are full of hopelessly conflicted heroes. The fictional knights themselves wanted at one and the same time to be military heroes, to be courteous and admired by the ladies, and to be Christian enough for a decent shot at heaven at the end of an active life. Churchmen probably had the clearest ideal image: they wanted knights to protect the churches and kill the infidel, but they did not call this chivalry, and they did not write romances. The ladies do not seem to have had much say at all, except to accept or reject the men who came to them, fresh from victorious battle or tournament and armed with learned and courtly arguments as to why they should love them.

If, as the churchmen believed, anything like a normal knightly life could not really be Christian, there was still hope for such knights. They could, preferably, give it all up and join the church, or at least they could spend some of their considerable power and wealth helping individual churches. As will be seen in the next chapter, even if churchmen saw nothing to admire either in killing or in pursuing the ladies, the churches of the High Middle Ages needed the nobles and courted their friendship.

༄

CHAPTER FIVE

Nobility and the Church

The relationship between the high medieval nobility and the church is a fairly new scholarly topic. The view of medieval society as divided into three orders once made it easy for scholars to treat the aristocracy and the church as separate concerns, even though the majority of the documents through which one learns about either of these "orders" in fact include mentions of both, generally engaged in some joint activity.[1] Even though churchmen beginning in the eleventh century tried to draw sharp distinctions between cleric and layman, in the High Middle Ages there was a large and growing gray area in between. It has long been recognized that members of the same social group, indeed, often the same families, constituted the rulers of both secular society and the church hierarchy. But only in recent years have scholars begun examining the complex ways in which nobles and churchmen interacted, each side borrowing from the other and responding to the other, even though for most of the time their goals were very different.[2]

It should first be pointed out that it is no more correct to speak of "the" church in the Middle Ages than it is of "the" nobility. Churchmen (and churchwomen) were an extremely diverse group, and a group that changed dramatically over the course of the Middle Ages.

---

[1] Constance Brittain Bouchard, *Sword, Miter, and Cloister*, pp. 24–26. John Howe, "The Nobility's Reform of the Medieval Church."

[2] Jean Dunbabin, "From Clerk to Knight: Changing Orders," in Christopher Harper-Bill and Ruth Harvey, eds., *The Ideals and Practice of Medieval Knighthood II*, pp. 26–39. Marcus Bull, *Knightly Piety and the Lay Response to the First Crusade*, pp. 115–203.

The High Middle Ages, the period when knights appeared and castles, chivalry, and centralized kingdoms developed, was also a period in which both laymen and churchmen reexamined and redefined the spiritual life with enormous enthusiasm.[3]

In the twelfth and thirteenth centuries, the chief division within the church was between the so-called "secular" clergy, those who dealt with the secular world on a daily basis, and the "regular" clergy, those who lived secluded from the world, following the strict dictates of a rule (*regula* in Latin). The secular clergy included bishops and parish priests, the canons who served cathedrals as well as many small churches (canons were priests who lived and served their churches in a group, rather than individually), papal representatives, university professors, and many of the officers in royal courts. This branch of the church was often in at least latent conflict with the regular clergy, a group made up primarily of monks and nuns but also of "regular" canons, that is, bodies of priests who followed a stricter rule than the so-called secular canons.

The tensions between secular and regular clergy went back to the early Middle Ages; the bishops always considered themselves the institutional heirs of the apostles, deriving their authority ultimately from Christ, but the monks, believing that their way of life more closely reflected that of the apostles, persisted in considering *themselves* Christ's chief followers.[4] Women could be members of the regular clergy but not the secular clergy, as they were not authorized to administer the sacraments (any more than they can in the modern Catholic Church); in consequence, the number of women in the high medieval church was only a small fraction of the number of men.

Even within these two main branches, there was never anything approaching uniformity. Different bishops often had different views (and indeed often different from the pope, the bishop of Rome, who became the head of Christendom in any meaningful way only in the later eleventh century), and they could become involved in power struggles with members of university faculties or royal officials. Bishops' attempts to educate, much less control and monitor, the parish

[3] André Vauchez, *The Spirituality of the Medieval West*, pp. 75–143. John Van Engen, "The 'Crisis of Cenobitism' Reconsidered."

[4] For the conflicts at Tours over whether the bishops who succeeded Saint Martin, the monks of the monastery the saint had founded, or the canons of the basilica where he was buried were his true "heirs," see Sharon Farmer, *Communities of Saint Martin*.

priests in their dioceses often led to unexpected complexities. Different monasteries contrasted their own rules and ways of life with those of other monks, generally to the others' detriment. Even the basic division between secular and regular clergy was complicated by the presence throughout high medieval Europe of hermits, men (usually) who lived a solitary life without a rule, and also wandering preachers, who tried to spread Christianity to the broader population without receiving formal priesthood training. These men claimed they were following the dictates of the Bible and the church Fathers, and might attain a widespread reputation for holiness, but bishops, parish priests, and cloistered monks all regarded hermits and wandering preachers with deep suspicion.[5]

This diverse group of people made the church a much larger presence within medieval society than are all the modern churches. It has been estimated that as many as 20 percent of adult males from the aristocracy were in the church, although this figure was much lower for noblewomen and for other sectors of society.[6] Because there were so many churchmen, much of their activity was directed toward the good of their own institution, which, they considered, glorified God, rather than toward serving broader society. And monks, who spent much of their life in secluded prayer, prayed for a society in which they did not participate and which they did not see

Noble Entry into the Church

It was once thought that noble parents regularly sent a son from each generation into the church, but closer examination of the sources indicates that the actual situation was much more complicated. Some aristocratic families never put any children, boys or girls, into the church, whereas in other cases a large number of family members, often including two generations, might all decide to enter together.[7]

---

[5] Herbert Grundmann, *Religious Movements in the Middle Ages.*

[6] John Van Engen, "The Christian Middle Ages as an Historiographical Problem." Bouchard, *Sword, Miter, and Cloister,* p. 46.

[7] Michel Parisse called it a "classic rule" that at least one son per generation enter the church; yet his own evidence indicates that many families produced no ecclesiastics. "La noblesse Lorraine," pp. 340, 403. See also Joachim Wollasch, "Parenté noble et monachisme réformateur," pp. 7–11; and Theodore Evergates, "Nobles and Knights in Twelfth-Century France," in Thomas N. Bisson, ed., *Cultures of Power,* pp. 17–19.

Such examples are important because they indicate how highly variable were the factors that made someone from the aristocracy decide to give up a comfortable secular life for a life devoted to religion.

Nobles could theoretically enter the church at any time in their lives at which they felt a religious impulse, but in practice most made their conversion (as it was called) at one of only three points: childhood (between ages six and ten), young adulthood, or old age. Childhood entry was the most common sort in the early Middle Ages, but the new monastic orders of the twelfth century, especially the Cistercians, actively discouraged it, and by the thirteenth century other monasteries too were trying to limit their recruits to those old enough to know what they were doing. My discussion focuses primarily on boys because nuns were so much rarer, but girls' entry into the religious life followed similar patterns.[8]

Those who entered religious life as children did not of course make their own decision; their parents decided for them. As noted in Chapter 3, boys whom their parents destined for an ecclesiastical life might be sent off to begin their training at about the same point that modern boys begin elementary school. The parents would have to decide whether they wanted their child to grow up to become a monk, in which case they would send him to a monastery, or a member of the secular clergy, in which case they would send him in the High Middle Ages to a house of canons or to the cathedral school. In either case, the boy was given the chance, probably in his teens, to make his own final decision on his career, but someone who had been brought up in the church would rarely have considered leaving it for a secular life.

A well-documented example of a boy being set in the church by his relatives is that of Bishop Hugh of Lincoln, who was born to a castellan family of the region of Grenoble. After his mother's death, when Hugh was about eight, his father set him into a small house of regular canons for training and shortly became a canon there himself. Hugh seems never to have considered any other career than the church, and he was appointed to the responsible position of prior of a cell (a church dependent on his church) when still a young man.[9]

Boys given to monasteries were called "oblates," from the Latin

<hr />

[8] Penelope D. Johnson, *Equal in Monastic Profession*, pp. 13–34.
[9] Adam, *Magna Vita Sancti Hugonis*, 1:6–7, 18.

word meaning "that which is offered" (*oblatus*).[10] The gift of a child was considered very precious indeed, and the monastic customaries that describe the process make it clear that it was seen almost as a bloodless sacrifice offered by the parents.[11] Thus the oblation itself was expected to have a positive effect on the parents' hoped-for salvation. Additionally, of course, it would be spiritually beneficial in the future both for the child, who would retain his virginal innocence, and for his relatives, who would have someone in the cloister praying for them. Moreover, it cannot be overlooked that the church could provide an excellent opportunity for upward social mobility for these oblate boys. Thus in the first half of the twelfth century someone such as Suger, who came from a simple knightly family but entered the church early, could end up as abbot of the French royal monastery of St.-Denis and friend and confidant to two kings.[12]

The gift of a child to a monastery or other church was generally accompanied by a gift of property. The twelfth-century account of an aristocratic boy who decided to become a monk at age seven indicated his parents' acceptance of his decision by noting that they gave the monastery four mills. The rulings of church law and councils made it clear in the High Middle Ages that a monastery could not *demand* an entry gift, because such a thing would be simony, that is, an attempt to buy salvation. But in practice no noble family would have considered giving a child to a monastery without such a gift.[13] The amount of this gift, however, varied widely, with wealthier families being expected to give more.

In giving their children to the church parents were not simply disposing inexpensively of excess offspring; rather, it is clear, much more than economic or demographic considerations went into the decision to make a child an oblate.[14] Some noble families might send no one into the church at all for generations, and these were not always the

---

[10] For the training and education of these oblates, see Patricia A. Quinn, *Better Than the Sons of Kings*.

[11] Maria Lahaye-Geusen, *Das Opfer der Kinder*.

[12] John F. Benton, "Suger's Life and Personality," in *Culture, Power, and Personality in Medieval France*, pp. 387–91.

[13] Herman of Tournai, *The Restoration of the Monastery of Saint Martin of Tournai* 62, p. 90. Joseph H. Lynch, *Simoniacal Entry into Religious Life*.

[14] Bouchard, *Sword, Miter, and Cloister*, pp. 60–63. Bull, *Knightly Piety*, pp. 116–25. John Boswell, in using the term "abandonment" to characterize child oblation, unfortunately perpetuated this stereotype, even though he clearly realized that the principal spiritual and social reasons behind oblation were unrelated to issues of family

small families. Other families, by contrast, committed what might be called "dynastic suicide," sending so many children into the church that the family failed to reproduce itself. Indeed, one study suggests that in over 10 percent of the cases a monastic oblate was the only son.[15] Boso, abbot of Bec in the early twelfth century, was one of three sons, *all* of whom were intended for the church by their castellan parents. A few years later, the knightly couple Ralph and Mainsendis decided to convert to the monastic life after Ralph nearly died of a fever, and they decided to make all of their young sons monks at the same time.[16]

If the parents' chief purpose was to reduce potential heirs to the patrimony in order to preserve it intact, one would not have expected them to give their children to the church so young, before it was clear how many would survive the dangers of childhood. Nor is it easy to understand why they would diminish that patrimony by granting with each oblate substantial property that would not be returned if the child died. Nevertheless, both early oblation and accompanying gifts of large fractions of the family wealth were quite common. When Hugh of Lincoln's father was widowed, he divided his property into three equal parts and gave a full third of it to a house of regular canons along with his young son Hugh.[17]

Had parents' only concern been economics, in many ways it would have made *more* sense to keep their children in the world rather than send them into the church. As noted, many noble families made arrangements by which a younger son was given a piece of the family patrimony to hold for his lifetime, with the understanding that it revert to his nephews on his death, so that the family's patrimonial property would not be permanently divided. Property given to the church, however, was gone for good, no matter what happened to the boy. And since a boy sent into either the cathedral school or the

---

size. *The Kindness of Strangers*, pp. 228–29. On this point see also Mayke De Jong, *In Samuel's Image*, pp. 1–15.

[15] Lynch, *Simoniacal Entry into Religious Life*, p. 43. Alexander Murray, *Reason and Society in the Middle Ages*, pp. 346–47.

[16] Milo Crispin, "The Lives of William and Boso," in Sally N. Vaughn, *The Abbey of Bec and the Anglo-Norman State*, p. 126. Herman of Tournai, *The Restoration of Saint Martin of Tournai* 61, p. 87.

[17] Adam, *Magna Vita Sancti Hugonis*, 1:6. A recent study suggests that entry grants for nuns as well were large enough to cover a lifetime of expenses; Sharon K. Elkins, *Holy Women of Twelfth-Century England*, p. 98.

monastery was often named for an older relative (generally an uncle) who was already an established member of that church, the decision to send him must have been made by the time of his baptism.

It should also be noted that the children whom their parents sent into the church were not necessarily any weaker or more likely to be crippled than the children left in the world. It did of course happen that parents, realizing that a particular son would never make a good knight, might decide that the church was a more appropriate career for him; and the religious life might become the final option for a child who did not seem to fit in anywhere. One such boy was Astrolabe, son of Abelard and Heloise, a child of distinguished origins but no sustainable social position, for whom the abbot of Cluny offered to find a suitable prebend in some cathedral after his father died and his mother became an abbess.[18] But by far the majority of boys and girls sent into the church seem to have been neither socially unplaceable nor unhealthy. The monk Guibert of Nogent commented at the beginning of the twelfth century that he himself had been so athletic as a child that if his father had not died young, he might have regretted his decision to put his son into the church; but note that Guibert *did* still become a monk.[19]

It is especially noteworthy that it was the girls who might most easily be considered "excess" children, and yet they rarely entered the church in the High Middle Ages. Even though there were more women than men looking for spouses in this period, parents did not respond to this problem by relegating their daughters to nunneries. Instead, until the late Middle Ages the boys, about whom the parents always worried, hoping they would safely grow to maturity and inheritance in a time when life was very dangerous for someone with a sword on his hip, far outnumbered their sisters within the church.

Once sons had grown into young adulthood, parents quite clearly did *not* want them entering the church. And yet in the High Middle Ages young adulthood was one of the stages at which conversions to the religious life were likely to be made. Hugh, abbot of Cluny in the second half of the eleventh century, had been destined for a knightly life by his parents according to his *Vita*, but as a young man he slipped off to join Cluny without his father's knowledge. Later, after

[18] Peter the Venerable, Letter 168, *The Letters*, 1:401–2; translated in *The Letters of Abelard and Heloise*, pp. 286–87.
[19] Guibert of Nogent, *Memoirs* 1.4, p. 14.

he had become abbot, according to a story told after his death, Hugh visited a noble couple who had been hoping for a son and announced that they would have a boy who would become a monk. The couple was delighted to learn the wife was pregnant but brought their boy up for a military life; he had to make the decision himself to become a monk, as he eventually did at Cluny.[20]

If the devout young man who turned his back on military training for a monastic life was a *topos* of eleventh-century Cluny, it became a painful reality for many aristocratic parents in the twelfth century. Guibert of Nogent commented that in his day "nobles became attracted to voluntary poverty" and "spurned" their possessions as they entered monasteries.[21] The *juvenes*, the young men who had finished their training and been knighted but who were not yet ready to inherit, contributed the bulk of the converts to the new, rigorous religious orders of the twelfth century. The men who made such conversions, it should be noted, almost never became parish priests or canons or joined a house of relaxed discipline; rather, they entered the most demanding of the new houses, the ones where the deliberate embrace of poverty was considered a sign of special holiness.

The Cistercian Order, founded in 1098, was the best known and most successful of these austere new orders. From the beginning, Cistercian monks consciously tried to make their way of life more difficult and more rigorous than the life in other monasteries.[22] They specified that they wanted no oblates, only those old enough to make up their own minds that this was the path they wanted to follow to salvation. And within a few decades they were flooded with converts, largely young men of noble and knightly families who often had to overcome stiff parental resistance.[23]

The example of Bernard of Clairvaux, the best-known monk of the Cistercian Order, is strikingly illustrative. He came from a large family, six sons and a daughter; yet his knightly father had never intended to send any of them into the church. Bernard himself decided to become a monk in 1113. Once he had taken the habit, Bernard ultimately persuaded his sister and all his brothers—even the ones who were al-

---

[20] Gilo, "Vita Sancti Hugonis Abbatis" 1.2–3, in H. E. J. Cowdrey, "Two Studies in Cluniac History," pp. 49–50. Hugh, "Epistola ad Domnum Pontium Cluniacensem abbatem," ibid., pp. 113–14.

[21] Guibert of Nogent, *Memoirs* 1.11, p. 33.

[22] Louis J. Lekai, *The Cistercians.*

[23] Orderic Vitalis, *The Ecclesiastical History* 8.26, 4:327.

The Cistercian monastery of Fontenay, located in Burgundy, flourished because of the financial support and conversions of knights from the region. Cistercian architecture was deliberately kept simple; knights who became monks of the order left luxury behind. Here the pillars of the twelfth-century cloister of Fontenay were done without any of the decorative capitals often found in other churches built at the same time. Giraudon/Art Resource, NY.

ready married—to enter the church as well. His biographer tells the charming story of his youngest brother, who had been designated as the one to remain in the world and continue the family after all his relatives became monks. He complained that he had been deprived of heaven and shortly followed his brothers into the monastery. Bernard's neighbors, the biographer indicated, had a very real fear that he might similarly entice all *their* sons and brothers into the cloister, thus ending their lineages as he had ended his own. By the end of the twelfth century, Bernard's appeal to young aristocrats had become a mocking story in which he had "carts driven round through the towns and castles, in which to carry off his converts to the cloister."[24]

[24] William of St.-Thierry, *Vita Prima Sancti Bernardi* 1.3, PL 185:235–36. Walter Map, *De nugis curialium* 1.24, pp. 77–79. Bouchard, *Sword, Miter, and Cloister*, pp. 329–31.

Young women, too, might decide to enter the cloister against their parents' wishes in this period. In the first half of the twelfth century, for example, an English noble named Christina pursued her vocation for a religious life in direct opposition to her parents, who tried to marry her to a suitable young man and forbade her to visit monastic houses. Her parents told her they wanted grandchildren and that if she resisted their authority, "We shall be the laughingstock of our neighbors." They tried bribery, reproaches, threats, and punishments, invited those given to "worldly amusement" to their house, brought in "old crones" to give her love charms, and made her attend elegant banquets—all in an unsuccessful attempt to make her change her mind. Interestingly, Christina's fiancé became so exasperated with waiting that he offered to pay her entry gift into a nunnery if her parents would agree to release him from his promise to marry her. But Christina was able to become a religious recluse at last, according to her *Vita*, only by running away from home after years of unsuccessfully trying to convince her parents of her desire to convert, and then she long had to remain concealed in a hermitage while they tried to find her and bring her back.[25]

Yolanda, the daughter of the count of Vianden, underwent a similar experience a century later. She decided to become a nun at age twelve, when her parents were arranging a marriage for her. According to her *Vita*, her parents first promised she could become a nun in just a little while, hoping that if she continued to take part in her family's courtly life—and was married soon—she would forget about the plan. When instead she ran away and joined a convent, the count of Luxembourg, a relative of her fiancé, ordered the nuns to return her to her family. Her mother continued to try to make her dance and sing to entertain visitors, but it was no use, for she behaved like a nun even while dressed in her finery. Yolanda's brother, a cathedral canon at Cologne, was called in to talk sense into her but ended up supporting his sister's vocation. Even after Yolanda's fiancé got tired of waiting for her to change her mind and married someone else, her mother kept insisting—and calling on other family members to support her view—that the girl must not become a nun. It was not until five years after her initial attempt to convert that Yolanda was able to gain her

[25] *The Life of Christina of Markyate*, esp. pp. 59, 69, 93.

mother's approval and enter a nunnery.[26] Though both Christina and Yolanda were finally successful, their stories were told as examples of unusual determination; most young women would long since have given in to family pressure.

The third and final stage at which nobles were likely to enter the church was old age. In the first half of the eleventh century, a man who decided in active adulthood to leave the knightly life for the monastery was ridiculed by a friend, who expressed the more common opinion that conversions were more suited for the old than for youths or those in middle years. This friend said that *he* would become a monk only "after he had grown weary of arms and satiated with worldly pleasure." Indeed the old, weary, and widowed often did seek to live out their lives in the quiet of the monastery. It was possible for someone whose spouse still lived to convert, but because religious houses normally demanded that *both* spouses convert in that case, the widowed convert was more common.[27]

Lord Guichard III of Beaujeu decided to become a monk at Cluny in the 1130s "in the decline of his old age," in order to "concentrate his mind," until then distracted by a knightly life. (Interestingly, it was said fifty years later that Guichard then created new distractions for himself, taking up writing vernacular poetry, and at one point riding out again to help his son fight against his enemies before returning peacefully to the cloister.) In the twelfth-century epic of William of Orange the hero is inspired by an angel immediately after his wife's death to go become a monk. But such mature conversions were not for all. King Philip I of France had reached what was regarded as an appropriate age in 1106 when the abbot of Cluny tried to persuade him to become a monk, telling him that the surest path to penitence was the monastic profession, but the king chose to remain in the world and take his chances.[28]

Both men and women might convert in widowhood, the women

[26] Yolanda's story is told by Joachim Bumke, *Courtly Culture*, pp. 355–56.

[27] Gilbert Crispin, "Vita Sancti Herluini," PL 150:699, 703; trans. Vaughn, *Abbey of Bec*, pp. 68, 74. For an example of an aristocratic husband and wife converting together, see Herman of Tournai, *The Restoration of Saint Martin of Tournai* 57, p. 81.

[28] Walter Map, *De nugis curialium* 1.13, pp. 37–39. "William in the Monastery" 2, in *Guillaume d'Orange*, p. 282. Hugh of Cluny, Letter 7, in Cowdrey, "Two Studies," pp. 153–54. For Lord Guichard of Beaujeu, see Bouchard, *Sword, Miter, and Cloister*, pp. 292–93.

probably younger than the men because they had married, on the average, appreciably younger. Even Yolanda of Vianden's mother, in her own declining years after her husband died, took the veil in the same house where her daughter was now a nun. The early thirteenth-century Old French *Lancelot of the Lake* has the hero's mother decide to become a nun as an explicit alternative to suicide, after her husband has died. Because there were many fewer nunneries than male monasteries, widows who intended to convert might find no nearby house to which to retire; some, especially in the eleventh and early twelfth century, ended up as recluses or anchorites living near a monastery. In a few cases, wealthy widows founded nunneries specifically to serve as their own places of retirement. In one of the *Lais* of Marie de France, a wife rather compliantly founds a nunnery and becomes an abbess there, so that her husband can marry his young mistress.[29]

When men and women sought the monastery in their later years, they usually did not want to join one of the rigorous houses favored by the young knights who swelled the ranks of the Cistercians, for example. But they did want a monastery with a reasonably high reputation for holiness. After all, the purpose of such mature conversion was to prepare oneself for death, although some of the women who became nuns may well have also wanted a little respite from a life spent dealing with men. The noble father of Bishop Hugh of Lincoln, who became a canon regular near Grenoble for the last decade of his life, said, according to Hugh, that ordinary retirement would not have done, because that would have given respite from military fatigue but no assurance of salvation.[30]

Those men and women who joined the monastery while still vigorous, although in their mature years, might acquire positions of responsibility and authority.[31] Even bishops might decide to convert to monasticism in their declining years. In many cases, however, both bishops and their castellan brothers and sisters might put off conversion as long as possible, so that they had to be rushed to the monastery to don the habit at the last minute.

[29] Bruce L. Venarde, *Women's Monasticism and Medieval Society*, pp. 11–13. Johnson, *Equal in Monastic Profession*, p. 34. Sally Thompson, *The Founding of English Nunneries after the Norman Conquest*, pp. 167–79. *Lancelot of the Lake*, p. 23. Marie de France, *Lais* 12, p. 125.

[30] Adam, *Magna Vita Sancti Hugonis*, 1:7.

[31] Penelope D. Johnson, *Prayer, Patronage, and Power*, p. 40.

Nobles as Church Leaders

It was taken for granted, both by the nobles themselves and by broader society, that the leaders of the church should come from the same aristocracy that ruled in the world. Because the nobles sent a much higher proportion of their children into the church than did any other social group (an additional indication, incidentally, that the church was not just a dumping ground for children the family could not support, for nobles were certainly in the best position to support their children), there were naturally more noble churchmen available to take up church office. But even more important, it was simply considered natural that the ecclesiastical brothers and cousins of counts and castellans should become bishops and abbots.[32]

For most bishoprics, the lists of bishops for the High Middle Ages are unbroken strings of men from at least knightly and often castellan or comital background. Additionally, the majority of these men were from the immediate local region. Often the only men who cannot be said to be from the local aristocracy are those whose family connections are simply unknown. When someone from a less exalted background *did* become bishop, very unfavorable remarks were usually made about him. Alternatively, if there was a dispute over who should be elected to church office, a candidate's noble birth might be offered as a reason why he was the best possible candidate. When Ivo of Chartres, a noted canon lawyer, was explaining to the pope's representative why he supported a particular candidate for archbishop of Sens at the end of the eleventh century, he emphasized the aspirant's noble blood as well as his regular election.[33]

And yet the nobles who became church leaders were not an undifferentiated group. Just as first castellans and then knights began to act as the social and political equals of the counts and dukes with longer-established power, so over the course of the High Middle Ages bishops came increasingly from the lower strata of the aristocracy, in large part because of a change in how bishops were chosen. In the eleventh century, very powerful regional lords had often selected bishops, who, by no coincidence, were frequently their close relatives. By the

---

[32] Bouchard, *Sword, Miter, and Cloister*, pp. 65–67. Wilhelm Störmer, *Früher Adel*, pp. 311–81. Saints, too, usually came from the aristocracy in the High Middle Ages. André Vauchez, "Lay People's Sanctity in Western Europe," pp. 21–32.

[33] Ivo of Chartres, Letter 59, PL 162:70.

twelfth century, however, elections of bishops had been reformed, and the decision usually rested in the hands of the local cathedral chapter, made up mostly of the sons of the lords of nearby castles. Not surprisingly, these men usually elected one of their own.[34]

Nunneries, like bishoprics, were most commonly headed by members of the high aristocracy, especially in the eleventh century. The monastic chronicler Herman of Tournai found it remarkable that the noblewoman Ida actually did not want to take up a position of authority in the convent after she converted, "although she was the noblest of the nuns." Peter Abelard commented that it was best if an abbess not be of a noble family "powerful in the world," lest she become "presumptuous because of the proximity of her kindred"—an indication that this was the common pattern.[35]

The situation was slightly different in the male monasteries, where the leaders were also normally of noble origins but rarely, if ever, from the highest levels of the aristocracy. Abbots of reformed houses were from castellan families in the eleventh century and continued to be in the twelfth. As knights came to be considered a part of the nobility, they too provided abbots and bishops for French churches.[36] Only at the end of the thirteenth century, when the popes, rather than the local ecclesiastics, began to choose these church leaders, was there a change in their social origins.

Bishops (and, to a lesser extent, abbots) also exercised many of the same functions within the surrounding society as great nobles. Like counts, they administered justice to their regions and controlled large tracts of land themselves, and by the twelfth century they had a number of castellans as their vassals. When monks and nobles came into conflict, resolutions were commonly negotiated by bishops. During the course of the twelfth century, in most cities, counts and bishops had to work out mutually acceptable agreements on their relative jurisdictions.[37] After all, the cities, which had been the centers of episco-

[34] Constance B. Bouchard, "The Geographical, Social, and Ecclesiastical Origins of the Bishops of Auxerre and Sens in the Central Middle Ages." Jean-Pierre Poly, *La Provence et la société féodale*, pp. 269–71.

[35] Jean Verdon, "Les moniales dans la France de l'Ouest aux XIe et XIIe siècles," pp. 249–50. Elkins, *Holy Women*, pp. 2, 99. Herman of Tournai, *The Restoration of Saint Martin of Tournai* 56, p. 78. *The Letters of Abelard and Heloise*, p. 202.

[36] Johnson, *Prayer, Patronage, and Power*, p. 44. Bouchard, *Sword, Miter, and Cloister*, pp. 67–78.

[37] Constance Brittain Bouchard, *Spirituality and Administration*, pp. 54–55.

pal power since the time of the Roman Empire, had also become the centers of counties not much later. In a few cities, however, such as Langres and Reims, the bishops had also been the titular counts since the tenth century, combining both episcopal and comital functions.[38]

But bishops were much more than secular lords, and those bishops who seemed to forget this truth were severely criticized by their contemporaries. For example, Hugh of Noyers, bishop of Auxerre at the end of the twelfth century, was castigated by other priests for devoting so much of his time and energy to improving the fortifications of the family castle he administered for his nephew.[39] Despite bishops' often extensive lordly activities, their principal functions in the twelfth and thirteenth centuries were generally considered to be spiritual: overseeing the liturgy in the cathedral, making sure that both parish priests and monks followed exemplary lives, dispensing charity to the poor, and mediating between the Christians of the diocese and the great saints to whom their churches were dedicated. It was very difficult to balance the conflicting demands of spiritual leadership and temporal administration, but bishops were expected to try. And those secular lords who counted on their friendship or blood relationship with a bishop for favoritism in a dispute might find themselves sadly disappointed by his insistence on at least appearing impartial—and often genuinely being so.

Nobles and the Monasteries

At the same time as castles spread across France and banal lordship appeared in the eleventh centry, monasticism underwent rapid expansion. This was no coincidence. There had been monasteries in Gaul since the fifth century, including a large number founded during the sixth and seventh centuries, and Charlemagne and Louis the Pious in the eighth and ninth centuries had extended their protection to monasteries and ordered them all to follow the Benedictine Rule.

---

[38] The combination of comital and episcopal functions was even more common in German lands, where bishops might become the heads of important principalities. See Benjamin Arnold, *Count and Bishop in Medieval Germany.* For the somewhat different situation in contemporary Italy, where the bishops also functioned as local princes but received their greatest opposition from local communes, not the counts, see Maureen C. Miller, *The Formation of a Medieval Church,* pp. 142–74.

[39] Bouchard, *Spirituality and Administration,* pp. 13–15, 109–14, 141–44.

But the late ninth and tenth centuries had been a difficult period for the monks, with wars often disrupting their lives, the local counts sometimes appropriating the office and revenues of the abbot, and the Vikings considering the monks' wealth and wine cellars tempting prizes. There were, nevertheless, a very few new monastic foundations in this period, most notably Cluny, founded in 909 in Burgundy; this house became an island of stability in a troubled landscape.[40]

But in the early eleventh century many of the old, ruined, or dissolute monasteries began to be refounded and rebuilt, and regular life was established in them once again. The chronicler Raoul Glaber, describing Burgundy shortly after the year 1000, said that the countryside had been covered with a "white mantle of churches."[41] Cluny was an important focus in this renewal but by no means the only monastery that inspired such reforms or sent monks to settle in newly refounded houses. Even within Burgundy, the independent monastery of St.-Bénigne of Dijon, after being reformed to Cluny's way of life in 990, became a separate center for the renewal of other monasteries.[42]

And formerly derelict monasteries, in Burgundy and elsewhere, were reformed or founded by the nobility. Although monastic reform has sometimes been characterized as a struggle between idealistic monks and recalcitrant and greedy nobles, the evidence assembled by recent scholarship makes clear that the spread of monastic reform would have been impossible without the goodwill and indeed active participation of the local aristocracy.[43] At the end of the tenth and beginning of the eleventh centuries, well before the Investiture Controversy pitted church and state against each other, old, ruined churches began to be reformed by the regional dukes and counts—and often

[40] Barbara H. Rosenwein, *Rhinoceros Bound*. Idem, *To Be the Neighbor of Saint Peter*. Constance B. Bouchard, "Merovingian, Carolingian, and Cluniac Monasticism."

[41] Raoul Glaber, *Historia* 3.4.13, pp. 115–17.

[42] Niethard Bulst, *Untersuchungen zu den Klosterreform Wilhelms von Dijon*. The older view that Cluny was somehow the fountainhead of all eleventh-century monastic reform has long since been discredited. In different regions different houses became the chief centers of reform, as Kassius Hallinger first demonstrated for Lorraine in 1950 (*Gorze-Kluny*).

[43] Bouchard, *Sword, Miter, and Cloister*, pp. 87–89. Joachim Wollasch, *Mönchtum des Mittelalters zwischen Kirche und Welt*.

their episcopal brothers and cousins—the same men whose families had often controlled these churches for several generations.[44]

These lords gave their ruined churches to already established monasteries (such as Cluny), giving up their own rights over these establishments and generally making them generous gifts as well. Castellans, seeking to imitate the longer-established nobility in this as in so many areas, also became important monastic patrons. In fact, they were soon to exceed those they emulated, for by the late eleventh and twelfth centuries, when large numbers of completely new monastic foundations began to be made for the first time in centuries, it was usually the castellans who established such houses. And the knights of the twelfth century in turn became especially important as donors to the houses of the new Cistercian order.[45]

This generosity should not by any means suggest that nobles were always or even routinely helpful to their monastic neighbors. True, one of the chief roles for secular nobles in the monastic world was that of the advocate, whose responsibilities included protecting "his" monks from other members of the aristocracy. Sometimes, however, a new regional lord, count or banal lord, would come to power expressing friendship for the local monks, but relations would then deteriorate. In other cases a young lord would come into his inheritance and simultaneously start raising claims against the very monks his parents had patronized. Because many nobles considered themselves better suited than the churchmen themselves to judge holy behavior, they might try to impose their own version of monastic virtue on reluctant monks. Such an attitude found an echo in literary works; the epic hero William of Orange, for example, faced stiff opposition in the monastery he joined when he ate more than any other monk but was also much more assiduous in attending mass.[46]

The whole relationship between monastery and local lord was in fact imbued with ambiguity. Nobles trying to consolidate their power also wanted to exercise power over the monks of their region, even

[44] Bernard Chevalier, "Les restitutions d'églises dans le diocèse de Tours du Xe au XIIe siècles," pp. 129–43. Jacques Boussard, "Les évêques en Neutrie avant la réforme grégorienne."

[45]Constance Brittain Bouchard, *Holy Entrepreneurs*, pp. 165–77. For parallels with English nunneries, see Elkins, *Holy Women*, p. 61.

[46] Johnson, *Prayer, Patronage, and Power*, pp. 69–102. Bouchard, *Holy Entrepreneurs*, pp. 160–82. "William in the Monastery" 11, in *Guillaume d'Orange*, p. 288.

the same monks they sometimes protected from other laymen's influence. These monks in turn could not have survived without the assistance of the nobles, though they epitomized the worldly wealth and self-will the monks were trying to escape. Over the generations—and even in a single generation—monks and a powerful local family could both aid and attack each other. In the middle of the twelfth century, for example, the Benedictine abbot of Vézelay, a distant cousin of the count of Nevers, acted as regent for the county while the count was on the Second Crusade, but soon after his return, only a few years later, the count began plotting "strategems" to seize the monks' property.[47]

The reason that such connections persisted, in spite of the alternation of friendship and feud, was that nobles and monks needed each other.[48] Without gifts from the wealthy, the monasteries would not have had the property they needed to support their life of prayer and contemplation. The spread of religious orders, with new foundations where enthusiastic converts could be set, was possible only if nobles gave the land; after all, monks could scarcely settle where they were not wanted. Even monasteries' membership throughout the Middle Ages was made up primarily of the brothers and cousins of their powerful aristocratic neighbors.

And the nobles also needed the monks, for just as important if perhaps less obvious reasons. First of all, the nobles wanted the monks' prayers. By the twelfth century the aristocracy was well enough educated in Christian morality to have realized that life as a warrior was not the life recommended in the Bible.[49] If one did not want to take the radical step of actually giving up such a life, one was going to have to find some other path to salvation. Of course, as noted, some idealistic young nobles *did* take the radical step of becoming monks, but for the majority the best way to assuage their worry about their souls was to make generous gifts to saints who they hoped had God's ear and to monks who would include them in their prayers. As Guibert of Nogent put it, those "who were unable to renounce their possessions fully [by becoming monks themselves] . . . supported those who had made a full renunciation with frequent gifts. . . . Unable to

[47] Hugh of Poitiers, *The Vézelay Chronicle*, pp. 165–66.
[48] For the network of ties between monks and their powerful neighbors, see, most recently, Martha G. Newman, *The Boundaries of Charity*, pp. 171–90.
[49] C. Stephen Jaeger, *The Origins of Courtliness*, pp. 211–35.

imitate the prayers and embrace the pious way of life of the others, they attempted to provide the equivalent with material help."[50]

Nobles appear to have realized fairly early that capturing monks and forcing them to pray was not going to work; instead, they tried to win the friendship of the monks and the saints they served. This friendship was won especially through generosity, making "friends in heaven" through the "mammon of unrighteousness," as many charter prefaces put it (Luke 16:9). Such prefaces often spelled out the spiritual benefits that would result from gifts to monks, and it would be wrong to read these as simple rhetoric or meaningless clichés. It is not coincidence that the largest proportion of donations to monasteries took place at times of death, either the donor's own imminent demise or the death of a close relative.[51] The reformed houses, those where the monks' ascetic way of life seemed to indicate especial closeness to the saints, always received the most donations.

And yet gifts should not be seen as a simple payment for prayers, for a great many gifts made no specific mention of any liturgical activities, often instead mentioning that the donor would enter the "society and community" of the monastery. In this sense, donations should be seen more as interactions that formed an associative bond between monks and secular lords than as commercial transactions (so much land for so many prayers). As well as giving the monks property they needed to maintain themselves, gifts acted symbolically to bind monks and nobles into a single community.[52]

Even when they made their gifts while in full vigor, the nobles who patronized monasteries looked ahead toward death, their relatives' or their own. In the medieval church, the dead were just as much a part of the community as the living—indeed, one of the most important parts. The biographer of Hugh of Lincoln singled out as a special mark of his subject's saintliness that no one since the biblical Tobias had equalled him in his zeal for burying the dead.[53] At the monastery of Montmajour outside of Arles, built on solid rock so that there was no soil nearby for burials, the church was surrounded by graves cut

[50] Guibert of Nogent, *Memoirs* 1.11, pp. 33–34.

[51] Joseph Avril, "Observance monastique et spiritualité dans les préambules des actes," pp. 5, 17–27. Bouchard, *Sword, Miter, and Cloister*, pp. 190–92.

[52] Megan McLaughlin, *Consorting with Saints*, pp. 138–65, 247–49. Constance B. Bouchard, "Community." Rosenwein, *To Be the Neighbor of Saint Peter*, pp. 47–48.

[53] Adam, *Magna Vita Sancti Hugonis*, 2:1.

At the gates of hell, demons overthrow pride, here represented allegorically by a knight in chain mail being thrown from his warhorse. Pride was very commonly represented as the characteristic sin of the aristocracy. This early twelfth-century carving from the facade of the basilica of Conques also represents the sin of lechery by a well-endowed woman next to the fallen knight, and shows the consequences of slander by having a man's tongue ripped out by demons, above.

directly into the rock. A shortage of soil was clearly not going to keep the church from having a burial ground where the pious dead could be buried near the pious living. At Arles itself, the vast Alyscamps cemetery, used since the time of the Roman Empire, received the dead not only from the town itself but from upstream communities along the Rhône River.[54] Excavations of old churches such as St.-Laurent of Grenoble have discovered thousands of skeletons of people buried in and under the church over the centuries. Medieval churches were thus quite literally built on the dead.

Among the best ways for nobles to be associated with monks after death was to be buried next to them or to have the monks establish anniversary observances for them.[55] Monks routinely buried their noble patrons; even houses of the Cistercian Order, which initially resisted burying laymen in the monks' cemetery, made exceptions in the case of their most generous donors. Indeed, nobles were virtually never buried anywhere except a religious establishment, and monasteries were much more popular burial places for them and their families than were cathedrals, houses of canons, or the parish churches in whose graveyards the mass of the population was buried.[56]

An anniversary observance, which could be established whether or not one was actually buried at a particular monastery, was an annual remembrance, usually on the date of the person's death. On this day the monks would pray specifically for the deceased and, if he or she had left some property for this purpose, perhaps have a special meal or even a new set of shoes in his or her honor. It would take a fairly spectacular gift to establish not just annual but daily masses for someone's soul; Lancelot's queenly mother gave "great wealth, gold and plate, and jewelry" for such daily service in the early thirteenth-century *Lancelot of the Lake.* Monasteries compiled memorial books, *libri memoriales,* sometimes enormous tomes that listed, date by date,

---

[54] Jean-Pierre Poly and Eric Bournazel, *The Feudal Transformation,* p. 312.

[55] Bouchard, *Sword, Miter, and Cloister,* pp. 192–97. Idem, *Holy Entrepreneurs,* pp. 73–74, 121–22. Bull, *Knightly Piety,* pp. 146–53. For English parallels, see Brian Golding, "Anglo-Norman Knightly Burials," in Christopher Harper-Bill and Ruth Harvey, eds., *The Ideals and Practice of Medieval Knighthood,* pp. 35–48. Townsmen often imitated the aristocracy in making gifts for their souls; in fact, in Castile and Aragon in the twelfth and thirteenth centuries, testamentary legislation assumed a man would give 20 percent of his worth in *pro anima* gifts. James W. Brodman, "What Is a Soul Worth?"

[56] McLaughlin, *Consorting with Saints,* pp. 44–54, 117–26.

the special friends of the monastery whom the monks would remember that day.[57]

But the monastery was not just a place where nobles went when thinking about their souls' welfare in the world to come. It was also a vital part of the community of the living, one of the elements that bound different noble lineages together. A patrilineal family that had never before been associated with a particular monastery, for example, might begin to make gifts to it after the current lord married a woman from a family that *did* have long association with that house.[58] Similarly, a feudal lord might encourage his vassals to make gifts to the same monastery he patronized. Such affinities, once established, could continue for generations, forming an ongoing link between the families involved.

Part of a monastery's links with its noble neighbors might in fact have nothing to do with gifts or salvation. By the twelfth century, nobles often undertook complicated financial transactions with the local monasteries. Although mortgaging, pawning, and the like have usually been considered urban activities, in France, primarily rural in the High Middle Ages, these sorts of financial transaction began in the countryside, between aristocrats and the monasteries. When aristocrats needed money, the easiest way to obtain it was by selling, pawning, or leasing some of their property to the monks. The gifts from generous donors which the monasteries had long received and, in the case of the Cistercians, the monks' own economically successful system of agriculture, meant that in many instances twelfth-century monks provided the best source of ready cash. Crusaders especially, preparing for an arduous and expensive expedition, often pawned property to the monks for needed funds in the rather hollow hope that they would return alive and, ideally, loaded with plunder, and thus be able to redeem the land within a few years.[59]

Such financial transactions occurred simultaneously with the more pious transactions. Whereas to the modern eye there may be something rather startling about a noble mortgaging his land to the same

---

[57] *Lancelot of the Lake,* p. 23. Karl Schmid and Joachim Wollasch, "Die Gemeinschaft der Lebenden und Verstorbenen in Zeugnissen des Mittelalters." McLaughlin, *Consorting with Saints,* pp. 90–101.

[58] Bouchard, "Community." Idem, *Sword, Miter, and Cloister,* pp. 142–48.

[59] Bouchard, *Sword, Miter, and Cloister,* pp. 220–23. Idem, *Holy Entrepreneurs,* pp. 31–65.

ascetic monks whom he wanted to pray for his soul, such a perception owes more to the twentieth century than to the twelfth. Gifts in alms to reformed monasteries continued and indeed multiplied at the same time as financial transactions with these same monasteries became common, indicating that the aristocrats themselves saw no discordance between these two roles. Monks formed part of the nobles' broader social context, which included concern for their families, their finances, and their salvation. Those leaving on dangerous trips, borrowing money from the local monks to pay expenses, asked these same monks for their prayers if they did not return.

Conflict Resolution

A more negative, yet recurring aspect of the relationship between monks and nobles was the outbreak of quarrels, usually quarrels over property. In many cases powerful laymen simply found the lands and goods of their monastic neighbors too tempting to pass up, but it must also be noted that a great many conflicts arose because laymen genuinely thought the monks had something that belonged to them.

Faced with forceful claims or outright attacks on their property, the monks could not, of course, simply oppose physical strength with strength, although one of the functions of the monastic advocate in the eleventh century was supposed to be to discourage such attacks with his own authority. The church of Orléans was fortunate in having the youthful Louis VI come to their aid to attack the castellan who they felt had taken away their rights.[60] But churches often did not have such powerful protectors and had to find other methods. Sometimes it was hoped that flaunting the very weakness of a religious house might discourage the powerful from taking advantage of it. In the epic *Raoul de Cambrai*, a group of threatened nuns tells Raoul, "You can easily slaughter and destroy us." Raoul, mollified, agrees on the spot not to harm them. Nevertheless, he does come back the next day and burn down their nunnery anyway, suggesting the flaw in counting on weakness as a defense.[61]

One of the few weapons the monks had at their disposal was to call down the wrath of the saints on their enemies when no secular judge

[60] Suger, *The Deeds of Louis the Fat* 6, p. 36.
[61] *Raoul de Cambrai* 66, p. 87.

could help them. Many eleventh-century books of miracles are collections of stories in which knights and nobles attacked monks or their possessions, but were then killed or maimed by the saints the monks served.[62] Liturgical cursing by the monks helped make sure the saints moved quickly against their enemies. "May they be cursed in town and cursed in the fields," one malediction ran. "May their barns be cursed and may their bones be cursed. May the fruit of their loins be cursed as well as the fruit of their lands."[63] In other cases monks might even turn their anger against their own saints, "humiliating" the saints' relics by putting them on the ground or placing thorns around them, in some cases pounding on the altars with their fists to recall the saints to the duty of protecting the monks who served them.[64] Both malediction and humiliation of relics were examples of spiritual weapons, the only ones at the monks' direct disposal, used against enemies in a period without a regular or centralized legal system to help them.

During the eleventh and twelfth centuries, conflicts between monks and laymen were most commonly settled by compromise. Since it might be difficult to say whether a layman who, for example, had not given his permission when his father had donated property to a monastery really did have a legal right to it, it was easier to compromise than attempt a ruling on a point of law where the law itself was very murky. The weakening of the power of kings and counts after the end of the tenth century meant that it was also harder to enforce a ruling—part of the reason that monks sometimes turned instead to ritual cursing. Additionally, a layman might be more willing to accept a compromise to which he had agreed beforehand than a ruling against him. Hence, even when judges were used they were often essentially arbiters, or at most would confirm an agreement the two parties had already worked out privately.[65]

Here it is important to stress that there was no single method that monks used to deal with their enemies—or potential enemies. In

[62] See, for example, *The Book of Sainte Foy.*

[63] On such curses, see, most recently, Lester K. Little, *Benedictine Maledictions.* This particular curse is found on p. 36.

[64] Patrick J. Geary, *Living with the Dead in the Middle Ages,* pp. 95–124.

[65] Stephen D. White, " 'Pactum . . . legem vincit et amor judicium.' " Stephen Weinberger, "Cours judiciaires, justice, et responsabilité sociale dans la Provence médiévale."

some cases, as at the very wealthy house of Cluny, the same families (and often the same individuals) who quarreled with the monks were also their closest friends and most generous benefactors. Indeed, in a certain sense one advantage of quarreling with the monks, even aside from (potentially) gaining some property, was being able to make up with them afterwards, a process that always involved an integration or reintegration into the spiritual society of the monks. At other houses, in contrast, the monks, through friendship with a powerful layman such as the king, were often able to win resounding victories over their enemies. In still other cases, monks considered other clerics, especially the local bishop, their chief rivals, and turned to powerful lay patrons for assistance. In all these cases, it is clear that the boundary between friend and enemy was not the same as the boundary between clergy and laity.[66]

Of course, from the monks' point of view it was often simpler to avoid conflict in the first place. Especially in the High Middle Ages, as I have suggested, many of the miracle stories that monks composed to celebrate the power and holiness of their patron saints functioned especially to protect monastic property. In these stories, men and women who help the saints benefit from the association, while those who attack the saints by attacking the property of the monks who serve those saints are severely punished. When monks could back up the wrath of their saintly "fathers" with the protection of local political authorities, they could enjoy relatively peaceful relations with their secular neighbors.[67]

Monks could also hope to reduce or avoid future conflicts over property by gaining the consent of all a donor's close relatives when he or she made the gift in the first place. Since the single most common claimant arriving at the doors of most monasteries was the heir of an earlier donor, the monks hoped that obtaining the heir's consent, the *laudatio*, ahead of time could reduce the incidence of such claims. From the point of view of the donor's family, the *laudatio* had value even if the heirs had no intention of appropriating a gift in the future because, by being present at the property transfer and having

[66] Barbara H. Rosenwein, Thomas Head, and Sharon Farmer, "Monks and Their Enemies." Bouchard, "Community," pp. 1037–38. Stephen D. White, *Custom, Kinship, and Gifts to Saints*, pp. 172–76.
[67] Thomas Head, *Hagiography and the Cult of Saints*.

their names transcribed in the donation charter, they could share in the spiritual benefits the donor obtained.[68]

Conflicts between nobles and churchmen in high medieval France, then, were most commonly resolved not by legal judgment in a formally constituted court of law but through an attempt by both sides to avoid disagreement in the first place and to find a mutually acceptable resolution to those conflicts that inevitably occurred. Here it should be noted that, even though most nobles probably quarreled with monks at least once in their lives, the connection between going to the monks and finding some sort of agreeable resolution to a dispute was so strong that nobles normally took even secular quarrels before ecclesiastical arbiters. The war in the epic *Raoul de Cambrai*, which seems impossible to end, is resolved when the abbot of St.-Germain-des-Prés intervenes.[69] The church was not just a career, a source of prayers that could make the difference in the life to come, or a wealthy moneylender who could be counted on to deal honestly. The church was also the embodiment of peace.

Just as members of the aristocracy did not live entirely separate from the peasants who raised their food and the townsmen who bought their agricultural surplus and provided them with luxury imports, so they were not separated from a church that could, without having to concentrate hard, list dozens of ways that the normal knightly life of warfare, ostentation, and extortion was sinful. This church was not a unified body standing over to one side, observing knights and nobles and their behavior. Rather, it was a complex conglomerate of men—and some women—virtually all the leaders of which were from aristocratic backgrounds. Indeed, in the twelfth century especially, the most vocal and admired church leaders, men such as Bernard of Clairvaux, knew very well what they meant when they criticized the knightly life, because it was a life they had been trained for themselves.

[68] White, *Custom, Kinship, and Gifts*, pp. 46–54. Emily Zack Tabuteau, *Transfers of Property in Eleventh-Century Norman Law*, pp. 113–95. Bouchard, *Holy Entrepreneurs*, pp. 135–40.
[69] *Raoul de Cambrai* 239, pp. 315–17. For examples from chronicles and charters, see Geoffrey Koziol, "Monks, Feuds, and the Making of Peace in Eleventh-Century Flanders," in Thomas Head and Richard Landes, eds., *The Peace of God*, pp. 239–58; Geary, *Living with the Dead*, pp. 125–60; and Stephen D. White, "Feuding and Peace-Making in the Touraine around the Year 1100," pp. 204–9.

The church could not simply dismiss the aristocracy, for the clergy needed the nobles—as a source of converts in general, as a source of leaders in particular, for protection against other enemies, and for the gifts that made the material existence of rural monasteries possible. Nobles needed the church as well—as a place to go out of world-weariness in old age or spiritual disgust in idealistic youth, as a source of ready cash when they were beginning an expensive and dangerous enterprise, and as a source of prayers when they saw their close friends and family dying or decided their own behavior had gone a little too far past any semblance of the Christian life.

Relations between churches and their noble neighbors were certainly not uniformly harmonious. In fact, they were often strained, especially by property disputes or when the occasional banal lord decided that his authority should extend over *everyone* in his castellany, including the churchmen. But these were the same kinds of disputes that occurred within noble families. And just as nobles, when external enemies threatened, needed and relied on the very same close relatives with whom they fought when not facing enemies, so they needed and relied on a church with which they could never completely agree. By providing a focus in many cases for kin consciousness when relatives were all buried at the same monastery, by helping bind together the knights of a region in shared generosity to the same monks, and in providing the judges and mediators for their quarrels with other nobles, churchmen became a key part of the community network that linked the knights and nobles of a region to each other. If the extended family, with its frenetic infighting and shared cause against outsiders, was the most obvious model for the aristocracy's social interactions, then the church was part of that family.

CONCLUSIONS

Anyone who might have come to this book hoping that it would provide clear and unambiguous definitions of the abstract nouns nobility, knighthood, and chivalry must by now be disappointed. Certainly there are medieval terms—*nobilitas, militia, chevalerie*—that correspond to these modern English words. Thus it is at least worth attempting to find a definition, whereas in trying to pin down such recently created constructs as "feudalism" or "courtly love" one ends up discussing not medieval authors but ones from the nineteenth and twentieth centuries. But the unwillingness of modern historians to be pinned down, to give, say, "the ten commandments of chivalry," is due to the very ambiguity and lack of agreement in the primary sources.

Previous generations of historians looked at disorderly and contradictory medieval definitions and tried to create simplicity, in the rather patronizing (though probably unconscious) assumption that we can define for the people of the past what their governing structures and ideals were, even if they were incapable of doing so themselves. Lately, however, scholars have been more willing to take seriously the attempts by people of the past to discuss what was, after all, their own society. The advantage of this procedure has been to encourage an appreciation of how complicated were the structures and ideals of the eleventh through thirteenth centuries and how rapidly they changed. Even if one were able to create a definition of, say, knighthood valid in one particular decade and one particular place, it would not necessarily be a useful definition elsewhere or at another time.

Even more important, by taking seriously the very diversity in the sources, rather than treat it as a hindrance to a comprehensive definition, one comes to realize how much of a dialogue was the attempt during the High Middle Ages to come to terms with these concepts. That is, even at the same time, different individuals might have very different ideas of what were the key elements of a particular institution. This is true even for nobility and knighthood, where the modern reader can glimpse some sort of developing consensus, but it is especially true for chivalry. At exactly the same time as the concept of the chivalrous knight was developing and taking on a variety of attributes, there was a growing realization, pointed out quite explicitly in the literature, that these attributes were inherently contradictory.

Who then *were* the knights and nobles of high medieval France, and what was this chivalry that they increasingly claimed they wanted to follow? Here it is easiest to begin by treating *nobilitas* not as a social class but as a personal status denoted by a collection of attributes and recognized by behaviors that could differ over time and space or even in the view of different individuals. Those who shared in the attributes of "nobility" had in this period no juridic separation from the rest of society, but they were certainly elevated by their greater wealth, their power to command, and their ability to point to ancestors as "nobly born" as themselves. Increasingly, over the course of the eleventh and twelfth centuries, men with noble position also defined themselves militarily, so that any self-respecting wellborn and wealthy lord would also be a skilled fighter.

Could a man or woman lose noble status, or could a non-noble gain it? Here the quite deliberately ambiguous language of the period indicates a persistent unwillingness to be tied into a sharp definition. This can be seen most clearly in the familiar *topos* that someone was noble by birth and even more noble by spirit. Hence, someone who protected the defenseless and made gifts to the churches might be described (by churchmen) as "more noble," but this description did not mean that someone who did none of these things was "less noble." There was another *topos* of being "puffed up by nobility" to take care of such circumstances; nobility was good when a nobleman did good things, bad when he did not. The twelfth-century nobles who chose the religious life gave up their wealth and power, renounced the military life, and cut themselves off from their noble families, but those who joined traditional orders or houses of canons were still considered noble if they cared to be. On the other hand, the nobly born members of the new rigorous orders such as the Cistercians never called themselves noble.

Despite the difficulty of defining nobility, the knights of the High Middle Ages could recognize it well enough to know that they wanted to join it. The *milites,* men whose position derived from fighting on horseback, were originally in a position of service to the longer-established noble lords. Being a knight was in the eleventh century a description of a function, not of a social group; a servitor who stopped taking part in military activities stopped being a knight, and even a powerful lord, by the end of the eleventh century, was called a knight as long as he was armed and on horseback. But service knights gradually took on a certain social coherence, becoming a group one step down from the nobles but one step up from peasants and townsmen. Their military function made them less and less distinguishable from nobles who were increasingly stressing their own military abilities, and their carefully calculated marriages could give their children noble birth. By the time that either nobility or knighthood became a clearly defined social class, at the end of the thirteenth century, they were not two groups but one. Dubbing, the ceremony that marked a young noble's coming-of-age by giving him his first knightly weapons, became the criterion for nobility that had not before existed.

The aristocracy of knights and nobles did not exist within a vacuum but was an integral and extremely influential part of the society that surrounded it. Both the relationship between knights and nobles and the expansion and eventual rise of the knights themselves owe much to the rapid social changes that took place in France in the early eleventh century. At this point, the effective political power of central, royal authority was gone. Even some of the counts who had once served as the king's agents in the ninth century and then, in the tenth century, as essentially independent princes were losing their authority. But in the first half of the eleventh century new political structures emerged with the spread of castles, commanded by independent-minded castellans and staffed by the knights who served them. These castellans took on juridic and economic roles that local lords had not before held as they began to exercise banal rights over all the inhabitants of the regions around their castles.

If the eleventh century appears, however, to have been a period in which independent castellans were going to triumph, then the twelfth century was a period in which that independence was challenged. The kings, reestablishing central authority on a new basis, balked castellans' power to do whatever they wanted. The towns and villages, growing rapidly in a period of economic prosperity, sought and obtained charters of liberties from the local lords. Serfs, whose ancestors had been subject in the body to castellans' ancestors for generations, obtained their freedom, often by buying it. The development and spread of the new institution of fief holding tied nobles into tighter webs of obligation and interdependence with each other. And nobles themselves, even if many took advantage of economic opportunities to raise or extort more money and spend more ostentatiously, also were more likely in the twelfth century to abandon the secular life for austere prayer in the monastery. The growing power and independence of the castellans in the early eleventh century had been marked in part by their taking on the role of monastic founder, protector, and donor which had once been an important element of royal prerogatives. To this was increasingly added in the twelfth century the role of adult convert. Here too the knights followed the nobles. Knights, who had spent much of the eleventh century trying to emulate their lords, outdid them in many cases in the twelfth century in thorough rejection of the secular world, and they formed the chief pillar of support for the new, stricter monastic orders.

When expectations and obligations were constantly shifting, it is not surprising that the chivalric ethos, as portrayed in epic and romance, also constantly shifted. Far from describing a simple "code" to which knights and nobles might (or might not) measure up, the literature of the time kept showing, generally quite explicitly, that it was impossible for anyone, even the glorious knights and nobles of story, to find and successfully follow an idealized mode of conduct that was not inherently contradictory. "Chivalry" had been relatively straightforward when it involved only battlefield skills and raw courage; once it was also expected to include courtly behavior, service to ladies (perhaps from a distance, perhaps from sinfully close), and Christian morality—especially since most churchmen of the twelfth century saw no way that a fighting knight could also be a Christian unless he were fighting Muslims—it became an impossible mix to keep stable.

The French knights and nobles of the High Middle Ages were not the followers of the elaborate rituals that became attached to the idea of chivalry in the fourteenth and fifteenth centuries; nor were they the pure and true heroes of nineteenth-century Romanticism. They were people with more opportunities than the great mass of society for wealth and command, and also more opportunities—many of which they brought on themselves—for sudden violent death. With an education consisting of at least a smattering of the classics, a fair amount of Christian doctrine, an enormous amount of fighting, and tales of chivalric heroes, it should not be surprising that for a large number of young knights of the High Middle Ages, the only answer was to renounce it all and join a monastery, where the answers were in some ways harsher but at least there were fewer questions. As for the rest, many took refuge in developing sharper categories and definitions of nobility in the Late Middle Ages, using these newly created criteria to create for the first time unambiguous descriptions of their expectations and status.

BIBLIOGRAPHY

Primary Sources

The primary sources are cited, by preference, in easily accessible English translations where such exist. Some of the epics and romances appear in multiple modern translations; inclusion here of a particular translation is not meant to indicate any judgment on the quality and merits of one version over another, but only an indication of the edition I myself used.

Adalbero. "Carmen ad Rotbertum regum." Ed. Claude Carozzi. *Poème au roi Robert.* Classiques de l'histoire de France au moyen âge 32. Paris, 1979.

Adam. *Magna Vita Sancti Hugonis.* 2d ed. Ed. and trans. Decima L. Douie and David Hugh Farmer. *The Life of St. Hugh of Lincoln.* 2 vols. Oxford, 1985.

Andreas Capellanus. *The Art of Courtly Love.* Trans. John Jay Parry. New York, 1990.

Anselm of Canterbury. *Epistolae.* PL 159:9–272.

Aucassin and Nicolette and Other Medieval Romances and Legends. Trans. Eugene Mason. New York, 1958.

Bernard of Clairvaux. *Opera.* Ed. Jean Leclercq and H. Rochais. Rome, 1957–.

——. *Treatises III.* Trans. Conrad Greenia. Kalamazoo, Mich., 1977.

Beroul. *The Romance of Tristan.* Trans. Alan S. Fedrick. London, 1970.

Bertran de Born. *The Poems of the Troubadour Bertran de Born.* Ed. and trans. William D. Paden Jr., Tilde Sankovitch, and Patricia H. Stäblein. Berkeley, 1986.

The Book of Sainte Foy. Trans. Pamela Sheingorn. Philadelphia, 1995.

Le cartulaire de Marcigny-sur-Loire (1045-1144): Essai de reconstitution d'un manuscrit disparu. Ed. Jean Richard. Dijon, 1957.

The Cartulary of Flavigny, 717–1113. Ed. Constance Brittain Bouchard. Medieval Academy Books 99. Cambridge, Mass., 1991.

Chrétien de Troyes. *Arthurian Romances.* Trans. William W. Kibler. London, 1991.

Cowdrey, H. E. J. "Two Studies in Cluniac History, 1049–1126." *Studi Gregoriani* 11 (1978), 1–298.

The Death of King Arthur. Trans. James Cable. London, 1971.

Fulbert of Chartres. *The Letters and Poems.* Ed. and trans. Frederick Behrends. Oxford, 1976.

Galbert of Bruges. *The Murder of Charles the Good, Count of Flanders.* Trans. James Bruce Ross. New York, 1960.

Gilbert Crispin. "Vita Sancti Herluini." PL 150:695–714.

Gottfried von Strassburg. *Tristan.* Trans. A. T. Hatto. Harmondsworth, Eng., 1960.

Guibert of Nogent. *Memoirs.* Trans. Paul J. Archambault. *A Monk's Confession.* University Park, Pa., 1996.

Guillaume de Lorris and Jean de Meun. *The Romance of the Rose.* Trans. Charles Dahlberg. Princeton, 1971; rpt. Hanover, 1986.

Guillaume d'Orange: Four Twelfth-Century Epics. Trans. Joan M. Ferrante. New York, 1991.

Herman of Tournai. *The Restoration of the Monastery of Saint Martin of Tournai.* Trans. Lynn H. Nelson. Washington, D.C., 1996.

Hugh of Poitiers. *The Vézelay Chronicle.* Trans. John Scott and John O. Ward. Binghamton, 1992.

Ivo of Chartres. *Epistolae.* PL 162:11–288.

Jean Renart. *The Romance of the Rose or Guillaume de Dole.* Trans. Patricia Terry and Nancy Vine Durling. Philadelphia, 1993.

John of Salisbury. *Policraticus: Of the Frivolities of Courtiers and the Footprints of Philosophers.* Trans. Cary J. Nederman. Cambridge, 1990.

Lancelot. Trans. Samuel N. Rosenberg and Carleton W. Carroll. In Norris J. Lacy, ed. *Lancelot-Grail: The Old French Arthurian Vulgate and Post-Vulgate in Translation.* Vol. 2. New York, 1993.
　The story of Lancelot in the mid-thirteenth-century vulgate cycle version.

Lancelot of the Lake. Trans. Corin Corley. Oxford, 1989.
　The early thirteenth-century Old French version of the Lancelot story, later rewritten and incorporated into the vulgate cycle.

The Letters of Abelard and Heloise. Trans. Betty Radice. London, 1974.

Liber instrumentorum memorialium: Cartulaire des Guillems de Montpellier. Ed. A. Germain. Montpellier, 1884–86.

The Life of Christina of Markyate, a Twelfth-Century Recluse. Revised ed. Ed. and trans. C. H. Talbot. Oxford, 1987.

Mansi, J.-D., ed. *Sacrorum conciliorum nova et amplissima collectio.* Vol. 21. Venice, 1776.

Marie de France. *The Lais.* Trans. Glyn S. Burgess and Keith Busby. Harmondsworth, Eng., 1986.

Odo of Cluny. "The Life of St. Gerald of Aurillac." Trans. Gerald Sitwell. *St. Odo of Cluny.* London, 1958.

Odo of Deuil. *De Profectione Ludovici VII in Orientem.* Ed. and trans. Virginia Gingerick Berry. New York, 1948.

Orderic Vitalis. *The Ecclesiastical History.* Ed. and trans. Marjorie Chibnall. 6 vols. Oxford, 1969–80.

Otto of Freising. *The Deeds of Frederick Barbarossa.* Trans. Charles Christopher Mierow. New York, 1953.

Peter the Venerable. *The Letters.* Ed. Giles Constable. 2 vols. Cambridge, Mass., 1967.

Peters, Edward, ed. *The First Crusade.* Philadelphia, 1971.

The Quest of the Holy Grail. Trans. P. M. Matarasso. London, 1969.

Raoul de Cambrai. Ed. and trans. Sarah Kay. Oxford, 1992.

Raoul Glaber. *Historia.* Ed. and trans. John France. Oxford, 1989.

Richer. *Histoire de France.* 2 vols. Ed. Robert Latouche. Paris, 1930–37.

The Song of Roland. Trans. Glyn Burgess. London, 1990.

Suger. *The Deeds of Louis the Fat.* Trans. Richard C. Cusimano and John Moorhead. Washington, D.C., 1992.

———. "Epistolae." RHGF 15:483–532.

Teulet, Alexandre, ed. *Layettes du trésor des chartes.* 2 vols. Paris, 1863–66.

Three Arthurian Romances: Poems from Medieval France. Trans. Ross G. Arthur. London, 1996.

Vaughn, Sally N. *The Abbey of Bec and the Anglo-Norman State, 1034–1136.* Woodbridge, Eng., 1981.
Includes translations of the primary sources on the foundation and early history of Bec.

Walter Map. *De nugis curialium: Courtiers' Trifles.* Ed. and trans. M. R. James. Oxford, 1983.

William of St.-Thierry. *Vita Prima Sancti Bernardi.* PL 185:226–447.

Wolfram von Eschenbach. *Parzival.* Trans. A. T. Hatto. Harmondsworth, Eng., 1980.

Secondary Sources

This is not intended to be a complete bibliography of studies on medieval nobility and chivalry (which could easily surpass this entire book in length), only of those referenced in the text, a selection of the most important, most accessible, or most recent works. The notes and bibliographies in these works will give the interested reader access to the broader literature. If I cited several articles out of a book of collected articles, I here give the editor and title of the volume but not of the individual articles, which will be found in the footnotes. The most useful references are provided with brief annotations.

Airlie, Stuart. "Bonds of Power and Bonds of Association in the Court Circle of Louis the Pious." In Peter Godman and Roger Collins, eds. *Charlemagne's Heir: New Perspectives on the Reign of Louis the Pious (814–840)*. Oxford, 1990.

Allen, Peter L. *The Art of Love: Amatory Fiction from Ovid to the "Romance of the Rose."* Philadelphia, 1992.

Arnold, Benjamin. *Count and Bishop in Medieval Germany: A Study of Regional Power, 1100–1350*. Philadelphia, 1991.

——. *Princes and Territories in Medieval Germany*. Cambridge, 1991.

Avril, Joseph. "Observance monastique et spiritualité dans les préambules des actes (Xe-XIIe s.)." *Revue d'histoire ecclésiastique* 85 (1990), 5–29.

Bachrach, Bernard S. "The Angevin Strategy of Castle Building in the Reign of Fulk Nerra, 987–1040." *AHR* 88 (1983), 533–60.

——. "Charles Martel, Mounted Shock Combat, the Stirrup, and Feudalism." *Studies in Medieval and Renaissance History* 7 (1970), 47–75.
Effectively refutes the old idea that the stirrup and feudalism were somehow simultaneous inventions in the eighth century.

——. *Fulk Nerra: The Neo-Roman Consul, 987–1040*. Berkeley, 1993.

Baldwin, John W. *The Government of Philip Augustus: Foundations of French Royal Power in the Middle Ages*. Berkeley, 1986.

——. *The Language of Sex: Five Voices from Northern France around 1200*. Chicago, 1994.

——. *Masters, Princes, and Merchants: The Social Views of Peter the Chanter and His Circle*. 2 vols. Princeton, 1970.

Barber, Malcolm. *The New Knighthood: A History of the Order of the Temple*. Cambridge, 1994.

Barthélemy, Dominique. "La mutation féodale a-t-elle eu lieu?" *Annales: Économies, sociétés, civilisations* 47 (1992), 767–77.

——. *L'ordre seigneurial, XIe–XIIe siècle*. Paris, 1990.

——. "Qu'est-ce que le servage, en France, au XIe siècle?" *Revue historique* 582 (1992), 233–84.
A careful reassessment of the nature and development of serfdom, including a historiographic survey of scholarly opinions.

——. *La société dans le comté de Vendôme de l'an mil au XIVe siècle*. Paris, 1993.
The most important of the recent French local-history monographs, a massive work with implications far beyond Vendôme.

Bartlett, Robert. *Trial by Fire and Water: The Medieval Judicial Ordeal*. Oxford, 1986.

Bates, David. *Normandy before 1066.* New York, 1982.

Bautier, Robert-Henri. "Les foires de Champagne: Recherches sur une évolution historique." In Robert-Henri Bautier. *Sur l'histoire économique de la France médiévale: La route, le fleuve, la foire.* Aldershot, Eng., 1991.

Bean, J. M. W. *From Lord to Patron: Lordship in Late Medieval England.* Philadelphia, 1989.

Beech, George T. "Les noms de personne poitevins du 9e au 12e siècle." *Revue internationale d'onomastique* 26 (1974), 81–100.

——. "Prosopography." In James M. Powell, ed. *Medieval Studies: An Introduction.* 2d ed. Syracuse, 1992.
Broader than the title suggests, this article is a good introduction to how noble families are studied and reconstructed; includes an extensive bibliography.

Beitscher, Jane K. " 'As the Twig Is Bent . . .': Children and Their Parents in an Aristocratic Society." *Journal of Medieval History* 2 (1976), 181–91.

Benton, John F. *Culture, Power, and Personality in Medieval France.* Ed. Thomas N. Bisson. London, 1991.
The collected articles of a major scholar on nobility and chivalry who unfortunately did not live to produce a book tying his ideas together.

Bishop, Jane. "Bishops as Marital Advisors in the Ninth Century." In Julius Kirshner and Suzanne F. Wemple, eds. *Women of the Medieval World: Essays in Honor of John F. Mundy.* Oxford, 1985.

Bisson, Thomas N. "The 'Feudal Revolution.' " *Past and Present* 142 (1994), 6–42.

——. "Medieval Lordship." *Speculum* 70 (1995), 743–59.

——. "Nobility and Family in Medieval France." *French Historical Studies* 16 (1990), 597–613.
A review essay, vital for understanding how scholars' conception of the medieval nobility has developed in the last fifty years.

——, ed. *Cultures of Power: Lordship, Status, and Process in Twelfth-Century Europe.* Philadelphia, 1995.
Includes articles by many of the American and French scholars now working on medieval nobility and rule.

Bloch, Marc. *Feudal Society.* Trans. L. A. Manyon. Chicago, 1961.
Probably still the single most influential work on the topic of the medieval aristocracy, even though very few scholars now accept its conclusions. It should be read last, not first.

——. *The Royal Touch: Sacred Monarchy and Scrofula in England and France.* Trans. J. E. Anderson. London, 1973.

Bloch, R. Howard. *Medieval Misogyny and the Invention of Western Romantic Love.* Chicago, 1991.

Bonnassie, Pierre. *From Slavery to Feudalism in South-western Europe.* Trans. Jean Birrell. Cambridge, 1991.
A collection of this influential scholar's most important articles.

Bosl, Karl. "Freiheit und Unfreiheit: Zur Entwicklung der Unterschichten in Deutschland und Frankreich während des Mittelalters." *Vierteljahrschrift für Sozial- und Wirtschaftsgeschichte* 44 (1957), 193–219.

Boswell, John. *The Kindness of Strangers: The Abandonment of Children in Western Europe from Late Antiquity to the Renaissance.* New York, 1988.

——. *Same-Sex Unions in Premodern Europe.* New York, 1994. Includes a good deal of information on the West's developing view of heterosexual marriage.

Bouchard, Constance B. "The Bosonids: or, Rising to Power in the Late Carolingian Age." *French Historical Studies* 15 (1988), 407–31.

——. "Community: Society and the Church in Medieval France." *French Historical Studies* 17 (1992), 1035–47.

——. "Consanguinity and Noble Marriages in the Tenth and Eleventh Centuries." *Speculum* 56 (1981), 268–87.

——. "Family Structure and Family Consciousness among the Aristocracy in the Ninth to Eleventh Centuries." *Francia* 14 (1986), 639–58.

——. "The Geographical, Social, and Ecclesiastical Origins of the Bishops of Auxerre and Sens in the Central Middle Ages." *Church History* 46 (1977), 277–95.

——. *Holy Entrepreneurs: Cistercians, Knights, and Economic Exchange in Twelfth-Century Burgundy.* Ithaca, N.Y., 1991.

——. *Life and Society in the West: Antiquity and the Middle Ages.* San Diego, 1988.

——. "Merovingian, Carolingian, and Cluniac Monasticism: Reform and Renewal in Burgundy." *Journal of Ecclesiastical History* 41 (1990), 365–88.

——. "The Migration of Women's Names in the Upper Nobility, Ninth–Twelfth Centuries." *Medieval Prosopography* 9/2 (1988), 1–19.

——. "The Origins of the French Nobility: A Reassessment." *AHR* 86 (1981), 501–32.

——. "Patterns of Women's Names in Royal Lineages, Ninth–Eleventh Centuries." *Medieval Prosopography* 9/1 (1988), 1–32.

——. "The Possible Non-existence of Thomas, Author of *Tristan and Isolde.*" *Modern Philology* 79 (1981), 66–72.

——. *Spirituality and Administration: The Role of the Bishop in Twelfth-Century Auxerre.* Cambridge, Mass., 1979.

——. "The Structure of a Twelfth-Century French Family: The Lords of Seignelay." *Viator* 10 (1979), 39–56.

——. *Sword, Miter, and Cloister: Nobility and the Church in Burgundy, 980–1198.* Ithaca, N.Y., 1987.

Boulton, D'Arcy Jonathan Dacre. *The Knights of the Crown: The Monarchical Orders of Knighthood in Later Medieval Europe, 1325–1520.* Woodbridge, Eng., 1987.

Boureau, Alain. *Le droit de cuissage: La fabrication d'un mythe (XIIIe–XXe siècle).* Paris, 1995.

Boussard, Jacques. "Les évêques en Neutrie avant la réforme grégorienne (950–1050 environ)." *Journal des savants*, 1970, pp. 161–96.

Bradbury, Jim. *The Medieval Archer*. New York, 1985.

——. *The Medieval Siege*. Woodbridge, Eng., 1992.

Brodman, James W. "What Is a Soul Worth? *Pro Anima* Bequests in the Municipal Legislation of Reconquest Spain." *Medievalia et humanistica* n.s. 20 (1993), 15–23.

Brown, Elizabeth A. R. "The Tyranny of a Construct: Feudalism and Historians of Medieval Europe." *AHR* 79 (1974), 1063–88.
The fundamental article on why the term "feudalism" should be jettisoned.

Brundage, James A. *Law, Sex, and Christian Society in Medieval Europe*. Chicago, 1987.

Bull, Marcus. *Knightly Piety and the Lay Response to the First Crusade: The Limousin and Gascony, c. 970–c. 1130*. Oxford, 1993.

Bulst, Niethard. *Untersuchungen zu den Klosterreform Wilhelms von Dijon (962–1036)*. Pariser historische Studien 11. Bonn, 1973.

Bumke, Joachim. *The Concept of Knighthood in the Middle Ages*. Trans. W. T. H. Jackson and Erika Jackson. New York, 1982.
An important book that uses the sources of both history and literature to interpret the origins and ideals of chivalry.

——. *Courtly Culture: Literature and Society in the High Middle Ages*. Trans. Thomas Dunlap. Berkeley, 1991.
Almost encyclopedic in coverage, with the focus on Germany. Includes an extensive bibliography of works published before about 1980.

Bur, Michel. *La formation du comté de Champagne, v. 950–v. 1150*. Nancy, 1977.

Carozzi, Claude. "Les fondements de la tripartition sociale chez Adalbéron de Laon." *Annales: Économies, sociétés, civilisations* 33 (1978), 683–702.
A discussion of Adalbero's social theory by the man who edited his works.

Cherchi, Paolo. *Andreas and the Ambiguity of Courtly Love*. Toronto, 1994.
Argues that Andreas, far from being a proponent of courtly love, wrote his treatise to denounce it.

Chevalier, Bernard. "Les restitutions d'églises dans le diocèse de Tours du Xe au XIIe siècles." In *Études de civilisation médiévale (IXe–XIIe siècles): Mélanges offerts à Edmond-René Labande*. Poitiers, 1974.

Chickering, Howell, and Thomas H. Seiler, eds. *The Study of Chivalry*. Kalamazoo, Mich., 1988.
Contains a number of useful articles by historians and literary specialists.

Church, Stephen, and Ruth Harvey, eds. *Medieval Knighthood V: Papers from the Sixth Strawberry Hill Conference*. Woodbridge, Eng., 1995.

Constable, Giles. "The Structure of Medieval Society according to the *Dictatores* of the Twelfth Century." In Kenneth Pennington and Robert

Somerville, eds. *Law, Church, and Society: Essays in Honor of Stephan Kuttner*. Philadelphia, 1977.

Contamine, Philippe. *War in the Middle Ages*. Trans. Michael Jones. London, 1984.

Detailed and thorough, especially for the late Middle Ages; includes an extensive bibliography.

——, ed. *La noblesse au moyen âge: Essais à la mémoire de Robert Boutruche.* Paris, 1976.

Cowdrey, H. E. J. "The Peace and Truce of God in the Eleventh Century." *Past and Present* 46 (1970), 42–67.

Crook, J. A. *Law and Life of Rome, 90 B.C.–A.D. 212.* Ithaca, N.Y., 1967.

Crouch, David. *The Image of the Aristocracy in Britain, 1000–1300.* London, 1992.

——. *William Marshal: Court Career and Chivalry in the Angevin Empire, 1147–1219.* London, 1990.

Cummins, John. *The Hound and the Hawk: The Art of Medieval Hunting.* New York, 1988.

De Jong, Mayke. *In Samuel's Image: Child Oblation in the Early Medieval West.* Leiden, 1996.

Delort, Robert, and Dominique Iogna-Prat, eds. *La France de l'an mil.* Paris, 1990.

DeVries, Kelly. *Medieval Military Technology.* Peterborough, Ontario, 1992. A historian's look at a topic usually reserved to costumers and wargamers.

Droit privé et institutions régionales: Études historiques offertes à Jean Yver. Paris, 1976.

Duby, Georges. *The Chivalrous Society.* Trans. Cynthia Postan. Berkeley, 1977. This volume contains most of the articles that made Duby the premier French historian on the medieval aristocracy.

——. "The Courtly Model." In Christiane Klapisch-Zuber, ed. *A History of Women in the West: Silences of the Middle Ages.* Cambridge, Mass., 1992.

——. *The Early Growth of the European Economy: Warriors and Peasants from the Seventh to the Twelfth Century.* Trans. Howard B. Clarke. Ithaca, N.Y., 1974.

——. "Guerre et société dans l'Europe féodale." In Vittore Branca, ed. *Concetto, storia, miti, et immagini del medio evo.* Corso internazionale d'alta cultura 14. Venice, 1973.

——. *The Knight, the Lady, and the Priest: The Making of Modern Marriage in Medieval France.* Trans. Barbara Bray. New York, 1983.

——. *Medieval Marriage: Two Models from Twelfth-Century France.* Trans. Elborg Forster. Baltimore, 1978.

——. *Rural Economy and Country Life in the Medieval West.* Trans. Cynthia Postan. Columbia, S.C., 1968.

Still the best introduction to the medieval rural economy.

——. *La société aux XIe et XIIe siècles dans la région mâconnaise.* 2d ed. Paris, 1971.

This book (originally published in 1953) inspired all subsequent studies of individual French regions, which together have transformed the overall picture of the French Middle Ages.

——. *The Three Orders: Feudal Society Imagined.* Trans. Arthur Goldhammer. Chicago, 1980.

A somewhat dense but rewarding work on social theory in the eleventh and twelfth centuries.

——. *William Marshal: The Flower of Chivalry.* Trans. Richard Howard. New York, 1985.

Duby, Georges, and Jacques Le Goff, eds. *Famille et parenté dans l'Occident médiéval.* Rome, 1977.

The transactions of a 1974 colloquium which brought together some of the leading French, German, and Italian medievalists.

Dulac, Liliane. "Peut-on comprendre les relations entre Erec et Enide?" *Le moyen âge* 100 (1994), 37–50.

Dunbabin, Jean. *France in the Making, 843–1180.* Oxford, 1985.

——. "What's in a Name? Philip, King of France." *Speculum* 68 (1993), 949–68.

Elkins, Sharon K. *Holy Women of Twelfth-Century England.* Chapel Hill, N.C., 1988.

Evergates, Theodore. *Feudal Society in the Bailliage of Troyes under the Counts of Champagne, 1152–1284.* Baltimore, 1975.

A close study of Champagne documents is used as a base for a clear statement of the nature of both knighthood and peasantry.

Farmer, Sharon. *Communities of Saint Martin: Legend and Ritual in Medieval Tours.* Ithaca, N.Y., 1991.

Ferrante, Joan M. *The Conflict of Love and Honor: The Medieval Tristan Legend in France, Germany, and Italy.* The Hague, 1973.

Fichtenau, Heinrich. *Living in the Tenth Century: Mentalities and Social Orders.* Trans. Patrick J. Geary. Chicago, 1991.

Fleckenstein, Josef, ed. *Das ritterliche Turnier Im Mittelalter.* Göttingen, 1985.

Fleming, Robin. *Kings and Lords in Conquest England.* Cambridge, 1991.

Flori, Jean. "Amour et société aristocratique au XIIe siècle: L'exemple des lais de Marie de France." *Le moyen âge* 98 (1992), 17–34.

——. "Chevalerie, noblesse et lutte de classes au moyen âge." *Le moyen âge* 94 (1988), 258–71.

——. *L'essor de la chevalerie, XIe–XIIe siècles.* Geneva, 1986.

An expansion of the ideas first put forward in his essay "La notion de chevalerie" that "chivalry" was really only a development of the end of the twelfth century; the sources here are chronicles and treatises, rather than literary works.

——. *L'idéologie du glaive: Préhistoire de la chevalerie.* Geneva, 1983.

———. "La notion de chevalerie dans les chansons de geste du XIIe siècle: Étude historique de vocabulaire." *Le moyen âge* 81 (1975), 211–44, 407–45. The classic study that first demonstrated clearly, on linguistic grounds, that in the twelfth-century vernacular epics "chivalry" meant fighting on horseback, not a code of conduct.

———. "Les origines de l'adoubement chevaleresque: Étude des remises d'armes et du vocabulaire qui les exprime dans les sources historiques latines jusqu'au début du XIIIe siècle." *Traditio* 35 (1979), 209–72.

Fossier, Robert. *Peasant Life in the Medieval West.* Trans. Juliet Vale. New York, 1988.

Fournier, Gabriel. *Le château dans la France médiévale: Essai de sociologie monumentale.* Paris, 1978. Based on written records as well as archaeology, this work includes an extensive appendix of primary sources (translated into French) referring to castles.

Freed, John B. "The Formation of the Salzburg Ministerialage in the Tenth and Eleventh Centuries: An Example of Upward Social Mobility in the Central Middle Ages." *Viator* 9 (1978), 67–102.

———. *Noble Bondsmen: Ministerial Marriages in the Archdiocese of Salzburg, 1100–1343.* Ithaca, N.Y., 1995.

———. "Reflections on the German Nobility." *AHR* 91 (1986), 553–75.

Freedman, Paul. "Cowardice, Heroism, and the Legendary Origins of Catalonia." *Past and Present* 121 (1988), 3–28.

———. *The Origins of Peasant Servitude in Medieval Catalonia.* Cambridge, 1991. Includes a good deal of information on the meaning of serfdom outside as well as within Catalonia.

———. "Sainteté et sauvagerie: Deux images du paysan au moyen âge." *Annales: Économies, sociétés, civilisations* 47 (1992), 539–60.

Ganshof, F. L. *Feudalism.* Trans. Philip Grierson. Rev. ed. New York, 1964.

Geary, Patrick J. *Aristocracy in Provence: The Rhône Basin at the Dawn of the Carolingian Age.* Philadelphia, 1985. Includes an edition and translation of the eighth-century testament of Abbo.

———. *Before France and Germany: The Creation and Transformation of the Merovingian World.* Oxford, 1988.

———. *Living with the Dead in the Middle Ages.* Ithaca, N.Y., 1994.

———. *Phantoms of Remembrance: Memory and Oblivion at the End of the First Millennium.* Princeton, 1994.

Genicot, Léopold. *Études sur les principautés lotharingiennes.* Louvain, 1975.

———. *Les généalogies.* Typologie des sources du moyen âge occidental 15. Turnhout, 1975.

———. "La noblesse médiévale: Encore!" *Revue d'histoire ecclésiastique* 88 (1993), 173–201.

——. "La noblesse médiévale: Pans de lumière et zones obscures." *Tijdschrift voor Geschiedenis* 93 (1980), 341–56.

This and the preceding article are bibliographic essays on the study of the medieval nobility during, respectively, the 1970s and 1980s.

——. *Rural Communities in the Medieval West.* Baltimore, 1990.

Gies, Joseph, and Frances Gies. *Life in a Medieval Castle.* New York, 1979. Written for a popular audience but based on primary sources. Principally covers twelfth- and thirteenth-century England.

Gimpel, Jean. *The Medieval Machine: The Industrial Revolution of the Middle Ages.* New York, 1976.

Girouard, Mark. *Life in the English Country House.* New Haven, 1978. A discussion of upper-crust life from the late Middle Ages to the nineteenth century.

Goetz, Hans-Werner. "Serfdom and the Beginnings of a 'Seigneurial System' in the Carolingian Period: A Survey of the Evidence." *Early Medieval Europe* 2 (1993), 29–51. A thoughtful reassessment of the status of serfs, slaves, and *servi.*

Gold, Penny Schine. *The Lady and the Virgin: Image, Attitude, and Experience in Twelfth-Century France.* Chicago, 1985. Important for the changing role of women in chivalric society.

Goody, Jack. *The Development of the Family and Marriage in Europe.* Cambridge, 1983.

Grundmann, Herbert. *Religious Movements in the Middle Ages.* Trans. Steven Rowan. Notre Dame, 1995. Originally published in 1935, this remains the most influential work on the nature of heresy and religious poverty in the High Middle Ages.

Guerreau-Jalabert, Anita. "Sur les structures de parenté dans l'Europe médiévale." *Annales: Économies, sociétés, civilisations* 36 (1981), 1028–49.

Guillot, Olivier. *Le comte d'Anjou et son entourage au XIe siècle.* Paris, 1972.

Hajdu, Robert. "Castles, Castellans, and the Structure of Politics in Poitou, 1152–1271." *Journal of Medieval History* 4 (1978), 27–53.

Hallam, Elizabeth M. *Capetian France, 987–1328.* London, 1980.

Hallinger, Kassius. *Gorze-Kluny: Studien zu den monastischen Lebensformen und Gegensätzen im Hochmittelalter.* Studia Anselmiana. Rome, 1950. The first work to demonstrate clearly the existence of multiple centers of monastic reform in the tenth and eleventh centuries.

Harper-Bill, Christopher, and Ruth Harvey, eds. *The Ideals and Practice of Medieval Knighthood: Papers from the First and Second Strawberry Hill Conferences.* Woodbridge, Eng., 1986. The volumes in this series contain learned articles bringing together the specialties of the historian and the literary scholar.

——, eds. *The Ideals and Practice of Medieval Knighthood II: Papers from the Third Strawberry Hill Conference.* Woodbridge, Eng., 1988.

——, eds. *The Ideals and Practice of Medieval Knighthood III: Papers from the Fourth Strawberry Hill Conference*. Woodbridge, Eng., 1990.

——, eds. *Medieval Knighthood IV: Papers from the Fifth Strawberry Hill Conference*. Woodbridge, Eng., 1992.

Head, Thomas. *Hagiography and the Cult of Saints: The Diocese of Orléans, 800–1200*. Cambridge, 1990.

Head, Thomas, and Richard Landes, eds. *The Peace of God: Social Violence and Religious Response in France around the Year 1000*. Ithaca, N.Y., 1992. A collection of articles which brings together the latest scholarship on the topic.

Heinzelmann, Martin. "La noblesse du haut moyen âge (VIIIe–XIe siècles)." *Le moyen âge* 83 (1977), 131–44. A review article summarizing important studies of the 1970s.

Herlihy, David. *Medieval Households*. Cambridge, Mass., 1985.

——. "The Medieval Marriage Market." *Medieval and Renaissance Studies* 6 (1974), 3–27.

Hilton, R. H. *English and French Towns in Feudal Society: A Comparative Study*. Cambridge, 1992.

Holdsworth, Christopher J. "Christina of Markyate." In *Medieval Women*. Ed. Derek Baker. Oxford, 1978.

Howe, John. "The Nobility's Reform of the Medieval Church." *AHR* 92 (1988), 317–39.

Hunt, Tony. "The Emergence of the Knight in France and England, 1000–1200." *Forum for Modern Language Studies* 17 (1981), 93–114. A careful and useful summary of how historians' views have changed on the nature of knighthood.

Hurtig, Judith W. *The Armored Gisant before 1400*. New York, 1979.

Hyams, Paul R. *Kings, Lords, and Peasants in Medieval England: The Common Law of Villeinage in the Twelfth and Thirteenth Centuries*. Oxford, 1980.

Jackman, Donald C. *The Konradiner: A Study in Genealogical Methodology*. Frankfurt am Main, 1990.

Jaeger, C. Stephen. *The Envy of Angels: Cathedral Schools and Social Ideals in Medieval Europe, 950–1200*. Philadelphia, 1994.

——. *The Origins of Courtliness: Civilizing Trends and the Formation of Courtly Ideals, 939–1210*. Philadelphia, 1985. A convincing redefinition of the roots of chivalry.

Johnson, Penelope D. *Equal in Monastic Profession: Religious Women in Medieval France*. Chicago, 1991.

——. *Prayer, Patronage, and Power: The Abbey of la Trinité, Vendôme, 1032–1187*. New York, 1981.

Jordan, William Chester. *From Servitude to Freedom: Manumission in the Sénonais in the Thirteenth Century*. Philadelphia, 1986.

Kaminsky, Howard. "Estate, Nobility, and the Exhibition of Estate in the Later Middle Ages." *Speculum* 68 (1993), 684–709.

Katsura, Hideyuki. "Serments, hommages, et fiefs dans la seigneurie des Guilhem de Montpellier (fin XIe–début XIIIe siècle)." *Annales du Midi* 104 (1992), 141–61.

Kay, Sarah. *The "Chansons de geste" in the Age of Romance: Political Fiction.* Oxford, 1995.

Keen, Maurice. *Chivalry.* New Haven, 1984.
Learned and thorough; especially useful for the late Middle Ages.

Kelly, Douglas. *The Art of Medieval French Romance.* Madison, Wis., 1992.

——. "Courtly Love in Perspective: The Hierarchy of Love in Andreas Capellanus." *Traditio* 24 (1968), 119–47.

Konecny, Sylvia. *Die Frauen des karolingeschen Köngishauses.* Vienna, 1976.

Koziol, Geoffrey. *Begging Pardon and Favor: Ritual and Political Order in Early Medieval France.* Ithaca, N.Y., 1992.

Lahaye-Geusen, Maria. *Das Opfer der Kinder: Ein Beitrag zur Liturgie- und Sozialgeschichte des Mönchtums im Hohen Mittelalter.* Altenberge, 1991.

Landes, Richard. *Relics, Apocalypse, and the Deceits of History: Ademar of Chabannes, 989–1034.* Cambridge, Mass., 1995.

Le Jan, Régine. *Famille et pouvoir dans le monde franc (VIIe–Xe siècle): Essai d'anthropologie sociale.* Paris, 1995.
The most important recent study of early medieval family structure among the nobility.

Le Jan-Hennebique, Régine. "*Domnus, illuster, nobilis:* Les mutations du pouvoir au Xe siècle." In Michel Sot, ed. *Haut moyen-âge: Culture, éducation, et société: Études offertes à Pierre Riché.* Paris, 1990.

Lekai, Louis J. *The Cistercians: Ideals and Reality.* Kent, Ohio, 1977.

Lemarignier, Jean-François. *Le gouvernement royal aux premiers temps capétiens (987–1108).* Paris, 1965.

—— "Political and Monastic Structures in France at the End of the Tenth and Beginning of the Eleventh Century." In Fredric L. Cheyette, ed. and trans. *Lordship and Community in Medieval Europe.* New York, 1968.
This article, originally published in 1957, has been very influential on the scholarly vision of both government and monasticism in eleventh-century France.

Lewis, Andrew W. *Royal Succession in Capetian France: Studies on Familial Order and the State.* Cambridge, Mass., 1981.

Lewis, C. S. *The Allegory of Love: A Study in Medieval Tradition.* Oxford, 1936.
For sixty years this study has cast its shadow over all attempts to define or discuss courtly love.

Leyser, K. "The German Aristocracy from the Ninth to the Early Twelfth Century: A Historical and Cultural Sketch." *Past and Present* 41 (1968), 25–53.

Little, Lester K. *Benedictine Maledictions: Liturgical Cursing in Romanesque France.* Ithaca, N.Y., 1993.

Livingstone, Amy. "Kith and Kin: Kinship and Family Structure of the Nobility of Eleventh- and Twelfth-Century Blois-Chartres." *French Historical Studies* 20 (1997), 419–58.

Lynch, Joseph H. *Godparents and Kinship in Early Medieval Europe*. Princeton, 1986.

——. *Simoniacal Entry into Religious Life from 1000 to 1260*. Columbus, Ohio, 1976.

A thorough study of the gifts that accompanied converts into the cloister in the High Middle Ages.

Magnou-Nortier, Elisabeth. *La société laïque et l'église dans la province ecclésiastique de Narbonne (zone cispyrénéenne) de la fin du VIIIe à la fin du XIe siècle.* Toulouse, 1974.

One of the most important of the French regional histories that were inspired by Duby.

Martindale, Jane. "The French Aristocracy in the Early Middle Ages: A Reappraisal." *Past and Present* 75 (1977), 5–45.

Important for identifying the chief features of the nobility.

Il matrimonio nella società altomedievale. Settimane di studio del Centro italiano di studi sull'alto medioevo 24. Spoleto, 1977.

Includes several important articles on aristocratic marriage patterns.

McKee, Sally. "Households in Fourteenth-Century Venetian Crete." *Speculum* 70 (1995), 27–67.

McLaughlin, Megan. *Consorting with Saints: Prayer for the Dead in Early Medieval France.* Ithaca, N.Y., 1994.

McNamara, Jo Ann, and Suzanne Wemple. "The Power of Women through the Family in Medieval Europe, 500–1100." In Mary Erler and Maryanne Kowaleski, eds. *Women and Power in the Middle Ages.* Athens, Ga., 1988.

Miller, Maureen C. *The Formation of a Medieval Church: Ecclesiastical Change in Verona, 950–1150.* Ithaca, N.Y., 1993.

Miyamatsu, H. "Les premiers bourgeois d'Angers aux XIe et XIIe siècles." *Annales de Bretagne* 97 (1990), 1–14.

Moi, Toril. "Desire in Language: Andreas Capellanus and the Controversy of Courtly Love." In David Aers, ed. *Medieval Literature: Criticism, Ideology, and History.* New York, 1986.

Monson, Don A. "Andreas Capellanus and the Problem of Irony." *Speculum* 63 (1988), 539–72.

——. "The Troubadour's Lady Reconsidered Again." *Speculum* 70 (1995), 255–74.

Mullally, Evelyn. *The Artist at Work: Narrative Technique in Chrétien de Troyes.* Transactions of the American Philosophical Society 78/4. Philadelphia, 1988.

Murray, Alexander. *Reason and Society in the Middle Ages.* Oxford, 1978.

One of the first works in English to treat seriously the relationship between nobles and reformed monasticism.

Nelson, Janet L. *Charles the Bald*. London, 1992.

Newman, Charlotte A. *The Anglo-Norman Nobility in the Reign of Henry I: The Second Generation*. Philadelphia, 1988.

Newman, Martha G. *The Boundaries of Charity: Cistercian Culture and Ecclesiastical Reform, 1098–1180*. Stanford, 1996.

Nichols, Stephen G., Jr. *Romanesque Signs: Early Medieval Narrative and Iconography*. New Haven, 1983.

Painter, Sidney. *French Chivalry*. Baltimore, 1940.

Parisse, Michel. "La noblesse Lorraine, XIe–XIIe s." Diss., Université de Nancy II, 1975.

Paterson, Linda. "Knights and the Concept of Knighthood in the Twelfth-Century Occitan Epic." *Forum for Modern Language Studies* 17 (1981), 115–30.

——. *The World of the Troubadours: Medieval Occitan Society, c. 1100–c. 1300*. Cambridge, 1993.

Perroy, Edouard. "Les châteaux du Roannais du XIe au XIIIe siècle." *Cahiers de civilisation médiévale* 9 (1966), 13–27.

Poly, Jean-Pierre. *La Provence et la société féodale, 879-1166: Contributions à l'étude des structures dites féodales dans le Midi*. Paris, 1976.

Poly, Jean-Pierre, and Eric Bournazel. *The Feudal Transformation, 900–1200*. Trans. Caroline Higgitt. New York, 1991.
This book, originally published in 1980, brings together much of the French scholarship of the preceding generation.

Pounds, N. J. G. *An Economic History of Medieval Europe*. New York, 1974.

——. *The Medieval Castle in England and Wales: A Social and Political History*. Cambridge, 1990.

Quinn, Patricia A. *Better Than the Sons of Kings: Boys and Monks in the Early Middle Ages*. New York, 1989.

Reuter, Timothy, ed. and trans. *The Medieval Nobility: Studies on the Ruling Classes of France and Germany from the Sixth to the Twelfth Century*. Amsterdam, 1978.
Translations of articles by most of the European scholars who redefined during the 1960s and 1970s the concept of nobility.

Reynolds, Susan. *Fiefs and Vassals: The Medieval Evidence Reinterpreted*. Oxford, 1994.
A reexamination of the nature and role of fief holding, arguing cogently that fiefs were much less central an institution in the High Middle Ages than they have been considered.

——. *Kingdoms and Communities in Western Europe, 900–1300*. Oxford, 1984.
A successful effort to create a theoretical framework for medieval society, from kings to peasants, without invoking "feudalism."

Rivers, Theodore John. "The Manorial System in the Light of 'Lex Baiuvariorum' I, 13." *Frühmittelalterliche Studien* 25 (1991), 89–95.

Robertson D. W. Jr. "The Concept of Courtly Love as an Impediment to the Understanding of Medieval Texts." In F. X. Newman, ed. *The Meaning of Courtly Love*. Albany, 1968.

This indictment of the term "courtly love" is as relevant now as it was thirty years ago.

Rogers, R. *Latin Siege Warfare in the Twelfth Century*. Oxford, 1992.

Rösener, Werner. *Peasants in the Middle Ages*. Trans. Alexander Stützer. Cambridge, 1992.

Rosenwein, Barbara H. *Rhinoceros Bound: Cluny in the Tenth Century*. Philadelphia, 1982.

This book and Rosenwein's *To Be the Neighbor of Saint Peter* have refocused Cluniac studies for the abbey's first century.

——. "St. Odo's St. Martin: The Uses of a Model." *Journal of Medieval History* 4 (1978), 316–31.

——. *To Be the Neighbor of Saint Peter: The Social Meaning of Cluny's Property, 909–1049*. Ithaca, N.Y., 1989.

Rosenwein, Barbara H., Thomas Head, and Sharon Farmer. "Monks and Their Enemies: A Comparative Approach." *Speculum* 66 (1991), 764–96.

Scaglione, Aldo. *Knights at Court: Courtliness, Chivalry, and Courtesy from Ottonian Germany to the Italian Renaissance*. Berkeley, 1991.

Scammell, Jean. "The Formation of the English Social Structure: Freedom, Knights, and Gentry, 1066–1300." *Speculum* 68 (1993), 591–618.

Schmid, Karl. "Zur Problematik von Familie, Sippe und Geschlecht, Haus und Dynastie beim mittelalterlichen Adel." *Zeitschrift für die Geschichte des Oberrheins* 105 (1957), 1–62.

Schmid, Karl, and Joachim Wollasch. "Die Gemeinschaft der Lebenden und Verstorbenen in Zeugnissen des Mittelalters." *Frühmittelalterliche Studien* 1 (1967), 365–405.

Schnell, Rüdiger. *Andreas Capellanus: Zur Rezeption des römischen und kanonischen Rechts in "De Amore."* Munich, 1982.

Southern, R. W. *The Making of the Middle Ages*. New Haven, 1953.

Spiegel, Gabrielle M. *Romancing the Past: The Rise of Vernacular Prose Historiography in Thirteenth-Century France*. Berkeley, 1993.

Ste. Croix, G. E. M. de. *The Class Struggle in the Ancient Greek World from the Archaic Age to the Arab Conquests*. Ithaca, N.Y., 1981.

Stephenson, Carl. *Feudalism*. Ithaca, N.Y., 1942.

Störmer, Wilhelm. *Früher Adel: Studien zur Politischen Führungsschicht im Fränkisch-Deutschen Reich vom 8. bis 11. Jahrhundert*. Stuttgart, 1973.

Strickland, Matthew. *War and Chivalry: The Conduct and Perception of War in England and Normandy, 1066–1217*. Cambridge, 1996.

Structures féodales et féodalisme dans l'occident méditerranéen (Xe–XIIIe siècles). Paris, 1980.

The papers of a colloquium attended by most of the important European scholars working on the medieval aristocracy.

Les structures sociales de l'Aquitaine, du Languedoc, et de l'Espagne au premier âge féodal. Paris, 1969.
Although focusing especially on southern France, the papers of this seminal colloquium have implications for a wider area.

Tabacco, Giovanni. "Su nobilità e cavalleria nel medioevo: Un ritorno a Marc Bloch?" *Rivista storica italiana* 91 (1979), 5–25.
A summary of the scholarship on knighthood and nobility in the 1970s.

Tabuteau, Emily Zack. *Transfers of Property in Eleventh-Century Norman Law.* Chapel Hill, N.C., 1988.

Tellenbach, Gerd. "Zur Erforschung des hochmittelalterlichen Adels (9.–12. Jahrhundert)." In Comité internationale des sciences historiques. *XIIe Congrès international des sciences historiques.* Vol. 1. *Rapports, Grands thèmes.* Vienna, 1965.

Thomas, Heinz. "Zur Kritik an der Ehe Heinrichs III. mit Agnes von Poitou." In Kurt-Ulrich Jäschke and Reinhard Wenskus, eds. *Festschrift für Helmut Beumann zum 65. Geburtstag.* Sigmaringen, 1977.

Thompson, M. W. *The Rise of the Castle.* Cambridge, 1991.

Thompson, Sally. *The Founding of English Nunneries after the Norman Conquest.* Oxford, 1991.

Turner, Ralph V. "The Problem of Survival for the Angevin 'Empire': Henry II's and His Sons' Vision versus Late Twelfth-Century Realities." *AHR* 100 (1995), 78–96.

Van Engen, John. "The Christian Middle Ages as an Historiographical Problem." *AHR* 91 (1986), 519–52.

———. "The 'Crisis of Cenobitism' Reconsidered: Benedictine Monasticism in the Years 1050–1150." *Speculum* 61 (1986), 269–304.

Vauchez, André. "Lay People's Sanctity in Western Europe: Evolution of a Pattern (Twelfth and Thirteenth Centuries)." In Renate Blumenfeld-Kosinski and Timea Szell, eds. *Images of Sainthood in Medieval Europe.* Ithaca, N.Y., 1991.

———. *The Spirituality of the Medieval West. The Eighth to the Twelfth Century* Trans. Colette Friedlander. Kalamazoo, Mich., 1993.

Venarde, Bruce L. *Women's Monasticism and Medieval Society: Nunneries in France and England, 890–1215.* Ithaca, N.Y., 1997.

Verdon, Jean. "Les moniales dans la France de l'ouest aux XIe et XIIe siècles: Étude d'histoire sociale." *Cahiers de civilisation médiévale* 19 (1976), 247–64.

Warlop, E. *The Flemish Nobility before 1300.* 4 vols. Trans. J. B. Ross. Kortrijk, Belgium, 1975–76.

Weinberger, Stephen. "Cours judiciaires, justice, et responsabilité sociale dans la Provence médiévale, IXe–XIe siècle." *Revue historique* 542 (1982), 273–88.

——. "The Ennoblement of the Aristocracy in Medieval Provence." *Medievalia et humanistica* n.s. 20 (1993), 1–14.

Wemple, Suzanne Fonay. *Women in Frankish Society: Marriage and the Cloister, 500 to 900.* Philadelphia, 1981.

Probably still the best book by a single author on medieval women.

Wenskus, Reinhard. *Sächsischer Stammesadel und fränkischer Reichsadel.* Abhandlungen der Akademie der Wissenschaften, philologisch-historische Klasse 3, 93. Göttingen, 1976.

Werner, Karl Ferdinand. "Missus—Marchio—Comes: Entre l'administration centrale et l'administration locale de l'Empire carolingien." In Werner Paravicini and Karl Ferdinand Werner, eds. *Histoire comparée de l'administration (IVe–XVIIIe siècles).* Munich, 1980.

——. "Die Nachkommen Karls des Großen bis um das Jahr 1000 (1.–8. Generation)." In Wolfgang Braunfels, ed. *Karl der Grosse, Lebenswerk und Nachleben.* Vol. 4. Dusseldorf, 1967.

All Charlemagne's descendants for eight generations, detailed and documented.

——. "Untersuchungen zur Frühzeit des französischen Fürstentums (9.–10. Jahrhundert)." *Die Welt als Geschichte* 18 (1958), 259–89; 19 (1959), 146–93; 20 (1960), 87–119.

The clearest statement of the themes that have animated all of Werner's scholarship.

——. *Vom Frankenreich zur Entfaltung Deutschlands und Frankreichs.* Sigmaringen, 1984.

A collection of some of Werner's most important articles.

White, Stephen D. *Custom, Kinship, and Gifts to Saints: The "Laudatio Parentum" in Western France, 1050–1150.* Chapel Hill, N.C., 1988.

A thoughtful work that reexamines many issues on the relations betwen the church and secular society.

——. "Feuding and Peace-Making in the Touraine around the Year 1100." *Traditio* 42 (1986), 195–263.

——. " 'Pactum . . . Legem Vincit et Amor Judicium': The Settlement of Disputes by Compromise in Eleventh-Century Western France." *American Journal of Legal History* 22 (1978), 281–308.

Wickham, Chris. "The Other Transition: From the Ancient World to Feudalism." *Past and Present* 103 (1984), 3–36.

Witt, Ronald G. "The Landlord and the Economic Revival of the Middle Ages in Northern Europe, 1000–1250." *AHR* 76 (1971), 965–88.

Wollasch, Joachim. *Mönchtum des Mittelalters zwischen Kirche und Welt.* Munich, 1973.

——. "Parenté noble et monachisme réformateur: Observations sur les 'conversions' à la vie monastique aux XIe et XIIe siècles." *Revue historique* 535 (1980), 3–24.

INDEX